Praise for *That Librarian*

"Book bans are spot fires breaking out all across the country, and bold-faced lies alleging prurient sexual content in children's literature are the accelerant. Lucky for us, debut author Amanda Jones has embraced the role of town bellringer, warning our national village of impending disaster and calling for the bucket brigade to fight these fires and douse these flames.

With book challenges in America multiplying at a dizzying rate, *That Librarian* is not only timely, but essential. Jones, a veteran classroom teacher and award-winning librarian, is uniquely suited to separate fact from fiction when it comes to what age-appropriate books are actually on school and public library shelves accessible to children and young adults, titles designed to help—not harm—the youngest library patrons. Here, she breaks down the politics behind the bans, and the library policies already in place to protect readers of all ages.

As an author who has devoted 45+ years to crafting such titles, it heartens me to know that Amanda Jones is fighting to keep my picture books, poetry, middle grade, and teen novels on the shelves where young readers who want or need my stories can find them.

Book banners really poked the proverbial bear when they came after Jones for daring to speak out against censorship at a public library board meeting in her Louisiana hometown. The personal and public smear campaigns and death threats that followed—and that persist—have been brutal. But like most librarians, Jones has turned out to be a badass, and this is a memoir of grit and grace. This is a rallying cry for the protection of intellectual freedom. And about that much needed bucket brigade: Tag! We're it."

—**Nikki Grimes, author of the frequently banned memoir in verse *Ordinary Hazards***

"As an author whose novels have been banned in hundreds of school districts after falsely being cited for explicit content, I have been waiting for a book like this one. We writers are well aware that the foot soldiers in this spreading civil war are librarians, who are threatened personally and profoundly by those who call for widespread book bans. Amanda Jones clearly outlines how we got here, who's leading this false charge against qualified educators, media specialists, and authors—and most importantly, she explores the steps we all must take to make the voice of truth and reason louder than their caterwauling."

—**Jodi Picoult, #1** *New York Times* **bestselling author**

"Deeply important and compelling, this book about one heroic librarian's fight against book bans will help all of us who care about books and our freedom to read."

—**Ellen Oh, author and CEO of We Need Diverse Books**

"Read this absorbing book to understand the conspiracy-driven war on public education—from inside the schoolhouse library. Amanda Jones takes us into the trenches and offers deft portraits of the people and organizations waging this war on democracy—as well as the heroes standing up for freedom and education."

—**Katherine Stewart, author of**
The Power Worshippers **and** *Money, Lies, and God*

That Librarian

That
Librarian

The Fight Against Book Banning in America

AMANDA JONES

BLOOMSBURY PUBLISHING

NEW YORK · LONDON · OXFORD · NEW DELHI · SYDNEY

BLOOMSBURY PUBLISHING
Bloomsbury Publishing Inc.
1385 Broadway, New York, NY 10018, USA

BLOOMSBURY, BLOOMSBURY PUBLISHING, and the Diana logo are trademarks of
Bloomsbury Publishing Plc

First published in the United States

Bloomsbury Publishing Plc does not have any control over, or responsibility for, any
third-party websites referred to or in this book. All internet addresses given in this book
were correct at the time of going to press. The author and publisher regret any inconvenience
caused if addresses have changed or sites have ceased to exist, but can accept no
responsibility for any such changes.

ISBN: HB: 978-1-63973-353-8; EBOOK: 978-1-63973-354-5

LIBRARY OF CONGRESS CATALOGING-IN-PUBLICATION DATA IS AVAILABLE

2 4 6 8 10 9 7 5 3 1

Typeset by Westchester Publishing Services
Printed and bound in the U.S.A.

To find out more about our authors and books visit www.bloomsbury.com and sign up
for our newsletters.

Bloomsbury books may be purchased for business or promotional use. For information
on bulk purchases, please contact Macmillan Corporate and Premium Sales Department at
specialmarkets@macmillan.com.

To Jason and Josie—because they are my everything

To Judy Blume and Michelle Obama (in the unlikely event that they read my book)

To my parents (in the likely event that they would disown me if I dedicated this to Judy and Michelle but left them out)

For the librarians. Invictus.

CONTENTS

Chapter 1

Liars and Buzzards and Trolls, Oh My

Amanda, you are indoctrinating our children with perversion + pedophilia grooming. Your evil agenda is getting print + national coverage. Congrats. Continue with your LGBT agenda on our children cause we gunna put ur fat evil commie PEDO azz in the dirt very soon bitch. You can't hide. We know where you work + live. . . . you have a LARGE target on your back. Click, click . . . see you soon . . .

[DEATH THREAT RECEIVED ON AUGUST 14, 2022,
SUBJECT LINE: ALPHABET AGENDA]

When I opened this email on August 14, 2022, my hands started to shake and I immediately began gasping for breath. The absurdness of it also crossed my mind, and I had the fleeting thought that my preteen students could write better emails than this. But there is nothing funny about receiving a threat on your life. I began again to wonder what possessed someone to send another human being such an email. Sadly, I'd been spending a large portion of the previous weeks pondering why random strangers go online to put down, troll, threaten, and defame people who they've never met. Do they wake up and think to themselves, "I wonder who I can ruin today to make myself feel better to fill the hole in my life?" I believe that anyone who does this kind of thing suffers from some type of trauma, or that something elemental is missing from their lives.

I am a middle school librarian in a small town called Watson in the southern Louisiana parish of Livingston. I have lived here all my life and have never thought of leaving. I bought the house next door to my childhood home and am lucky to have my parents as my closest neighbors. Watson sits some twenty miles southeast of Baton Rouge on what folks consider part of the Delta. The land is flat and the sky is big and in the summer the air is like a steaming wet blanket. The town isn't much to look at, and in the flood of 2016 much of it was leveled. Now, that was something. But generally, Watson is a place with few surprises, and that's a lot of what I love about it. Life has its regular rhythms, and I love those rhythms, love my job, my friends, my family. I take great satisfaction in being a school librarian, which puts me in the heart of the community, all the kids and their families and the rituals of the calendar year. I still feel like Livingston Parish is a good place, but I was not prepared for the surprise it threw at me.

I never imagined that I would receive an email in which someone writes "we gunna put ur fat evil PEDO azz in the dirt." It put chills down my back and scared me to the depths of my being. Reading a death threat—*my* death threat—has left me changed. I am scared to open emails from unknown senders. Seeing notifications on social media does not feel the way it used to. The email I opened did not feel anonymous. It felt personal. To mention that they knew where I worked added another layer of fear. The thought that someone might harm a child while coming to attack me made my heart race. Holding my phone in my trembling hand, I felt physically jolted and woozy. I thought I was having a heart attack. I now know it was a panic attack. I think about the words "click . . . click . . . see you soon" often. Too often. And I wonder if I am going to be attacked every time I step outside my home.

You might be asking yourself, "Why did Amanda receive this email? Surely, she did something heinous?" My parents asked the same question. My huge crime was speaking out against censorship at my local public library board meeting on Tuesday, July 19, 2022. In retrospect, it was a pretty tame statement, compared with the reaction it elicited.

On the night I spoke up at the library meeting, I was one of almost thirty speakers who registered their concerns about possible censorship and book banning. The meeting was held at Livingston Public Library, not my middle school library. I went as a citizen. The seven-member library board was seated up front, and there was a good crowd of locals. Two men, one from out of town and one local, also attended the meeting, and they are at the root of the attack on me. After I dared to speak, and after the others dared to speak, these two men zeroed in on yours truly. It took a few days, four to be precise, but on that fourth day, a Saturday, I opened social media to a barrage of hate.

I am here to tell you that being on the receiving end of an online hate campaign absolutely sucks. I do not recommend it. Two thumbs down. Zero out of five stars.

The hate started with two posts on social media that were shared hundreds of times. Imagine getting up on a Saturday morning, thinking about all the plans you have with your family for the day, but instead you wake to a full-fledged campaign created to discredit you and your years of service to your community. I did what I normally do during the summer off from my job as an educator: wake up a bit late, prop myself up on my pillow, and open social media to see what everyone is up to. I take a quick look at Facebook and Twitter before getting a cup of coffee and reading the newspaper at the kitchen table. I usually join my husband and child, and we hang out or watch an episode of some half-hour sitcom. Not that morning. That day I stayed in bed crying hysterically, glued to my phone as two men got busy attempting to damage my reputation.

The first post was made on Facebook by a local group called Citizens for a New Louisiana, a group that has wreaked havoc on public libraries across Louisiana. Citizens is led by Executive Director Michael Lunsford. I often think of him as a cartoon villain. Think Boris from *Rocky and Bullwinkle*, Gargamel from *The Smurfs*, or a villain from some current cartoon that I don't watch—someone with no redeeming qualities and instantly dislikable. Thinking of Michael Lunsford as a cartoon villain may be a coping mechanism because what he does is so much more serious than anything you or I would see on a Saturday morning show. Citizens is a dark-money nonprofit group in Louisiana whose director often posts the usual conspiracy theories about "the jab," hate rhetoric toward the LGBTQIA+ community, and your typical far-right nonsense. But it's nonsense that is believed by a lot of people. They published my name and said that I was fighting hard to "keep sexually erotic and pornographic materials in the kid's section" of our public library. They identified me as a school librarian and questioned what kind of nefarious influence I had over six-year-olds. They posted a picture of me with a target around my head. According to them, it's just a circle, but who are they kidding? Post after post from them left me dumbfounded. How could anyone come to that conclusion from my statement opposing censorship? Sexually erotic and pornographic material in the kids' section?! Six-year-olds?! What if people actually believed this nonsense?

I started to read the comments to the posts. Maybe I shouldn't have. But I needed to know if these lies were being believed. I found complete strangers were suddenly experts on what type of person I was and what I had said at the meeting. People were making so many assumptions about me. Everyone in the comments had an opinion, and they were in agreement. According to them, I was some type of deranged miscreant who needed to be kept away from children. I have devoted twenty-two years of my life to the children of our community. So much time outside regular work hours, time that often came at my family's expense. At that moment those twenty-two years didn't seem to matter to anyone, including me. Tears began rolling down my face. You see, the people commenting weren't just strangers. They were people I knew. People I grew up with. The hurt was almost more than I could bear that morning.

When I first saw the posts, I ran into the living room to show my husband. Jason, a man who is rarely on social media, had already seen them.

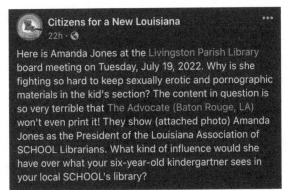

Citizens for a New Louisiana
22h · 🌐

Here is Amanda Jones at the Livingston Parish Library board meeting on Tuesday, July 19, 2022. Why is she fighting so hard to keep sexually erotic and pornographic materials in the kid's section? The content in question is so very terrible that The Advocate (Baton Rouge, LA) won't even print it! They show (attached photo) Amanda Jones as the President of the Louisiana Association of SCHOOL Librarians. What kind of influence would she have over what your six-year-old kindergartner sees in your local SCHOOL's library?

Amanda Jones, president of the Louisiana Association of School Librarians, speaks in opposition of potential restrictions on youth literature at a Livingston

He happened to stumble on them on his own that morning because of how quickly the posts traveled. And that meant more people were seeing them than I first realized. As I stood before my husband, my gut reaction was to be embarrassed for him to see them. It might have been irrational for me to be embarrassed, but I was. I had done nothing wrong. Jason knows me. He knows what I stand for and has always been supportive, but I did somehow feel those feelings. Discussing the posts out loud made them real, and I didn't want them to be real. I wanted them to disappear. I wanted to act like it wasn't happening. I wanted the posts to go away.

We both just stared at our phones in disbelief. I didn't know what to say to the man that I had been with for twenty-three years. This wasn't like anything we had faced before. What do you say when someone is posting lies about you online? We both knew they weren't true, but that didn't make it any less painful. Jason has thicker skin than I do, and he told me to ignore it. My eyes narrowed and I stared at him. How do you ignore something like this?

I looked at him incredulously, and he realized that that was not the thing he should have said. I feel bad now for narrowing my eyes and giving him the stare down. In all honesty, I don't think there was anything he could have said or done to make me feel better, but he did try. He made a joke about the imbeciles posting comments. He told me nobody would believe the lies. He seemed to not understand the full depth of my distress. I think that he, too, was just as confused about what was happening, but his confusion turned the corner to anger when I pointed out to him that it didn't matter if it wasn't true. I work with children, and there was a direct threat to my job by these men posting these lies. The pain got to be too much. I looked at him with tears in my eyes, chin trembling as I tried to hold it together, and then I retreated into the dark bedroom and shut the door. I wanted to crawl into a hole and die.

———

Right after seeing the post by Citizens for a New Louisiana, someone texted me about another post on Facebook. I received so many texts that morning that I don't remember who it was that sent the first text. The Facebook post was done by a local named Ryan Thames. Ryan is the type of average middle-aged white guy I like to refer to as a keyboard warrior. He is a self-professed "asshole" who in the same breath will tell you what a Christian family man he is and then turn around and mock someone whom he finds "less than." Who am I kidding? Ryan doesn't actually say these things to anyone's face. He hides behind his keyboard. He has for years.

Ryan posted a meme on this Facebook page he had created that he apparently found quite hilarious. He stole a picture from my professional website and added the words, "After advocating teaching anal sex to 11-year-olds, I had to change my name on Facebook. Amanda McKee Jones now identifies as Amanda Beth." He also identified my school and mocked the fact that I had won librarian of the year. You only mock people who have awards when you have no real accomplishments of your own.

Again I was flabbergasted. I knew what I had said that night at the library board meeting. At no point did I speak about anal sex. I certainly didn't advocate teaching children about it at the library or at my school. Where were these lies coming from? What were they rooted in? It made no sense to me then. In the year since, I have spent countless hours looking at where this nonsense is happening to librarians across the country. Sadly, my experience is by no means unique.

The worst part was it wasn't just him. Many of our community members—people I knew—shared his post. I was upset at the post and the comments, but I was devastated that people believed his lies. I had worked hard to build a reputation as a dedicated educator to my students. Parents of former students who knew me as a professional, who had once talked and joked around with me on field trips and school events, were now helping to spread the lies by sharing the posts. One parent in particular whose child I had helped with getting services for a learning disability was especially vicious. When I taught her child, she told me I was the best teacher they'd ever had. Now I was a person she wouldn't want around her child. The sense of betrayal was overwhelming. When you live in a small, two-red-light town like I do, everyone knows everyone. People whom I thought knew me, whom I had known since childhood, were suddenly turning on me.

To top it off, Ryan was a moderator of our local Facebook rants page, which at the time had forty-three thousand members. In case you aren't lucky enough to have a local community Facebook rants page, let me explain. This is a Facebook group where people in the community can share things they love or air their grievances. When you hear "airing of grievances," you might think of the famous *Seinfeld* Festivus episode. This Facebook page isn't that. Instead, it's all the grievances with none of the humor. Want to express your horror at the baked potato lunch served in the school cafeteria? Rant about it. Want to share the best places to buy horse dewormer because you think it cures COVID? Rave about it. Want to spread lies that

the local school librarian advocates giving pornography to children? We have the group for you! Ryan Thames's meme was shared to that page. The moderators turned off any ability I had to comment in that group, not that I would have, and blocked me from even viewing the post and comments. Then the dogpile really commenced.

At first I laughed, because grown adults weren't seriously posting things like that about me, were they? It was a hollow laugh that I tend to do when I'm angry, a defense mechanism. My "you've got to be effing kidding me" laugh. A laugh that's filled with anger and sadness, with disbelief, not mirth. Did adult human beings really think that it was okay to completely make up lies about me and post them on social media? But the proof shone brightly on my phone's screen in the dark of my curtains-drawn bedroom. I became petrified that I would lose my job. Ryan's claims that I had changed my name for advocating the teaching of anal sex were blatantly false, but I'd seen so many lies get traction in the blink of an eye. Of course I would fear for my future years as an educator.

I knew that social media was a vicious place. I just didn't know how diabolical it could be. I had made the decision to change my Facebook page before I went to the meeting. I had seen several librarian colleagues harassed after speaking out about censorship in their own towns, and I took preemptive measures to protect myself. I knew that there could be backlash for standing up for the LGBTQIA+ and BIPOC communities in my conservative town. But I never would have dreamed that strangers and friends would stoop so low with their lies and personal attacks.

I now realize that I went into some type of shock when the first waves of social media hate crashed over me. I've always heard that you shouldn't read the comments on posts like those, but I was unable to look away. There were moments when it became hard to swallow. It felt like there was a permanent lump in my throat and I was gasping for breath. I stared at those posts and obsessively refreshed the comments over and over the entire weekend. With every refresh of the screen, another wave of hate drowned me, leaving me open-mouthed as I saw what people I have known my entire life were commenting. The unfairness of it all made me want to scream at the top of my lungs. But how could that happen when I could barely breathe? I wanted to scream, though. I wanted to punch something. I wanted to write back on social media and explain what I actually said, even though I knew that no good would come of engaging.

The comments kept coming. Refresh. Cry. Try to breathe. Refresh. Cry. Try to breathe. Refresh. Cry. Try to breathe.

That was my weekend, and it was a dark one. I never knew that it was possible to cry so much that your eyes bruise and swell shut. I never knew you could work yourself up to the point of not being able to draw breath in your lungs, and cry so much that your sinuses close for a solid week. I never knew you could cry so much that you can soak the entire front of your shirt and a pillowcase.

That weekend I discovered that all those horrible things and so much more are possible.

———

Jason and I have a teenage daughter whom we cherish and whose character and accomplishments we are unabashedly proud of. The cliché is that raising a child in a small town is kind of ideal. And I'd certainly say that I loved growing up with two loving parents and my siblings in Livingston Parish. But if the air is fresher, the community more tightly knit, and kids can get from here to there on bikes and go swimming at the local creek, a change has come in my lifetime that I worry about, especially for my daughter.

Like so many rural communities across the country, Livingston has become redder and redder over the last decade or so. Not just red, but extremely alt-right and conspiratorial. My parents were and still are conservative. I was raised conservative, and for most of my life I voted as a registered Republican. I believe to the bottom of my heart that all sides deserve to be heard, unless hate is at play. If I have had a change in direction, my daughter was always going to go her own way. She is a strong young woman with a mind of her own, and her mind tends toward ideas that can be regarded as progressive. She has found a great group of like-minded kids, and they form a supportive Gen Alpha pack that is far more empathic than generations before them. Still, given the tilt of the place, Jason and I sometimes worry and wonder if we should be more protective.

On that Saturday and for the rest of the weekend, I desperately did not want my teenage daughter to know that anything was wrong. I didn't want her to see me cry. I definitely didn't want her to see the posts and comments. I don't know how we did it, but we kept her in the dark almost the entire weekend. We made up some excuse that I was sick and needed to stay in bed. There was some truth to that.

There are some details of that nightmarish weekend that I have blocked out, but I still feel the pain. Thinking about it, talking about it, even writing about it, can be helpful. But if I allow myself to *feel* that weekend, my heart races and I get sick to my stomach. To say that weekend was the worst weekend of my life is an understatement.

Eventually, we had to sit down and talk to our daughter. I knew that if she hadn't already been sent the posts, she soon would. Fortunately, my child doesn't use social media, but she's a teenager, and teenagers love a good community drama. Apparently so do adults.

We picked a moment and I sat her down on the couch and said, "I need to show you something. Remember how I went to the library meeting the other night? Well, some people did not like what I said and they are posting lies online, along with some hurtful memes." I handed her a copy of my speech and let her read them herself. She looked at me and said, "What's wrong with this? This seems like common sense."

I then showed her the online posts. We all three sat on the couch, and I handed her my phone. She looked at them a little shocked. I told her what was being posted was not true, and that I do not give pornography and erotica to children. I do not advocate teaching children about anal sex. She said, "Well, no crap. I was one of your students. I think these people are jerks. Is this illegal? Because it looks like cyberbullying that kids do, and that's illegal." I didn't show her the comments about violence or the name-calling beneath the original posts. Jason and I asked if she had any questions. She took it in stride and made a face, commenting, "Well, this is just dumb." She asked why someone would post those things, and I didn't have any answers for her. She wanted to know what I was going to do about it. That hit me hard. I've always taught her to stand up for herself, and here I was being tested to do the same thing. That comment would come into play later when I had decisions to make.

It's a dreadful thing to have to sit down with your child and show them lies and online harassment and explain to them that they might be bullied themselves because of it. I feared that when school started in two weeks, she would be shunned or made fun of at school. Even though it seems ridiculous now, I feared that she'd believe what was posted and be ashamed of me. I feared that she'd hate me for speaking out against censorship and complicating her social life. And I was scared to know what Jason was truly thinking of the posts. Did he wish for a wife who just stayed home and kept her thoughts to herself? I know that's not true, but you'd be surprised at the things that run through your head when faced with something traumatic.

Ryan Thames and Michael Lunsford, the self-appointed protectors of children, sure didn't think about protecting mine. I do wonder if they thought of my daughter. I imagine them sitting in a dark corner, laughing maniacally and rubbing their hands together like imbeciles, while I'm having to show my daughter a meme that says I teach children how to perform anal sex. I imagine them laughing at my humiliation. The thought angers me to the point that it scares me to feel a hatred so strong.

———

Both those two initial posts contained complete fabrications about me, embraced comments laced with hate, and grew wild with speculation. They were seen by thousands on the multiple feeds where they were shared. The algorithms were working overtime. I was called a groomer and a pedophile. Someone commented that I needed to be purged. It was said someone needed to "bring the heat" on me for pushing sexual content to preschoolers. I was labeled a sicko, pig, trash. One person wrote, "Maybe she is one of them child porn people with her sick self," while another posted, "This TRASH does not belong in a school. Period! Disgusting!" Someone else wrote, "Slap her in the back of the head so she will pay attention and shut up." Not everyone expressed such hate, but their support for me just brought hate onto themselves. When people defended me in the comments, Ryan Thames posted, "You pedophiles can kick rocks and take your leader with you." I wondered how people could believe whatever they saw on social media and think it was true. I wondered if they even thought it was true or if it just made them feel good to spread hate.

Citizens for a New Louisiana commented, "Don't worry about that teacher's school. We're going to be scheduling a visit tomorrow," and "We are headed to [my school] to see what this woman has in the library that she controls completely." What did that mean? Was that a veiled threat to harm me? My worry shifted away from me and my family. I started to worry that they would harass my co-workers and students at my school. I immediately notified my administration, school board representative, and leadership at our district office.

A day or two later, a new comment from Citizens for a New Louisiana appeared under the original post. A neighboring school's gym had burned down the day before. I believe that the fire department determined that it was an electrical fire from old wiring, but the new post claimed, "After Amanda's testimony, her school was struck by lightning and portions of it

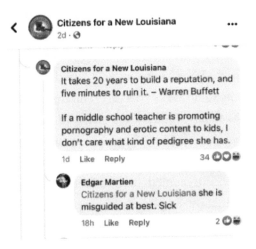

burned down. Not kidding." Were they trying to insinuate that I had caused lightning to strike a school's gym? That one threw me for a loop. Were they suggesting that God was smiting our community because I spoke out against censorship? You have to wonder at the logic of white Christian nationalists. This was the first of many comments or suggestions that would attempt to bring religion to the library discussion in our community. It was a roller coaster of emotions that weekend: shock, hate, disbelief, fear, and sadness.

As the commenters gassed each other up, the focus shifted from basic censorship at a public library meeting to a moral panic that I was handing out erotica to my students. People were having full conversations about me online. Each comment seemed to build in intensity and evolved into something more hateful, and each lie grew more far-fetched. It was a viral contagion. Citizens for a New Louisiana posted, "This is what happens when teachers push this type of material into little kids' hands." What material? Whose hands? All I did was make a statement on censorship, but people were posting like I was handing out copies of *Hustler* magazine at my school.

Although I had spoken out for our public library, the references to my job as a school librarian, and the insinuation that I was giving children sexual content, confused people. Many demanded that I be fired. I was fearful of being dismissed from the job I love with every fiber of my being. I hoped my school system would see that I had done nothing wrong. I started sweating and hives broke out on my neck. Did my students' families think that I was some sort of pervert? Did the school system?

If my story has villains, it also has plenty of heroes. I will forever be grateful to the man at our district office who reached out to me that weekend through a phone call and text messages to make sure I was okay, and who continues to send encouragement to me all these months after. He is a true leader and cares about the employees of our parish. I sent him my speech, and he reassured me that I had said nothing wrong. He reminded me that I was exercising my rights as a citizen and never mentioned in my public comments that I worked in our parish and never mentioned our school.

I remember wanting him to understand that I was not a danger to children, but he already knew this. I was shaking when we began speaking, but his practical advice calmed me down. I truly did not want this man whom I admire so much to think ill of me. I will not name him publicly for fear that he, too, will be targeted, but I wish that I could share with the world his name and how appreciative I am. He was a light in the darkness and made me feel that I was not alone. I wish other leaders had shown even a fraction of the empathy he showed me.

———

At the meeting, I had spoken about censorship only in general and didn't mention a single particular book, but Citizens for a New Louisiana posted, "It's an instruction manual. Teaching an 8-year-old how to perform a sex act is a criminal offense." What instruction manual? I never spoke about a specific book or listed any book titles. From the sadness, a rage started to emerge.

In eleventh grade, we read *The Crucible*, by Arthur Miller, about a Puritan town in New England so consumed with the hysteria of witch hunts that the people killed their own neighbors when accusations from other residents spiraled completely out of control. What was happening to me reminded me so much of the fear and hysteria in that play. "I saw Goody Amanda giving smut to kids."

As someone who has devoted thousands of hours to becoming the best educator I could be for the children of our community, and spent years solidifying myself as a community member dedicated to helping my students succeed, it was devastating to see it all come crashing down in the span of a few hours because of lies posted about me online. Citizens for a New Louisiana gleefully posted the Warren Buffett quote "It takes 20 years to build a reputation and five minutes to ruin it." Their goal was loud and clear, and nothing less than a public burning at the stake would be good enough.

Author
Citizens for a New Louisiana
Jacob Bourgeois **this book is in the kids section of the Livingston public library. We're headed to live oak middle to see what this woman has in the library she controls completely - if they'll let us in. After Amanda's testimony, her school was struck by lightning and portions of it burned down. Not kidding.**

3m   Like   Reply

My supporters in the posts were my angels. Some were friends and family, and some were strangers who immediately saw what was happening and voiced their concern. Each positive comment lessened the blows in some small way. The former students who stood up for me kept me going that weekend. But the people defending me on social media were also being attacked online—neighbors, family, and people I still viewed as students, under my protection. I didn't want them to suffer for standing up for me. I worried that my friends and family would be targeted next. Spoiler alert: they were. My sadness was palpable, but the rage intensified.

Well-meaning friends and family took screenshots of the posts and comments and texted them to me. It didn't take long for me to dread every notification from my phone. Ping. Negative post. Ping. Slanderous comments. Ping. Judgmental comments. Ping. Back to the post. I know that they were doing it to support me and make sure that I was aware of everything happening. But those well-meaning pings were constant reminders that I was the target of a full-on assault of hate. I couldn't ignore it. Even if I hadn't looked at the posts myself, they were being hand-delivered to me. When even the well-meaning people in my life were resurfacing my pain, it was too easy to feel like there was no escape.

My friends, colleagues, and family were wonderful, though. School librarians across the nation got wind of what was happening and showed up to defend me in the posts. My friend Sherri Jones, a school librarian from Washington, D.C., wrote, "This is a false and misleading meme. Amanda understands that every child should see him/herself represented. To insinuate that she is teaching anal sex is disingenuous and disheartening," and my lifelong friend Rachelle posted, "The ignorance here is painful." It felt like the cavalry had arrived. The texts from my friends on the Louisiana Association of School Librarians Executive Board that weekend mean the world to me. My friend and 2022 *School Library Journal* Librarian of the Year, K.C. Boyd, contacted people in multiple organizations to help me. My sisters constantly checked on me. I am incredibly fortunate to have such supportive friends and a network of colleagues from across the globe.

Over the ensuing days the coordination of hate quickly grew evident. I noticed that the same eight or nine people were commenting on the pages where the posts had been shared. When I looked at their social media profiles, they were all related to or friends with the two men. They might be ignorant in many ways, but they knew how social media works. Citizens for a New Louisiana began tagging the Louisiana Association of School Librarians, of which I was the current president, and someone commented, "They will answer my questions or not walk the streets without security of some type." I became afraid to step outside my own home. I'm still hesitant to do so a year later.

The buzzards wanted to circle my dead carcass and make sure I was ruined, all for the crime of speaking out against censorship at my public library. My state representative weighed in with her opinion on social media and perpetuated the lie that children needed to be protected from our library and children must be kept safe from the books on the shelves. Several months after the fact, I discovered via public records that many of the people defaming me donated to her reelection campaign around the same time of her posts that fall. They can deny it all they want, but it's my opinion that an all-out war was being waged against me, and it was a concerted, coordinated effort directed by several people.

I'd like to make one thing clear. I had never spoken to these people, in person or online. I didn't know them then and I do not know them now. They merely chose me out of all the other speakers that night to target. I have my suspicions as to why they chose me. Who better to take down than the award-winning school librarian? These men wanted to make an example out of someone and scare the community into silence.

It worked to some extent.

The large crowd that showed up to defend intellectual freedom on July 19, 2022, dwindled to only a few at the next public library board meetings. Nobody wanted to speak out if it meant becoming the next target. If they could take the first steps to completely ruin my reputation with just a few online posts, they could ruin anybody's. People told me outright they were scared to speak up and support me publicly for fear of retribution. I spoke well on July 19 and showed up the anticensorship crowd. I was able to help rally the troops for the July 19 public meeting, and they had expected a cakewalk.

Men like Michael and Ryan are intimidated by strong women, and when people have nothing of value to contribute to the conversation, they turn to personal attacks.

In a way, it was a small relief that I was the chosen target. I don't say that to act like a martyr, but I'm more aware than ever of the privilege I hold. Many others who spoke that night were sexual assault victims and members of the LGBTQIA+ community. A few were newer educators or teens. Members of the group Citizens for a New Louisiana laughed when several of the sexual assault survivors spoke out at the meeting. The people from Citizens are horrible examples of humans, but I was still shocked that someone could laugh at another person's trauma. I don't have some savior complex, but I don't wish this type of hate campaign on anyone, particularly on groups historically vilified and who have already been put through enough.

Michael Lunsford of Citizens for a New Louisiana did indeed contact my place of work. He didn't go to my school, but he submitted public records requests for my work emails, my personnel record, and the complete list of books in our school library. He knew that he wasn't going to be given my personnel record. It was an intimidation tactic.

I kind of wish that the school had given it to him. He'd see a glowing review of near-perfect evaluations and accolades. He wanted to view my disciplinary records. There are none to see. If he's searching for dirt on me, he will be searching forever because there is nothing. The funny thing about him requesting a title list of the books in our school library is that there was no need to do so. Our online library catalog is posted on the internet for anyone to view. I have nothing to hide. This notion that I'm purchasing erotica and putting it on our school library shelves is not only ridiculous but can be proved false by anyone with internet access.

After two days of crying myself dry, the pity party morphed into fury. A burning animosity began to replace the sadness. Through the slits of my swollen, puffy eyes, I began to think about ways to combat these online attacks. Every gasp of breath from hyperventilating made my right eye twitch with anger, and I was literally seeing red. The resentment was so strong that my blood pressure spiked. My husband forced me to stay in bed with my legs elevated. Instead of shaking with panic, I shook with bitterness and hatred. I realized that I had started to mumble audibly and began to be anxious about my mental state. Through all of this, I had to pretend like everything was fine so that I didn't upset my child. It was so hard to hide it.

I fantasized about revenge and the ways in which it would take place. I pictured my husband knocking the ever-loving crap out of Michael Lunsford's smug face and thought about how good it would feel to see Ryan Thames escorted to the police station in handcuffs. I thought about what I would do if I saw these people in public. Would I lose my shit and lash out? Maybe it seems odd to some of you for me to want to harm those that have harmed me. Truth be told, I knew that harm would never happen. I knew

Ryan Thames
1d · 🌐

These people are trying to normalize sex to children.

They feel justified in doing so because if they normalize it in children maybe they wont carry trauma when they are grown.

The reality is they are grooming an entire generation so that "they" can feel comfortable and so children will be less resistant to inappropriate advances.

"They"... are working in your schools and librarys to push this agenda.

Your children are being sexually targeted.... each step and action may seem harmless. But the collective of actions are deliberately taken to take advantage of vulnerable children.

👎😦 7   1 comment

I wouldn't take those steps and neither would the people who cared about me. We are not violent people, nor are we hateful.

But it does show how much I loathed what they did to me. How dare they tell these lies about me. This is *my* community of forty-four years. I have devoted half of my life to my school and my students. I thought about the hours and years of going above and beyond in my job as an educator because I love my school almost as much as I love my family. I decided that I'd be damned if I sat back and allowed these two men to destroy my life. I wasn't the first to be targeted this way, and I knew I wouldn't be the last.

Not unless I did something about it.

I decided to take matters into my own hands and reclaim my reputation. I filed police reports, hired an attorney, and started the process of taking back my life.

Chapter 2

How We Got Here

A man dies when he refuses to stand up for that which is right.
A man dies when he refuses to stand up for justice. A man dies
when he refuses to take a stand for that which is true.

—Martin Luther King Jr.

Libraries have always been places of wonder to me, and I am fiercely protective of them. We now have five amazing library branches in our parish, but I remember back when I was a child, before our community properly funded our library system, how our local branch was in a room next to a washeteria. It was so small and tiny, yet it held ideas so large. There's a certain smell that books have, and even now when I'm opening a book, the smell brings me back to those days of visiting the library as a child. The possibilities were endless. My mother allowed me to pick out whatever I wanted, and I would load a bag full of books. I was so proud to have my very own library card. When I was growing up, we would also visit the libraries in neighboring Baton Rouge. Back before cable television, streaming services, and the internet, libraries were one of the only places to get books and information. Today's libraries have pivoted over the years. They're still the place to find books and information, with the guidance of trained professionals, but they now include programs such as tea parties for teens, science experiments, and anime clubs. I can check out telescopes and cake pans and pick up free cultural passes to area museums. I can explore the world of virtual reality in our Idea Lab and print objects with 3D printers.

Libraries are important to our society, with the American Library Association reporting that there are more than sixteen thousand public libraries in the United States. *Smithsonian* magazine reported that more Americans go to libraries than the movies, and "visiting the library was 'by far' the most common cultural activity among Americans in 2019." Libraries are important to small towns like mine because they support cultural heritage and history, provide services many in our community could not otherwise afford, and are safe spaces for the most vulnerable. We use the library as a meeting space and to access Wi-Fi if we live in rural areas without internet, and there are even programs to provide snacks and meals for community members in need. The books are free, and I can check out as many as I need or want.

Books have always been important to our family. My mother would read to us almost every night: stories of Sleeping Beauty, the elves and the shoemaker, and *The Poky Little Puppy*. Before I could read on my own, my mother purchased Read-Along Book and Record titles. My sisters and I would listen to stories on our Fisher-Price record player and entire books on vinyl records. We would wait for the ding to turn the pages. It feels like we had hundreds of those and the Little Golden Books. Not everyone is as fortunate as me, to have parents who placed high value on books and could afford to purchase them.

I also grew up on the "Street." *Sesame Street*, that is. Not only did I learn things such as *ichi, ni, san* was one, two, three in Japanese, but I learned that our differences should be embraced and celebrated. With the help of LeVar Burton, I was raised to believe that I could grow up and be anything, travel anywhere, and learn anything. "Take a look, it's in a book, a Reading Rainbow." Fred Rogers taught me that it is our responsibility to take care of the most vulnerable, through his program *Mister Rogers' Neighborhood*. And, yes, Lady Elaine Fairchilde was a puppet that filled me with nightmares, but I learned things about the world that I would not have otherwise been exposed to in rural south Louisiana. Mister Rogers taught me that we can make a difference, and I watched his show daily.

My parents fostered a love of wonder and fun. When Mary Lou Retton competed in the 1984 Olympics, my mom fashioned a "balance beam" on the floor with masking tape so that my sisters and I could perform right alongside her in our living room. They also instilled a sense of patriotism. We were from the U S of A, damn it, and should be proud. We began school each day with a whole school sing-along of "This Land Is Your Land" and "My Country 'Tis of Thee." It wasn't until I was into my forties that I realized that some aspects of our country weren't so great. If my parents raised me in a conservative, religious, patriotic household, it wasn't a hate-filled home where they railed against "the left." It was a household that believed in learning, tradition, free speech, and the best aspects of America.

As I learned to read on my own, I was voracious, and my mother turned to the public library to keep me set up with books. We would go together to the library, and she introduced me to the Bobbsey Twins, the Boxcar Children, and Heidi. We often picked up my friend Rachelle for our library visits. Rachelle and I would take our time, in what seemed like hours, but was probably only ten minutes, trying to decide which Choose Your Own Adventure books we would check out. She was a fan of Trixie Belden; I was a fan of Nancy Drew. A shared love of books can grow bonds, and Rachelle and I are still friends to this day. My childhood revolved around books and reading, which is why libraries mean the world to me.

––––––––

Because libraries were at the center of my life, I had been paying close attention to attacks on the Lafayette Public Library, a parish one hour from my own of Livingston. That library system had seen a significant loss of funds and librarians after a push from Michael Lunsford of the group Citizens for a New Louisiana. I was nervous that our parish would be targeted.

In 2018, Lafayette voters failed to renew one of three property taxes that funded the Lafayette Parish library system, costing it about $3.5 million a year. A political action committee spent at least $21,500 urging voters to defeat a Lafayette Parish library tax renewal, and one of those spearheading the drive was Michael Lunsford. Michael was an administrator of the Facebook page called Lafayette Citizens Against Taxes. According to Claire Taylor, a Louisiana journalist, "Residents received in the mail slick flyers with graphics and messages similar to those used on the Facebook page. The flyers were paid for by Citizens for a New Louisiana."

The Citizens website proudly wrote, "During the April, 2018, election cycle, our research efforts exposed the library's ever-growing $42.3 MILLION surplus. This is perhaps the single largest contributing factor to their losing one of three dedicated property taxes. That defeated tax breathed its last in 2018 and will no longer be collected moving forward." In truth, the "surplus" they wrote about was the budget for the following fiscal year and was money already earmarked for the next year's expenses.

This group also managed to heavily influence library board decisions in Lafayette Parish and pushed to stop library book displays, including displays on Cajun heritage. Tom Aswell of the *Louisiana Voice* wrote, "Citizens for a New Louisiana managed to block a Black History presentation after Lunsford, through the Parish Council, managed to stack the Library Board of Control with his group's lap dogs, who took things a step further by banning *any* theme display at the library."

It's interesting to note that Michael does not live in Lafayette Parish but in St. Martin Parish, just like he does not live in my parish of Livingston, but his group's name was starting to pop up in reference to our parish's libraries. My big question was: Why?

When I saw that another employee of Citizens for a New Louisiana who didn't live in my town had started posting in our community rants page, it was a huge red flag. One day before the library meeting, she posted on that rants page that there was an upcoming library board meeting and encouraged people to attend. She also posted a page from a book, with no title or description. It said, "This is a page from a book your child may find in your public library. TAX FUNDED library. This isn't about gay vs straight vs trans. This is about what's age appropriate."

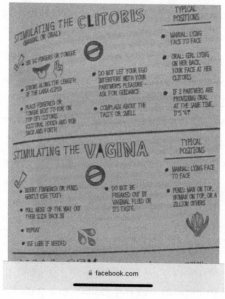

Our library is first-class, and I would do anything to protect it. Over the years, thanks to a tax millage, we have seen the library grow to five state-of-the-art branches. The Livingston Parish Public Library has accomplished wonders for our residents and is an award-winning system, which is why the Louisiana Library Association named Giovanni Tairov the 2019 Public Library Director of the Year. I fully trust his judgment and those of the other dedicated library employees. Our library has a solid collection development policy in place. Nobody is putting pornography in children's sections of the library, so someone pushing that false narrative made me suspicious. The librarians overseeing the collection have library science degrees and use professional reviews to make collection decisions. Like most libraries, we have a book challenge process if a community member doesn't like a particular book or the location of a book in the library. I also immediately wondered why, if it wasn't about gay and trans books, she felt the need to put that disclaimer in her post. She also said, "If you don't show up to and speak against this, you are okaying it." Those seemed like strong words for one page of a book. I now know that book is titled *Dating and Sex: A Guide for the 21st Century Teen Boy*. I have never read that book, but I have since looked it up on professional review sites. The book was published by the American Psychological Association and was reviewed for ages thirteen and up. I then looked at our library's online catalog and saw that our library contained one copy in just one of our five branches. It's shelved in the teen nonfiction section, not the children's section. The post was obviously made to rile people up. Why else would you take one page out of context and post it on Facebook and tell people to attend the library board meeting if you weren't trying to create some type of controversy?

Earlier in the summer, I had spoken to several friends of mine who worked at our public library. There was rumor afoot that a library board member had been making comments about LGBTQIA+ books and was questioning the purchase of certain books. These librarians all had an impending sense of doom that there would be a move to censor books with LGBTQIA+ characters. I told them if that happened, to let me know, and I would help get community members to speak out against it.

When I saw the post on Facebook, I got curious and pulled up the agenda of the Library Board of Control meeting. I saw that book content and signage were listed on the meeting agenda. From following censorship news and efforts across the United States, and particularly censorship in nearby Lafayette Parish, I knew that talks about "book content" almost always targeted LGBTQIA+ stories. The mention of signage sounded eerily similar to the display controversy in Lafayette Parish, which was created by Citizens for a New Louisiana.

I messaged my friends at our public library to ask what was going on. They were all very concerned about what this agenda item could mean. One said that she thought the signage agenda item could have been related to book displays for Pride Month. One said that he had received emails from the particular board member and feared censorship was coming, but he wouldn't go into detail about why he felt this way. He was afraid that if he spoke about it, he could lose his job.

My biggest concern after those discussions was that there would be a discussion at the meeting about censoring books with LGBTQIA+ and sexual health resources. Sexual reproduction is a taboo subject in my town.

There's virtually no sexual reproduction taught in our school system, and abstinence is preached around town. I grew up thinking that sex before marriage was an automatic ticket to hell, or genital warts at the very least. Children in our parish are not exposed to the dangers of sexually transmitted diseases, how to have safe sex, or how to stop pregnancy unless they are lucky enough to have honest parents. It's important that they have a place to find factual information like the library, rather than getting it from a random friend or internet website.

I was also upset at the thought that someone would want to censor books by LGBTQIA+ authors or protagonists, especially by a group that wasn't even from our parish. For several years, I had been alarmed by the derogatory comments I had heard friends and family say about the queer community. Things like "They are pushing their agenda on us." And "the gays are cramming their lifestyle choice down our throats." The only gay agenda I have ever seen is one in which the LGBTQIA+ community wants to be treated equally and have people leave them alone. There was no way I was going to miss an opportunity to speak out at that public library board meeting. In fact, I felt an obligation to my LGBTQIA+ friends, family, and students to do so.

I called and messaged several of my friends, including school librarians, and told them I thought we should all be at the meeting as a show of support for our library system and our public librarian colleagues. I messaged friends in the LGBTQIA+ community and told them my fears and asked them to show up. I pressed on them the importance of being there for that meeting, even if they didn't speak. I remember telling my friend Heather, "These assholes are coming for our books and our libraries. I need to be there and make a statement."

Libraries are for everyone, but our community often makes it clear that the LGBTQIA+ community is not welcome. I wanted to go and speak about the harmful effects that censoring these books can have on our LGBTQIA+ students. I have taught queer students who have been mocked in our community. They are name-called, treated as unequal, and often shunned. I have taught queer kids who grew up and took their own lives due to the loneliness of ostracization and have watched dozens of our younger citizens move away from our parish to more inclusive environments because they are sick of their ill-treatment. I'll be damned if I'm going to stand in silence while we lose another kid because of something our community has done to make them feel less-than. But I also worried about the library in general and was concerned about where this was headed.

———

It took less than an hour to write my speech. I was so mad that I was banging on my computer's keyboard. My original version was very strongly worded. I think I used words like *fascist* and *authoritarian regime*. I waited an hour and decided to give it another look. After getting out a first draft, I ditched any language that I thought sounded inflammatory. I had originally written an accusation against the board member in my first draft but took it out, since I felt that was unfair to her. I wanted to hear what she had to say first. I added the statement, "I hope that what I am about to say is not needed, and that my fear that a member of the board is trying to censor books and signage is unfounded." I wanted to show that I hoped I had been misinformed about what was happening. I also added a reminder that our parish is composed of citizens from all walks of life.

Driving to the meeting, I was very nervous. I had given countless presentations and talks to roomfuls of librarians and educators, but I had never spoken at a public meeting. Speaking to a room full of people whose mindsets on libraries you're unsure of can be very intimidating. I didn't know what would happen or who would be there. The fear of the unknown had my hands a little shaky on the drive. It seemed like everyone was up in arms online over that Facebook post. I wondered if there would be protestors and yelling. I was definitely on edge.

It takes twenty-five minutes to get to the main branch, where our public meetings are held. It's a drive through winding, country back roads shaded by oak trees. I remember getting a bit nostalgic on the drive, thinking of our libraries and how much our parish had grown in the past few years. I passed by our local pizza restaurant, aptly named the Pizza Place, and remembered how we would sometimes get lucky and stop for pizza after a library visit when I was younger, and how I sometimes do that now with my own child. I was going over the speech in my mind and realized that I was making faces as I drove. I reminded myself to relax my face while I was speaking. I practiced deep breathing, but my heart was beating a mile a minute.

I drove in silence and remember thinking how loud it must have been when my mom brought the three of us kids plus our friends to the library when we were growing up. We are a family of screechers, who all talk over each other, so I'm sure those drives were not meditative like that night's drive was for me. I honestly don't know how my mother kept her sanity with all the noise, and I was thinking how quiet my only child was in comparison. I remember wondering if I should have brought my daughter. I'm glad I did not. I didn't ever want those people to see her or the taint of their viciousness to even be in the same room. My heart seemed to race faster with each turn on the road as I got closer to the library. I was hoping to see people I knew and was afraid that nobody would show up except people wanting to censor books.

———

I pulled up to the library about an hour before the meeting and parked right in front. Stepping out of the air-conditioned car, I was reminded how hot and humid a July day in Louisiana can be, even in the evenings. The air was thick. I broke a sweat the minute I opened the door, and I remember not wanting to walk in with a "sweatstache" (sweaty upper lip). Fortunately, I reconnected with my best friend the air conditioner when the library's sliding glass doors whooshed open and I was hit with a blast of cold air. And then that old familiar, comforting smell of books. I stepped through the doors and took a left into the meeting room, nervously wondering where to sit. I saw the library director, Giovanni Tairov, and asked him if I had to sign up to speak. He gave me a rundown of how the meeting would go and what to do when it was time to speak. Little did I know that that first in-person conversation with him would spark a friendship based on our love of libraries.

More people started to show up, and I knew several of them. When you grow up in a small community, you always know someone in the room. I cannot stop at a single store in my town without running into at least one person I know. If you don't know someone personally, you know their cousin's neighbor's best friend. I usually run into at least one person I attended school with and at least one former student or one of their family members. After teaching for twenty-two years, people are often in both of those categories. I used to love this about our community before July 19, 2022. Now it was something I feared.

Soon after I walked in, I saw a friend I'd known since elementary school, and she introduced me to her teenage daughters. It was so good to see her, and her friendly face was calming. To be around Kiesha is to be around pure happiness and joy. I saw my friend Jessica, whose children I teach, who I knew was a big library supporter. I always love talking to Jessica so that I can praise her parenting. I have never met more vibrant, self-assured children than hers, and I hope that her positive parenting style rubs off on me when I'm around her. Talking to everyone settled my fears a little. These were people I knew.

I walked around chatting with people, catching up. I saw a family with a sign that said, LIBRARIES ARE FOR EVERYONE, and it warmed my heart to see that those kids were from my school. I approached the mother, Catlin, and told her how wonderful her daughter Eden was and that I was looking forward to teaching Catlin's sons in the fall. I recognized a woman named Kelci whom I had seen comment on social media about the library agenda, and we bonded over her cardigan as we met for the first time. She told me she loved libraries and worked as a communications manager at LSU. My friends Tammy, Kristy, and Tiffany attended the meeting in moral support of me, but also because they are from our community and love libraries. They are on the executive board of the Louisiana Association of School Librarians with me. We discussed where to sit. All of us were attending a public library board meeting for the first time.

Everyone was wondering about the book content and signage items on the agenda. Were we worrying over nothing, or was there about to be a

censorship attempt on our library? Some people were mad at the woman who had posted the book page insinuating that our library carried inappropriate content for children. Everyone was concerned, but there was no negative talk. Discussions were very lighthearted until they suddenly weren't. A group of people walked in, and you could almost feel the temperature drop in the room.

The apparent leader of this contingent had a self-important air about him. He acted like everyone was dying to meet him and circled the room introducing himself and handing out business cards. I try not to judge a book by its cover, but this cover was smug with an air of arrogance. That man was Michael Lunsford from Citizens for a New Louisiana. He doesn't live or work in our community, and he came with a small entourage. In attendance with him was Jamie Pope, another employee of Citizens for a New Louisiana, also not a resident of our parish. Jamie was the woman who posted the book page on our local social media page. She likes to consider herself a journalist, because she often writes the blog for Citizens, but really all she writes is online snark with the spelling and grammar of a child of ten. Although I've never spoken to her in person, she seems to take pride in putting down anyone who disagrees with her. She has posted that she is persona non grata in the media section of our state legislature. It's easy to understand why.

It's funny when people say a hush can fall over a room, but it really can. Someone murmured, "Who is that plastic dickhead?" I snorted, because, yes, I can be snarky too. He did indeed look like he was made of plastic and had the vibe of a big jerk. The board members began arriving and sat behind the front tables. They smiled at each other and said hello. Everyone looked friendly except for that one group. We didn't have much time to discuss the arrival of "the Plastics," because the meeting began as the final board member arrived and took her seat. The house was packed.

I didn't know any of the library board members except one, who had been the librarian at my school before me. We are not friends, and I hadn't seen her in the years since she left our school. I knew that she had a library science degree, but I wasn't sure who anyone else on the board was or their thoughts on censorship. I wondered what her thoughts were or if she even knew why there were so many people at the meeting. I wondered if any of them knew. They all seemed quite taken aback by the crowded room, and one of the board members kept looking around in wonderment.

The board member who had listed the item on the agenda started off by saying she wanted to talk about book content. She had a few handouts she gave the other board members and apologized for not having enough copies to go around the room. She said that she was concerned about some of the books in the library and started flipping through her packet.

She stated, "I'm concerned about the content in regard to children and young adult section. I have found it to be inappropriate and I need the board to look at it. You probably have no idea where I'm coming from, so for us to have this discussion, I wrote some books down so that you can go home and look at it. There's more. There's just so many, I don't know how to track it or address it. It is very tedious and complex."

That's the basic gist of what she said. I could tell she seemed ill-prepared for the number of people who showed up and was nervous. She never really articulated what her concern was, just that there was a concern to be had.

The floor opened for public comment on the agenda, and I was the very first person to speak. I reminded the board that the citizens of our parish consist of taxpayers who are white, Black, brown, gay, straight, Christian, non-Christian—people from all backgrounds and walks of life, and no one portion of the community should dictate what the rest of the citizens have access to. Just because a select few don't want to read it or see it, it doesn't give anyone else the right to deny others or demand its relocation. If we remove or relocate books with LBGTQ or sexual health content, what message is that sending to our community members?

I said what I had come to say. I reminded the board that in our parish we are almost all taught that God is love. I told them that what I've come to realize is that what many people mean is that God is love only if you have the same religious and political beliefs as them. I told them I was a forty-four-year resident, a mother of a child in our school system, and a library card holder since 1983. I reminded them that our public library was one of our parish's biggest assets—something we can be proud of—and reminded them, regardless of their own beliefs on the topic of book content and location, to think about this: no one on the right side of history has ever been on the side of censorship and hiding books. I said, "Hate and fear disguised as moral outrage have no place in Livingston Parish."

My voice cracked as I talked, my mouth grew extremely dry, and my hands shook the paper I was holding. I rested my hands on the podium so nobody would notice. I felt all the eyes weighing me down and couldn't wait for it to be over. I glanced up, and one of the board members nodded at me reassuringly. I kept talking. I glanced back up and saw a glare coming from Erin Sandefur, the board member who had objections to content. I wished I had written less because I was starting to sound long-winded, even to myself. As I was speaking, I heard a female voice from the group sitting with Michael Lunsford say, "This isn't even about censorship." I briefly wondered how she knew what it was supposedly about when nobody else in the room seemed to know. I finally finished and had never been so glad to be finished with something in my life. I shakily returned to my seat with a sigh of relief.

I said nothing earth-shattering. I spoke from the heart and said what I needed to say about censorship in general. I tried to be fair to the board member who had placed book content on the agenda. I didn't know her and wanted to give her the benefit of the doubt. Looking back, that was very naive of me. That woman makes Dolores Umbridge look like a saint, and, like Harry Potter, I must not tell lies. I said that she had once posted on social media that there are folks who do not agree with you and that we can be one of your greatest teachers. I told her that is an admirable statement and that I would love to teach her about how censorship, book policing, and agenda items like these affect our youth and historically marginalized community members.

I wasn't the only person who spoke. Many other people then got up and spoke. Some were heated. Some were calm. A grandmother said, "Despite whatever pretty words I think we've all heard about being concerned about what's in our collection, I want to make sure that we're being honest about what this discussion is. It's an attempt to remove content from the Public Library system and an effort to censor the voices of historically oppressed and marginalized communities. The board in this system has a responsibility to make decisions that align a library with mission and vision statements listed on the library website. I believe the content that Erin took offense to, and maybe some of the other parents and elected officials, are specifically LGBTQIA+. Those stories and voices are being targeted nationwide."

Another parent stated, "Before you discard my argument as just liberal propaganda, you may need to know I am a very conservative evangelical Christian. My family and I attend Live Oak Baptist Church every week. I've taught Sunday school for the past fifteen years, and I teach an inductive adult Bible class weekly. My personal views on homosexuality align with my conservative Southern Baptist faith and the Bible. However, my personal convictions are mine, while the Public Library is for everyone and is funded by everyone in the parish, conservative, liberal, Christian, and non-Christian alike. Our libraries are safe educational spaces for all within our parish."

Honestly, the testimonies were amazing. Our community was heartfelt, and the words were raw honesty. People spoke against censorship, spoke about the importance of books on sexual reproduction from the perspective of being sexual assault victims, and members of the LGBTQIA+ community talked of feeling safe and included at the library. Several brave women even spoke about their sexual assaults and why sexual health books were important. When several sexual assault survivors spoke, the group sitting around Michael Lunsford was making snide remarks and laughing. One speaker even stopped to call them out. She said, "I am ashamed of that board member over there. And the of two people sitting behind me who are rudely making comments. That is a shame on you."

I was seething. Who laughs at victims of sexual assault? The callousness shown during those testimonies was infuriating, but it goes to show you what type of human beings they are. Anyone who can mock a victim is not a kind person, but I've also seen their mocking blog and social media posts making fun of the LGBTQIA+ community. They put their hate on full display and do not even try to hide it. For the crowd who wants to "protect the children," they sure do set a bad example.

Nobody at that meeting, including myself, advocated for pornographic material to be kept in children's sections of the library. I mentioned in my speech that there was no pornography in our library. In fact, none of the books in our public library even contain sexually explicit material as defined by law. This is something important to note, because in the days after the meeting, it was insinuated that anyone who opposed censorship was for pornography being in the library, or sexually explicit material being available to children. Age-appropriate books on sexual reproduction in the teen section of our library is not giving children pornography.

In fact, almost everyone spoke along the same lines as me, or spoke on the importance of LGBTQIA+ and sexual health materials. Finally, Michael Lunsford spoke. He started out by saying, "This is an issue. It's going to be coming up all over the state of Louisiana and is actually coming up all over the country right now. I guess buckle up, I apologize, but it's just the way it's going to be." Kelci and I glanced across the room at each other with a knowing look. We both saw right through him, the man who had been a thorn in the side of the Lafayette Parish Library one parish over.

He wondered out loud why we were all even at the meeting, as if it wasn't his own co-worker who had posted on the community Facebook page. Michael stated, "I'm thinking to myself, Who in the world in the state of Louisiana in all sixty-four Parish Library board control meeting agendas that generally come out forty-eight hours ahead of time. Who can get together a large group of political activists to come here and fight? I could promise you it wasn't me. I did not tell a soul I was coming." Sure, Mikey.

Those comments really made me roll my eyes. He insinuated someone was trying to cause issues. Yes: him. His out-of-town group was trying to start a controversy. I know that I audibly sighed. Everyone in that room except for his group were residents. Referring to the concerned residents as activists also garnered a look to the heavens. The room was filled with local people. The only political activists in the room were his group. I wanted to shout that he could take his ass back to his own parish. I refrained. Michael suggested that there were explicit materials right next to *Green Eggs and Ham* on the shelves. As if. It was a bunch of bluster with no evidence.

The next speaker had something to say about Michael's insinuations. He said, "I am from Walker. I would like to address part of what the last gentleman was asking, which is why we're all here. In my mind, he made it very clear that there's a bizarre sort of implication that we are part of some grand conspiracy. My friend [redacted], who like me was a graduate of Walker High, tagged me on Facebook. It's a nefarious political machine that some of you may have heard about." I snorted so hard that snot came out, and I quickly tried to recover.

He went on to ask, "Ms. Sandefur, respectfully, at the beginning of this meeting, you indicated that you wanted some of these books to be looked at. Why? Could you give a specific reason? What do you find objectionable? It seems that most of the books had LGBTQIA+ content. Why do you find that objectionable? Do you have a problem with the fact that young people in this parish are being made to know that LGBTQIA+ people exist?" That indeed was the question of the evening, and she could not answer it.

I was so proud of my community for showing up, speaking, and shutting down the censors. Book censors will often say there are books containing pornographic or sexually explicit material in children's sections of the library to rile up public fear. They decry the need to protect children from the evil smut they say is next to Dr. Seuss books. As if a kid could be looking for *The Very Hungry Caterpillar* and whoops, there's *The Joy of Sex* or the *Kama Sutra* right next to it. That's never the case. Libraries have collection development policies for ordering books, and appropriate books are placed in the appropriate section. Public libraries do not purchase pornography. Adult books are not in the library's children section, and to suggest otherwise is ridiculous.

When the public commenting seemed to be closing down, I raised my hand like a student in school and said, "Can I ask a question of the board? I mean, we already have a reconsideration policy in place, so anyone who objects to these things can already do that. So I guess I'm just confused as to why there's a discussion when there's already a policy in place. I would think as a board member you would know there's already a policy in place."

Mrs. Sandefur replied, "I do want to say I said two words—book content. I don't know who took this and ran with it and turned it into censorship and banning. I feel like many of you have fallen victim to the polarization coming from the media. I said two words: *book content.* There's been lots of propaganda I've heard repeated back to me." We all looked around, confused, because it hadn't been in the media. Nobody knew what she was talking about, because there had been nothing in anything other than social media.

She then said, "What you see here is a spin that someone on social media put on this to turn it into banning and censorship. And that is not what it is. None of us have said that." The social media post was from her friend from Citizens for a New Louisiana. What propaganda was she talking about? And did she think we were stupid? Everybody started mumbling and rolling their eyes. Her comment reminded me of Donald Trump spewing conspiracy theories and then saying, "Do the research. It's fake news."

Erin had added book content to the agenda but really failed to articulate what she was trying to do that night. The discussion kind of petered out, and the board moved on. We thought that was it. I started to get happy inside, and Kelci and I glanced across the room again at each other with a smile. I leaned into my friend Kristy next to me and asked, "Is that it? Are we done?" We thought it was over, and I breathed a sigh of relief. Boy, were we wrong.

When the meeting was over, we all kind of looked at each other with hesitant smiles. There wasn't another library board meeting for two months, so we assumed we had kept off the censors and that was that. Right? People were rehashing some of the comments. Others were hugging, noticing friends in the room for the first time. Calls of "Tell your mom I said hello" were heard in the room. Several people were angry at Michael Lunsford. Everyone knew by his behavior and snide utterings during the meeting that he was not an ally of the LGBTQIA+ community, and I could tell by the other speeches that most people in the room were allies. Not only were we allies, but we were locals and he was not. The crowd started slowly dispersing.

Michael started the nonsense of walking around with his business cards again, like he thought we were all waiting to be thrown one like we were at a Mardi Gras parade. A friend of mine did snag one. For some reason, I took a picture of it for documentation. I didn't really know what I was documenting. I was also mystified that someone could have such little self-awareness that he didn't realize nobody wanted to talk to him. Maybe he just didn't care? He obviously felt disdain for our library and our community. It was easy to see that he'd been invited from out of town and was only at the meeting to further the agenda of censorship and chaos. I wondered who had invited him in the first place. Was it Erin Sandefur?

In my opinion, the censors really just wanted to target books with queer and BIPOC authors and characters. That became evident when the titles of five of the eight books on the list of books Erin had given to other board members were published the next day in the paper. But some of these people were also about using the library as a pawn to stir up drama for monetary or political reasons. It's been no secret that a small portion of our residents, and even a Livingston Parish council member, would like to take tax money from the library and use it for our parish's drainage issue. There was a

Citizens for a New Louisiana
13 hrs · 🌐

Kids shouldn't be exposed to pornography. People who say otherwise shouldn't be allowed near kids.

👍❤️ 698   68 Comments 48 Shares

👍 Like   💬 Comment   ↗ Share

meeting one year prior in which they tried to do that.

Ryan Thames himself has implied that he wants to see the library defunded because he doesn't believe in taxes going toward a public library. People like Michael and Ryan seem to think that none of us can see through hidden agendas and that we would fall for Michael's snake-oil-salesman pitch as if we were born yesterday. You might be asking yourself: Where was Ryan Thames during this meeting? He sat dead center of the room, one row back from me. He never spoke during public comment, which is ironic, since he would go on weeks later about how he was there to "protect the children." I guess protecting children means just sitting there, looking sullen.

A few days after the meeting, when I saw the onslaught of negativity and falsehoods being told not only about me but about the library, it seemed that some people in my town had indeed been born yesterday. Or at least, a very loud vocal minority had been. While the people in the library board meeting that night had been library lovers, readers, and allies, others in the community it seems, hadn't been not. They fell for the lies hook, line, and sinker.

But the people that night at the small-town library board meeting, who had showed up to defend it knew exactly what was going on.

Chapter 3

Here, There, Everywhere

A **challenge** is an attempt to remove or restrict materials, based upon the objections of a person or group. A **banning** is the removal of those materials. Challenges do not simply involve a person expressing a point of view; rather, they are an attempt to remove material from the curriculum or library, thereby restricting the access of others.

—AMERICAN LIBRARY ASSOCIATION

I t's hard to get people to see the truth when even your legislator piles on. I wonder about my local representative's character and how she thinks of herself when she so callously uses people for her own political gain. People willing to knock down others on a climb toward power are not the kind of people I want to be around. Regardless, people seem to believe everything they see on the internet these days, and there's nothing I can really do about it. So I watched helplessly as all the hard work I had done to build up a professional, positive reputation and a well-respected library program was washed down the drain as people misconstrued my speech and disregarded the fact that I had spoken at a public library board meeting and not about my school's library. The truth didn't really matter to them, and unfortunately this was happening to librarians across the country.

The fact is, it's not really about the truth, but truth is where I need to start. There are misconceptions these days about the purposes of libraries, and the reality that there are policies already in place to protect patrons and students often gets overlooked. There are lies being told about organizations such as the American Library Association, and people seem confused about the differences in materials found in an elementary versus high school library, as well as the differences between public libraries and school libraries. I'm going to attempt to dispel a few of the falsehoods being told by the alt-right talking heads who don't seem to have stepped into a library since they were children decades ago. So please pardon me while I put on my cardigan, push my glasses up my nose, and attempt to explain a few of the little-known intricacies of today's modern libraries.

First, there are vast differences between public and school libraries in regard to collection development and shelving. I don't expect the average citizen to know that all libraries have collection development policies, which describe how books are chosen for their library. These usually require guidance from professional review sources, and there are selection criteria that must be met. Professional reviews are found in journals like *Kirkus Reviews*, *Booklist*, *School Library Journal*, and *Publishers Weekly*. Librarians should never use crowdsourced reviews from Amazon, where anyone, including children, can write reviews. Those are okay for personal purchases but shouldn't be used to guide library selection decisions. Another source never to be used is BookLooks. This is a website created by a Moms for Liberty leader. This site takes book passages out of context, the rating system is questionable, and the majority of the books found objectionable are books with LGBTQIA+ characters and themes.

Librarians will read reviews to help determine purchasing and placement in public libraries. In public libraries, patrons can also request books to be purchased. In school libraries, librarians will often include students, teachers, and parents in the decision-making process for ordering books.

A public library serves patrons from birth to death, and the collection is usually broken into sections: children, young adult/teen, and adult. This means that books are ordered for all age ranges and then placed accordingly based on librarian expertise and professional review sources. In a school library, the school serves a certain age group of children, so books are ordered for the age relevancy of that school group.

For instance, my school is a fifth through sixth grade school. I would not have Stephen King's *It* at my school, because it's professionally reviewed for adults. Trust me, I've had many students request it. That doesn't mean I don't value the book if I don't have it in our school library. It means that I select books according to the ages of our students. Different books are written for different-age readers, and librarians always take that into consideration when making purchases. This is why library policies should be created by professional librarians who understand these differences and nuances. I get so frustrated when a member of our Parish Council, the local governing board, tries to say how libraries "should be." Not only are these critics not trained, but most have never stepped foot in our public libraries. They don't understand collection development and the purchasing decisions librarians must make.

Librarians cannot possibly read every single book before making a purchase, although we do try. Librarians are human, after all. Public librarians order thousands of books each year for their patrons. School librarians, those who are fortunate enough to have budgets, order hundreds if not thousands of books for their collections. Each year, I am given a very small budget. I must make decisions wisely. I ask for student and teacher suggestions, provide book catalogs so that students can make requests, and check all reviews for age relevancy before ordering books. I want our students to have input, and I want to select books they are going to read. Nothing makes me happier than to see a student's face light up when a book comes in that they requested. I try to make sure I order books to meet the needs of all teachers and students, maintain a diverse collection, choose books that will be popular and checked out from the shelves, and order new books as well as replacing older classics that are falling apart. There's a science to placing book orders, and there are entire classes in graduate school on how to create and follow collection development policies.

However, sometimes someone will not agree with a choice. That's why there are challenge and reconsideration policies. Challenge or reconsideration policies allow patrons (in public libraries) or the parents (in school libraries) to lodge complaints about a book and ask for it to be either relocated or removed. Some libraries will remove a book from the shelf while a book is being reconsidered. The American Library Association has created Guidelines for Reconsideration Committees, which states, "Challenged materials should not be removed from the collection while under reconsideration." Pro-censors will claim that a book isn't banned if it is returned to the shelf, but a book unavailable to readers even for a few days was still banned at one point. I get upset when I hear about libraries taking books off the shelves while going through the review process, because as a friend of mine named Marla pointed out at a recent library board meeting, books should be considered innocent until proven guilty, just like people.

Most public libraries also have guidelines for unaccompanied minors, which state that parents should accompany their children in the library. It is the responsibility of parents to monitor their own children and which sections they are allowed to browse in public libraries. At the 2023 Louisiana legislative hearing for SB7, then attorney general Jeff Landry said, "Parents should be able to drop off their children at the local library without them stumbling upon sexually explicit material." When it was time for me to speak, I countered, "Libraries are not daycare centers." A parent shouldn't just drop off their child at the local courthouse or Walmart, just like they shouldn't be dropping their minor children off at the library. Public libraries have adult sections because they also serve adults. If you don't want your child near adult material, you should monitor your own child.

At a recent Livingston Parish Public Library Board of Control meeting in my community, a board member suggested that we should not allow anyone under the age of eighteen in the library without a parent in case they go into the adult section. That was a new twist on our local library complaints. Our current policy is that anyone thirteen years old and younger should be with an adult. Our director said that there had been no issues in our library about this matter, other than a few younger students ages eleven and twelve walking unaccompanied to the library after school in one branch that was next to a school. Someone pointed out that sixteen- and seventeen-year-olds can drive, and that person would rather they go to the library to study or check out materials than go somewhere else where they could get in trouble. I asked John Chrastka of EveryLibrary his opinion, and he pointed out that in Louisiana sixteen-year-olds can get married. I hadn't even thought of that. Sixteen-year-olds can also have jobs. Wanting to ban a sixteen- or seventeen-year-old from entering the library without an adult when they can work and get married at that age is perverse to me. Kids younger than sixteen cannot drive alone. They wouldn't be in the library unaccompanied anyway unless they were dropped off. And again, libraries are not daycare centers. Monitor your own child. It is not the responsibility of the library to do so.

––––––––

The scene that played out at our public library board meeting in July 2022 is not unique to Livingston Parish. It's not even unique to Louisiana. In fact, it's happening all over the United States. Because I'm from the south, I thought that it was a "southern issue," but I soon discovered that it is happening coast to coast. It's not confined to Republican majority towns or states and it's happening in both rural and urban areas. However, censorship attempts are being pushed from the Far Right. I get dirty looks and comments when I mention to Republican friends that all book banners seem to be Republican, even if all Republicans don't agree with book banning. It is similar to the math concept that all squares are rectangles even if all rectangles are not squares. People don't want to hear that logic. I get angry that they refuse to admit it.

I had been eyeing my neighboring state of Texas, and following the work of the FReadom Fighters, a group of school librarians taking a stand in Texas. They organized a series of positive campaigns on social media and created a website with frequently asked questions that school librarians or parents might have about library procedures and policies. I had even previously presented at conferences on the topic of censorship and was a speaker on a panel with Britten Follett, CEO of Follett School Solutions, and the celebrated author Nikki Grimes, whose own books are often targeted by censors. I was ready for censorship attempts in our schools. I was not ready to confront the issue in my local public library, even though the war on libraries in Louisiana began in 2018 in Lafayette Parish.

In October 2018, Lafayette Parish announced plans to host a drag queen story hour at the public library. What ensued were protests, a lawsuit, a temporary moratorium for use of library meeting spaces, the resignation of the president of the library board, and public outcry at Lafayette City-Parish Council meetings. According to Melanie Brevis, a Lafayette resident, mother and anticensorship activist, "The library is an innovative, progressive beacon here in Lafayette. Its job is not to make everyone comfortable with every single program. If you don't like it, don't go, or just pretend it's not happening." The religious groups Warriors for Christ and Special Forces of Liberty filed a lawsuit to stop the event. The ACLU got involved, and eventually the Drag Queen Story Hour was held, but the event sent ripples through the parish's public library system, costing money and the addition of library board members with religious agendas.

A push by those in opposition, including Citizens for a New Louisiana, was successful in lobbying against a library property tax renewal, called a millage, which cost the Lafayette Public Library $3.5 million in funding. I was a little confused as to what exactly a millage was, so I turned to the Michigan Library Association's website, which states, "A millage is a tax on property, levied at the local, municipal level after being approved through a popular vote on a ballot initiative. The millage is the amount per $1,000 of the taxable value of property. For example, a 1 mill tax rate on a home valued at $100,000 would generate $100 in taxes."

The Lafayette City-Parish Council then failed to roll forward the millage, which cost the library an additional $1 million a year. If property assessments go up, the amount local government taxes you, a millage, gets rolled back so that you're not paying more. Local government can legally roll forward millages or choose not to do so. A loss of a millage, or the failure of a governing board to roll forward a millage, can be devastating to library budgets. Lafayette then had a vote passed to take an additional $8 million from the library's fund to put toward funding for drainage systems. Lafayette's Public Library System saw a huge loss in funding, which was soon felt in the halting of construction projects, loss of staff, fewer materials, and a cutback in programming events for the community.

Two people who had voiced public opposition to the drag queen story hour were then voted onto the library board, and one of them, Robert Judge, was voted president of the Lafayette Public Library Board of Control. People were concerned about his appointment, and rightfully so in my opinion. Robert Judge wears a giant cross around his neck and seems to think he's some sort of religious authority in Lafayette. I really had no thoughts on him one way or another until I found out about a post he made on a grieving mother's LinkedIn social media page.

During Pride Month, a mother posted the following about her child, a member of the LGBTQIA+ community who had taken his own life: "What I wouldn't give to be celebrating this with my son. Damn you, suicide." Robert then thought it appropriate to reply to her, "There is an internal struggle to attempt to justify an immoral and unhealthy lifestyle. The natural law is written on our hearts and no matter how we attempt to erase it with lies, the truth comes forth. Affirming one in a lifestyle that is sinful is mean and cruel and not loving at all." He wrote that on a grieving mother's post. That about sums up what type of person he is—the opposite of what he pretends to be in public.

Robert Judge allegedly violated open meeting laws in August 2023 when he spearheaded the firing of the library director in an executive session, which prompted a lawsuit and a petition by Lafayette Citizens Against Censorship to remove Judge from the library board. He also had a community member arrested at an earlier library board meeting for speaking out of turn, and hired security to have Melanie Brevis escorted out of a library board meeting for criticizing him. Judge told meeting attendees that they weren't allowed to make derogatory remarks against the board at meetings, thus prompting another lawsuit by Louisiana Citizens Against Censorship founders Lynette Mejia and Brevis and the Tulane First Amendment Law Clinic, for First Amendment rights violations. Lafayette continues to fight against censorship attempts to this day, and community members faithfully show up and speak on behalf of intellectual freedom and their public library.

———

Every day I wake up wondering who or where the next hate campaign will be launched. All across the country hate speech is running rampant, funding is being threatened, and our libraries are under attack. People are no longer hiding their racism. I don't know if I'm relieved, because at least they are showing their true colors so that we can identify them, or if I'm just sad and wish they'd go back to hiding it. Conservative groups have attacked both school and public libraries over "critical race theory," "porn," Drag Queen Story Hours, hosting LGBTQIA+ authors, antiracist messages, and more. A record number of books were challenged in 2022.

The American Library Association published its "State of America's Libraries 2023" report and noted that "since the fall of 2020, reports submitted to the ALA's Office for Intellectual Freedom document a precipitous rise in the number of attempted book bans in school and public libraries across the United States. In 2022, the Office for Intellectual Freedom received a record 1,269 book challenges, the highest number of demands to ban books reported to ALA since the association began compiling data about censorship in libraries. This nearly doubles the 729 book challenges reported to the Office for Intellectual Freedom in 2021.

Pro-censors challenged 2,571 books in 2022, a 38 percent increase from the 1,858 books targeted for censorship in 2021. Of those titles, the vast majority were written by or about members of the LGBTQIA+ community or by and about Black people, Indigenous people, and people of color." Many of those books were challenged from multiple people across the country. The ALA also reported that "the prevalent use of lists of books compiled by organized censorship groups contributed significantly to the skyrocketing number of challenges and the frequency with which each title was challenged. Of the overall number of books challenged, 90% were part of attempts to censor multiple titles. Of the books challenged, 40% were in cases involving 100 or more books." Those were just the number of challenges reported. We don't really even have an accurate depiction of how widespread these censorship attempts are, which is scary to me.

The groups challenging books are highly organized and well funded. As we have seen here in Louisiana, the challengers often have never even read the books. They copy and paste from erroneous websites, and the complaints are frequently rife with errors. Often the reasons listed in the challenges aren't related to the book being challenged. Someone in nearby St. Tammany Parish filled out a challenge form under the name Mickey Mouse.

Something even more frightening to think about is the number of book challenges that go unreported. The American Library Association believes that as many as 97 percent of challenges are not even being documented. America should be alarmed at the thought of books being pulled from shelves because of a few well-organized people with agendas that have more to do with divisive politics than books, education, and libraries. And we are seeing only the tip of the iceberg.

I know of a book that was removed from the shelves of a neighboring school by the school's principal because a parent came and complained. The parent did not file a formal book challenge. The principal did not follow the book challenge policy, did not consult the district, and forced the librarian to remove it from the school's library all at the request of one parent who admittedly hadn't read the book. The fact the book was professionally reviewed for that school's age group did not matter. The decision was made by a principal whose only experience in the classroom was as a PE instructor, who hadn't read the book, and who had no training in library science. The librarian was too scared to fight back or say anything. She was even too scared to report it to the Office for Intellectual Freedom, so I reported it anonymously for her. How many instances like this are happening across the country?

Everyone in the United States should stand up for intellectual freedom and stand against censorship, regardless of party line. You start banning one thing, and you're on a slippery slope to banning everything. We have seen this happen when groups angry at the banning of LGBTQIA+ books challenge the Bible to make a point of the hypocrisy of highlighting portions of a work out of context. One of my favorite quotes is from Deborah Caldwell-Stone, who once said, "Each attempt to ban a book by one of these groups represents a direct attack on every person's constitutionally protected right to freely choose what books to read and what ideas to explore. The choice of what to read must be left to the reader or, in the case of children, to parents. That choice does not belong to self-appointed book police."

I wish more people, particularly Republicans, would speak out against comments meant to push false narratives like Ben Shapiro's when he said, "What [Biden] really wants is for your local second grader to be able to walk into a school library and see graphic cartoon depictions of anal sex. That's really what Joe Biden wants." This outright lie by Shapiro also pushes the notion that there are these types of materials in school libraries, particularly at elementaries. There are not. Ben Shapiro is spreading lies about school librarians, and when he states these things to his followers, librarians' lives can be endangered by the type of fans he is seeking to enrage for money and views and political power.

Not only are books being challenged, but libraries as institutions, and the librarians who work there, are being threatened. The ALA's report went on to include the statement, "Books are no longer the sole target of attacks orchestrated by conservative parent groups and right-wing media. Both school and public librarians are increasingly in the crosshairs of conservative groups during book challenges and subject to defamatory name-calling, online harassment, social media attacks, and doxxing, as well as direct threats to their safety, their employment, and their very liberty."

Threats and challenges are happening everywhere, and they're spreading like wildfire. Armed protestors have shown up at children's events, and libraries across the country have received bomb threats. In 2019, the Idaho youth librarian Denise Neujahr began the Rainbow Squad Program, a monthly program for LGBTQIA+ youth and allies to connect, at her public library. Two years later, religious protestors began showing up and police presence was necessary. One man was arrested for alleged trespassing when he entered the property carrying a loaded gun and knife. A motorcycle group called the Panhandle Patriots allegedly targeted Denise, claiming that she was a groomer with a nefarious agenda. In June 2022, thirty-one members of the white supremacist group Patriot Front were arrested at a Pride event in northern Idaho. According to the Associated Press, five men of the group were found guilty of rioting charges after only an hour of deliberation. Jon Lewis, a George Washington University researcher who specializes in homegrown violent extremism, said in an article by the Associated Press that outrage directed at LGBTQIA+ people had been growing for months online. He stated, "A massive right-wing media ecosystem" has been promoting the notion that "there are people trying to take your kids to drag shows, there are trans people trying to 'groom' your children."

The hysteria spread to Roxbury, New Jersey, and targeted the school librarian Roxana Caivano to the point that, like me, Roxana filed a defamation lawsuit over insults on social media about the book *Gender Queer: A Memoir*, by Maia Kobabe. Roxana claims that three women who do not have children attending her school caused her emotional turmoil by insinuating that she's a child predator who attempts to lure children with sexually explicit material and had exposed minors to pornographic materials. Posts were made on social media and a blog about Roxanna, attempting to discredit her. Her husband, Anthony Caivano, who is acting as her attorney, told the journalist Anthony Johnson, "It affects someone's reputation and that's something that once it's taken, it's very difficult to get back." When I read about Roxana, I searched her name. Sure enough, I was able to find dozens of social media posts calling her a groomer and pedophile. I reached out to Roxana for a phone conversation, and her story eerily echoed my own.

Just like what was happening to me, the opposing lawyer in Roxana's case insisted that the case was about free speech and parental rights.

real GW Braun ❗ @BraunGeo · Apr 28   ...
@roxanacaivano only #PedophileDbags do this!
#StopSexualizingChildren or we will stop you.

According to the *Miami Herald*, the defendant's attorney, Corinne Mullen, stated, "The librarian's suit against the parents really, and ironically, attacks the First Amendment rights of the parents to have a voice." False. Roxana's lawsuit, like mine, is a defamation suit. Our lawsuits are not about stifling parental voices but stopping falsehoods from being spread in our communities in attempts to ruin our reputations. The lawsuits are not about books or parent rights but about people who feel free to go to school board meetings and profess lies about books and librarians or go online and make insinuations to rile up the community. People like those targeting Roxana and myself distort the truth and won't admit that our lawsuits are about bullying and defamation. Attorney Mullen also added, "That's a debate that should take place at the Board of Education meetings and that's a debate that should be robust." Nobody is shying away from debate, but librarians are absolutely right in denouncing defamations of their character. Those making the accusations aren't interested in civil debates.

This nationwide movement is exacerbating a teacher and librarian shortage, with many in the field switching careers or retiring early to avoid these threats to their lives and livelihoods. I took a leave of absence for an entire semester due to stress. After spending months trying to save my reputation in the public eye, dealing with a lawsuit, ignoring constant harassment, and trying to spread the word nationally about book banning efforts, all while trying to go to work each day with my head held high, I knew that I needed to take a break for both my physical and mental health. It was the right decision for me, and fortunately I was able to. Many are not.

One day I stumbled upon an article about the Utah school librarian Catherine Bates, and I was devastated after reading her story. Catherine announced her resignation after ten years in education because of the mental toll to her health after she voiced opposition to book banning in her school district. In an article by Martha Harris, Catherine stated with frustration, "If I could get to a point where I am not emotionally involved in the decisions that are being made, everything would be a little bit better. But I don't know how to do that when, like my entire life, I felt very strongly about what libraries are and how important they are." EveryLibrary associate director Peter Bromberg, also a librarian, stated it best when he said, "The accusations that someone, a teacher or librarian, is trying to harm a child is, really, it's indefensible and the emotional toll that it's taking is significant. We have people leaving the field. We have people who are staying in the field but can't sleep or are experiencing the ravages of chronic stress and are afraid to speak out about it."

Utah saw an uptick in censorship attempts and anti-library laws created by legislators with little to no library training, with schools immediately experiencing a precipitous rise in book challenges. There's a familiar pattern to books challenged in Utah. The majority of challenges have centered on books by or about members of the LGBTQIA+ community and people of color. But the pattern was all the starker because of Utah H.B. 374, a legislative bill titled "Sensitive Materials in Schools," which became law in March 2022. This bill gives schools the ability to circumvent the Miller test and disregard the artistic value or a book or intentions of the book as a whole.

When speaking about Utah, Peter Bromberg told Utah's KSL News-Radio, "It's not school libraries that parents need to be concerned about. It's their phones. If we're really concerned about the deleterious effects of pornography on children's brains, that's where we should be focusing. Not on books or literature."

One of my biggest frustrations is that the same people who are so hyper-fixated on our libraries will allow their own children unfettered access to phones, tablets, and devices where actual pornography is just a click away. If you point that out to them, they don't deny it. They'll just scream all the louder about taxes and libraries. I know very few parents who have parental filters on their children's devices or monitor their usage.

———

Don't confuse what I am saying, though. Neither public nor school libraries contain pornography. This is a false narrative told by politicians, keyboard warriors, people seeking to make themselves important by chasing clout, and sometimes well-meaning people swept up in the hysteria. Librarians do not purchase pornography, but if you believed everything you read on social media, you would think that there are issues of *Playboy* next to *Time* magazine. That's simply not true. However, public libraries do contain adult romances, in adult sections, as well as books on sexual reproduction.

When my daughter was eight years old, I took her to a class for kids ages eight to eleven at our local hospital. The class was about girls' bodies and went over the basics of puberty and menstruation. I sat in the back listening as the girls sat up front and the nurse showed them age-appropriate graphics and gave them simplified explanations about all of it. The girls got a cute little care package and were able to touch and feel different types of menstrual products. Josie asked many questions, all of which were very well-thought-out, and I was a little proud when the nurse kept smiling and finally asked, "Who in here is Josie's mom? Good job, Mom." After the class, Josie had even more questions. What did I do? I turned to our public library to help. I was able to find an age-appropriate book that would answer all her questions. I am thankful the library had this resource, because I really didn't know how to frame the conversation with someone so young.

There are many types of books written about sexual reproduction and sexual health in libraries, some that are even appropriate for elementary-age children and written in language for children to understand. Those books might be found in juvenile nonfiction because they're written specially for children. Books that go more in depth will be found in teen sections. Books on sexual reproduction found in young adult sections are books specifically on that topic written and reviewed for teens.

If you do not want your five-year-old to see books written for younger children on sexual reproduction, steer them away from those books. If you don't want them to see books on sexual reproduction for teenagers, parents should make sure their five-year-olds don't wander into sections of the library meant for teenagers and young adults. In fact, if you are a parent dropping off a minor, or not monitoring your own child, you are likely breaking library policy. It really is that simple.

Something that does seem to make Louisiana censorship attempts different is that so far we have experienced censorship attempts only at public libraries, whereas people and groups in other states tend to focus on schools or a mix of public and school book banning. In 2023, anti-library bills targeted library boards and materials deemed "sexually explicit" only in public libraries. This left our state a little underprepared for what was to come. School librarians had been discussing the importance of books, libraries, and reading for years, and I had been taking notes, examining library collection development policies, and gathering information on how school librarians could best stand up for intellectual freedom in the face of the growing trend of censorship attempts. It was unexpected that it would hit the public library first.

Though surprised, I was relieved that school libraries were not first up to bat. At the time, I was the president of the Louisiana Association of School Librarians, and the thought of having to fend off widespread book-banning efforts in both school *and* public libraries was overwhelming. I also think that this was a grave mistake on the part of the pro-censors.

It's hard to argue a book doesn't belong in a public library when public libraries are for people of all ages. That doesn't mean I don't think it's coming to our schools. It's only a matter of time, and I can only hope that years of solidifying collection development and reconsideration policies, as well as lessons learned from our public librarian counterparts, will help us. In fact, as the coming school year approaches, I fully expect my school to receive more complaints and a formal challenge or five. I am prepared. I have nothing to hide. I maintain that our library contains books age relevant for our student population.

Libraries and intellectual freedom go hand in hand, and I feel that it's important to point out policies and procedures already in place and how they work, which is what I did when I spoke at our public library board meeting and stated, "Just because you enter a library, it does not mean that you will not see something you don't like. Libraries have diverse collections with resources from many points of view, and a library's mission is to provide access to information for all users. All library users have the First Amendment right to borrow, read, view, and listen to library resources, according to the ALA. If an individual is concerned about a children's or young adult's resource or its location in the library, that individual has the right to go through the library's reconsideration policy that is already in place. Each family has the right to determine which library resources are acceptable for its own children, but individuals must also realize that they must afford the same rights to all other parents." I went to the meeting as a resident of my community to remind the public of the dangers of censorship and that our library should follow policies already in place.

Speaking out against censorship does not equate to the promotion of sexually explicit material or pornography to children. Speaking out against censorship means reiterating library policy and reminding the public that libraries are for everyone and that everyone in the community deserves the right to see themselves in the books at their local library. I didn't go to speak about any one book and didn't know that a list would be presented at the meeting. There is a time to voice concern about censorship attempts regarding particular books, and that's during public comment when individual titles are being reviewed. Getting mired in a debate about one or two books when it's not public comment time for those titles can confuse the situation, and that's what pro-censors want.

I guess in some ways I can see why my community would be concerned. Citizens for a New Louisiana, along with Ryan Thames of Bayou State of Mind, were posting pictures of cartoon characters engaging in sex from a book called *Let's Talk About It: The Teen's Guide to Sex, Relationships, and Being a Human*. Posting pictures of the book out of context was not telling the whole story of that book, and telling people it was in the children's section was simply not true. The book wasn't even brought up at the public library board meeting. But again, people were swallowing everything they saw on social media hook, line, and sinker. The social media posts merely echoed what was being said on alt-right news programs and by politicians pandering for votes.

Pro-censors like to post one page of a book out of context, for the shock and awe, and insinuate that it's on display for children to see or on the shelf next to picture books. The public must learn to investigate these posts and find out the truth for themselves. Most public and school libraries have an online catalog, and anyone can easily look up a book and find out the truth. Finding out the truth is no fun, and it's easier to believe a picture on social media. When in doubt, just call and ask your local librarian.

There are some books in the young adult sections that are targeted for older readers, because young adults are older teens, some of whom are in relationships. As noted, teenagers in Louisiana can get married at sixteen, so it stands to reason that they should be able to read about aspects of married life that include sex. And let's be honest, teenagers know what sex is. Reading accurate representations about relationships doesn't mean you're reading pornography. Reading books that include physical aspects of those relationships that many teens are involved in doesn't mean they're reading smut. I'd rather my teen read age-appropriate materials in a library book than turn to the internet. I understand that some parents don't want their teens to read about sex. Those parents need to police their own children's reading and stop policing mine.

It's also important to weigh the work as a whole. According to the American Library Association, "Passages or parts should not be pulled out of context. The values and faults should be weighed against each other, and the opinions based on the materials as a whole." For example, I understand that someone might not like the book *Gender Queer: A Memoir*, but the work taken as a whole doesn't meet the Miller test and doesn't constitute pornography. *Gender Queer* is a memoir told in graphic novel format and tells Kobabe's journey from childhood to becoming an adult and navigating gender identity and gender dysphoria, what it means to be transgender, and other topics. This book can be inspirational for anyone dealing with the same issues.

In 2022, *Gender Queer* was challenged in Jefferson County Public Schools, Kentucky, and the school board voted to allow it to remain on the shelves. In an official statement, the board wrote, "*Gender Queer* illustrates a lived experience that is not often represented in literature, especially in literature geared towards young adult or high school-aged students. Its inclusion in the libraries at Phoenix and Liberty serves a valuable educational purpose in the schools' efforts to educate the whole student. While reasonable people may differ as to what is offensive, this Board feels the few sexual passages in this material do not rise to the level that the average person, applying contemporary adult community standards, would find to be patently offensive."

———

I set out to find the truth in my parish through public records requests for challenged materials in our public library system. As both a librarian and a resident, I saw firsthand how our reconsideration policy worked, and I agreed with the decisions made by our librarians. On July 23, 2022, a patron challenged Sarah J. Maas's wildly popular fantasy series A Court of Thorns and Roses. I happened to have read this series twice but agree that it moves toward adult content after the first book. The challenger wrote, "Certain scenes in this book seem a bit mature" and asked that it be relocated to the adult fiction section. I agreed with the library's decision to house the books together in the adult fiction section, even if the first book is young adult.

Reconsideration policies have an important role in libraries. However, what we are currently seeing is the abuse and misuse of many of those policies. People are copying lists of "bad" books on websites like BookLooks and social media and then mass challenging the titles without reading them or making their own determinations. Sometimes books do need to be relocated if they are mistakenly placed in an unfavorable location of the library, as determined by trained librarians. When done correctly, and by following policies, community members can have books examined. When somebody who hasn't read a book challenges hundreds at a time, it costs the libraries time and money.

On August 8, 2022, a member of the public challenged the title *Let's Talk About It*, saying that "the book has several images of sexual acts" and "it encourages the reader to begin watching pornography and follow their favorite porn stars." *Let's Talk About It* was listed in the library system as being recommended for ages fourteen and up, and it was shelved in teen nonfiction. The book covers the topic of relationships, safe sex, friendships, gender, sexuality, and anatomy in graphic novel form. After a review, and not just taking one page they saw on the internet, the library determined that it would be appropriate to relocate the book in adult nonfiction. The committee wrote, "The author's suggestions that teens view pornography online, seek out kinks, and take nude photographs of themselves goes beyond sex education. Moving the work to the adult non-fiction collection will retain the work as available to patrons of the parish, maintaining the integrity of the system's collection, while adjusting the age threshold." The book was not removed from the collection but moved within the collection so that readers of a certain age would still have access to the title. I agreed with the librarians again and trusted their judgment of what was best for our library after they completed a comprehensive review.

In June 2023, a challenge was submitted for *Pride Puppy!*, by Robin Stevenson. The publisher describes the book: "A young child and their family are having a wonderful time together celebrating Pride Day: meeting up with Grandma, making new friends and eating ice cream. But then something terrible happens: their dog gets lost in the parade! Luckily, there are lots of people around to help reunite the pup with his family." In this case, the challenger wrote that this picture book was "gay propaganda being forced on kids who don't know better" and that the action taken should be to "remove it from the library completely." To completely remove a picture book from the public library simply for containing an LGBTQIA+ theme is the very definition of book banning and censorship. Fortunately, our library's Challenge Review Committee determined it should remain in the picture book section. Again, the process worked.

Around the same time that *Pride Puppy!* was challenged at the public library, I received an email about the same book. A random person I didn't know got confused and thought I was a librarian at our public library. She sent me an email to say, "My issue is this. As a Christian, the Bible tells us that marriage is between a man and a woman only. And that there are only 2 genders. Kids should be left alone to be kids. We, as adults, should be protecting them from things like this. I'm not saying that everything in the library like this needs to be banned, but it needs to be kept under lock and key." She then asked me to remove it from the library. In Louisiana public libraries, we have seen a huge rise in book challenges simply because they contain LGBTQIA+ characters.

In neighboring St. Tammany Parish, over 150 challenges have been lodged from only a handful of citizens. The challenged books, like picture books *Julián Is a Mermaid* and *A Costume for Charly*, are pulled until review and kept behind the circulation desk. This is a form of censorship. According to the journalist Piper Hutchinson, "Each challenge costs the St. Tammany library system about $400 and dozens of man-hours." Katie Schwartzmann, director of Tulane's First Amendment Law Clinic, wrote a letter to the board stating, "The Board's policy of holding challenged works behind the circulation desk pending review violates the Constitution because it removes protected works from the shelves. It provides a presumption in favor of censoring books, when actually the presumption should be that creative works are protected from government censorship except in extraordinarily rare circumstances. Federal courts have held that stigmatizing controversial books by hiding them behind counters or removing them from circulation is a First Amendment violation," she added.

In Llano, Texas, seven library patrons filed a federal lawsuit in April 2022 after seventeen titles were removed from the public library system and access to digital library books was suspended. According to journalist Alejandro Serrano, the books were removed after they were deemed inappropriate by a number of people in the community and Republican lawmakers. CNN reported that the lawsuit sparked retaliatory efforts to defund the public library system in April 2023. Thankfully, that discussion was dismissed, and as of now the Llano Public Library still has funding, but it took a judge's ruling to temporarily place the books back on the shelves for patrons.

The rise in book challenges, outright book bans, legislation, and attacks on authors, librarians, and the LGBTQIA+ community have caused a rise in soft, or silent, censorship. Soft censorship is when librarians do not

Kathy Irwin @BOBOWATO · Jul 2, 2022 ···
Llano Texas Independence Day Protest! Armed with books that have been challenged & removed from county **libraries**.
Quiet Opposition Reading to STOP right-wing Llano book bans, firing of a librarian and a federal civil rights **lawsuit** by residents.
HChronicle

purchase books for fear of reprisal, whether that comes in the form of personal attacks on social media, book challenges, or even losing their jobs. I would be lying if I said that when ordering books for our school library this past year, I second-guessed some of the titles requested by students. I followed our collection development policy and stood firm in ordering the books with LGBTQIA+ and BIPOC characters, but I did wonder if I would be opening myself up to further attacks on our collection or my character.

However, all our students deserve to see themselves and their families represented in the books on the shelves of our school and public libraries. I will not allow my fear of being targeted stop me from serving every student equally.

The current wave of book banning sweeping the country has created a chilling effect on our education system and the purchasing of books in our libraries, the effects of which will be seen for decades even if we somehow get it under control in the next year. This is a huge movement that has been in the works for a while. It is well funded and well coordinated. It is about marginalizing and erasing cultures and groups of people, it is about defunding public institutions, it is about dumbing down society for a more easily led population, and it is about using libraries for political gain. At the end of the day, the pro-censorship movement is about privatizing education and privatizing libraries for a group of people who are seeking to line their pockets. And to achieve those goals, otherwise well-meaning people have been enlisted in a social movement that goes against everything America stands for. That's the really sad and tragic thing.

Chapter 4

WWJD: What Would Judy Do?

How we handle our fears will determine where we go with the
rest of our lives.

—JUDY BLUME, *TIGER EYES*

In my small town of Watson, Louisiana, I grew up surrounded by books, po'boys, a strong emphasis on education, and a love of God in my lower-middle-class family of five. Watson is still unincorporated and officially classified as a village. Hillary Clinton famously once said, "It takes a village," and even though nobody in my village seems to like Hillary but me, I can attest that they do indeed feel this way about life. In our village, everyone knew everyone else. I knew I couldn't get away with any high school hijinks because someone in the village would immediately report me to my parents. We didn't have the internet or cell phones. We had Movieland Video and rented movies to watch each week as a family.

When I was growing up, we didn't have any red lights in Watson. We had a four-way stop, a gas station called the Village, a lone hardware store, churches, and our schools. Eating out meant ordering chicken from Linda's Chicken Hut or getting biscuits and gravy from Story's Grocery while saying hello to Mammaw Story or her children and grandkids. The whole village turned out each December for the elementary school's lighting of the community Christmas Tree at Live Oak Methodist Church and each spring for Amite Baptist Church's Easter play. We gathered on Sundays for worship and weekdays for T-ball and biddy basketball.

As I grew older, we saw a major population boom that can best be described as "white flight" from Baton Rouge, which is about twenty miles to the south. I remember we got our first red light when I was in high school and a little later our first Church's Texas Chicken. The local Village Food Mart was soon replaced by a Walgreens, and my graduating class of ninety-six students in 1996 is now a graduating class of over three hundred in 2023. We added three more schools, a Dollar General, and a Walmart. What was once a small community, where everyone knew everybody else, became a suburb. I still run into people I know when out on the "town," but it's not the same. One difference that I do love about our new community, though, is that we now have a top-notch library facility, a far cry from the small room next to the washeteria or the old bank that had previously housed our collections. It's hard to say that your community values libraries when the library shares a bathroom with the washeteria and a convenience store, so I was proud when we decided to pass a library tax to make improvements.

But in the beginning, there was Judy Blume and the books I found in that small, cramped room of our former library building. Judy was everything to me, and her books shaped my life. I began my journey with Judy when I stumbled upon *Tales of a Fourth Grade Nothing* in my school library around the age of eight. I imagined that I was Peter Hatcher, being blamed for every sibling spat, and that my sisters were Fudge. In my head, Fudge, aka my sisters Melanie and Colleen, were always cramping my big-sister style. I laugh thinking about that now, since they have been some of my biggest supporters over the past year. But at the time, I thought I had finally found a book character I could relate to! Then I read *Blubber*.

Blubber was the first book I ever read about anyone overweight and the first book I read from the point of view of a bully. My heart was filled with sadness as the narrator of the book, a fifth grader named Jill, felt conflicting emotions as she participated in the bullying of a classmate named Linda, but joined in anyway. As an overweight child, I cried reading that book. Although I was not bullied per se, thanks to wonderful friends, I could relate to being overweight. I was overly self-conscious at the age of eight that I was several sizes larger than most of my friends. Even at such a young age, I was aware that I was viewed as the funny one of the group, and not the prettiest, due to my size. It can seem like the end of the world in elementary school when you are five to six inches taller than most of the kids in your class and a good forty pounds heavier.

Blubber was my first foray into reading books I now realize helped shape who I am, and I credit Judy for making me more empathetic. In the past, I had participated in making fun of someone else, often for the same reasons as the main character Jill, so that I would not become a target. The book made me pause and reflect on my behaviors and their effects on others. When doing some internal reflection, I didn't necessarily like the kind of kid I was when I participated in bullying and I didn't necessarily like Judy pointing it out to me, even though I needed to read about it. As an overweight child, I sympathized with the character of Linda and prayed to God that I would never be the target of an entire group of people like she is in the book. The book was a roller coaster of emotions for me. In fact, it's the first book I can ever remember reading that actually made me emotional. That's the wonderful thing about books—their ability to shape who you are and make you think—and nobody has done it better in children's books than Judy.

Judy wrote about real issues that were easy to digest as a child, and I could not get enough of her stories. I devoured *Tiger Eyes, Iggie's House, Deenie,* and the rest of her books. I remember hiding while reading *Are You There God? It's Me, Margaret,* with a blush on my face, because I didn't want my parents to know that I was reading about periods. Yes, I learned about menstrual cycles from Judy! It was such a taboo topic and I wanted to know more. I checked out every Judy Blume book I could find at our school library, and when I wanted to read some of the "more mature" titles, I turned to our public library.

I was Sheila Tubman, from *Otherwise Known as Sheila the Great*, hiding my insecurities behind false bravado. I pretended to be brave, even when I was scared. I still do this. I also realized that I didn't want to be like Sheila, a very obnoxious personality, who often rubbed people the wrong way in social situations. I was a daydreamer like Sally J. Freedman, and got my first introduction to antisemitism when reading *Starring Sally J. Freedman as Herself.* I learned that boys also had a rough time with puberty from *Then Again, Maybe I Won't*. When I got a little older, I could relate to that book's main character Tony and his anxiety about his friend Joel's penchant for shoplifting when I was thrust into a particular situation with my own friend.

There's a saying that books shape lives, and I cannot imagine what type of person I would be if I hadn't grown up reading Judy Blume. Her books touched on topics that no other author at the time seemed to be writing about for kids, including racism, puberty, bullying, and anxiety. Her books were honest and raw, and they made me think about topics I hadn't thought about before. As I got older, I realized that not everyone liked her books as much as I did and that she is one of the most banned authors of all time. Those people are missing out. I am so very fortunate that I had parents who allowed me to explore life through literature and who never questioned the Judy Blume books I was reading.

My parents never actually questioned anything I read, and if I hid a book from them, it was more my own paranoia about taboo topics and nothing they ever said or did. I probably could have walked through the living room with *The Joy of Sex* and they wouldn't have noticed what I was reading. I'm not saying they were inattentive but that they seemed to accept they had an avid reader in their midst and trusted the value of a good book. When I was younger, I'd read a book or two a day during the summer and spend hours rooted to one spot, reading without moving an inch. As I got a little older, I discovered that my great-aunt had a treasure trove of adult romance novels. I'd sneakily borrow them and hide under the covers while I read next to my parents on the couch, looking around furtively when I got to the juicy parts.

In my opinion, allowing children to explore the world through books is one of the most precious gifts you can give a child. When my daughter turned five, I made a big deal of bringing her to the public library and letting her sign up for her very own library card. We took pictures and she was over the moon as she checked out the maximum number of titles, filling her book bag up to bursting. We paraded around the library like queens of the castle and I smiled at her taking ownership of her selections. How fortunate that we have a public library with rows upon rows of books and a brand-new facility.

To my chagrin, my child never picked out Judy Blume's books, but I cannot say I didn't try to talk them up. Turns out, Josie is a huge fan of graphic novels and manga, so I fostered her love of graphic novels with modern-day Judys like Raina Telgemeier, Svetlana Chmakova, and Shannon Hale. As a school librarian, I often encounter parents who worry about their children only wanting to read graphic novels. Reading is reading is reading. Foster what they love. Maybe they will expand to other formats. Maybe not. To me, fostering a love of literature is important no matter if the format is a novel, graphic novel, or audiobook.

Books are so much a part of my life that I named my daughter after a book character. In seventh grade, I read Louisa May Alcott's *Little Women*. I knew instantly that I wanted to raise a child like Jo March. A child who would be brave, sincere, loving, and headstrong. Lucky for me, seventeen years later, my husband was keen on the idea and we named our daughter Josephine. Try as I might, I have never persuaded her to read the original *Little Women*, but I mark it as a success that she's read many of the graphic novel adaptations.

So many books shaped my life growing up, and I can recall turning points in my life by the titles I was reading at the time. I remember reading about racism and realizing for the first time that not everyone had a happy childhood like me when Dr. Shirley McDonald, my high school librarian, introduced me to Maya Angelou's *I Know Why the Caged Bird Sings*. I remember the triumph of completing my first Stephen King novel, *It*, and being proud of reading a book so large in seventh grade. I remember the first time a book ever made me ugly cry when I read *The Thorn Birds*, and I remember the first time I realized how evil some people can be in this world when I read *A Tree Grows in Brooklyn*.

One of the most influential books in my life was *Harry Potter and the Sorcerer's Stone*. Knowing what I know now about the author, I hesitate to give her credit. I am vehemently against her attitude and comments about the trans community, but her books did reignite my passion for reading. In high school, I did what one does and tended to shift priorities from books to hanging out with friends, getting my first job, and probably partying too much. Reading was placed on the back burner.

My third year in college, as I was plugging along with getting my elementary education degree, I happened to take a literature class at Southeastern Louisiana University by Dr. Lori Brocato. She would often open class with a read aloud. At twenty-one, I sat enraptured like a kid on the reading carpet in a kindergarten class as I listened to her read *The Rainbow Fish*, *Where the Wild Things Are*, and *Cloudy with a Chance of Meatballs*. I had forgotten how much I loved books. In another literature class, I sat as if spellbound, glued to my seat, as Dr. Andrea Laborde read aloud a few chapters of *Hatchet* and *The Chocolate War* each week. It was around that same time that I discovered the wizarding world of Harry Potter.

Before classes one day, I happened to catch an episode of *The Rosie O'Donnell Show* featuring a new author named J. K. Rowling, whose first three books were numbers one through three on the *New York Times* Best Sellers list, and Rosie said, "These are amazing stories about magic and myth and integrity." I was intrigued and wanted to read them immediately.

The next day, I went to my university's library and checked out the first three Harry Potter books. I zipped through them. I read them a second time and wanted more. I talked about them nonstop. I remember showing them to a friend in my class named Kim and going on and on about these new Harry Potter books. Kim and I work together now, and we still talk about the amazing new books we read.

Maybe you think I'm being dramatic, but the first three Harry Potter books reignited a fire inside of me. That fire was the intense love I had for reading. I was in school to become an elementary education teacher, mainly because I wasn't sure what else to do. I figured my mom did it, I loved to play school, and I enjoyed working around children. I also had a sense of wanting to make a difference in the world, and what better way than to shape the minds of today's youth? After finishing the first three books in the Harry Potter series, I immediately wondered if I was meant to be a school librarian and about the steps I needed to take to achieve that goal. I spent a day researching the classes I needed to take in my student handbook. I booked an appointment with my college adviser to ask questions. I knew nothing about master's degrees or graduate classes. I learned that my university didn't have an MLIS program, whatever that was, but did offer school librarian certification. I asked special permission to take library science graduate courses as an undergraduate and took my first library science class the following semester. I knew the moment Dr. Laborde finished reading *Hatchet* to us, and then reading Harry Potter and rediscovering the joy I found in books, that I wanted to be a school librarian.

I recently rewatched that episode of *The Rosie O'Donnell Show* and heard again J. K. Rowling read a passage about dementors. I seem to have my own version of dementors. Men who hide behind computers like dementors whose heads are hidden beneath their hoods. Rosie asked, "What do the dementors do?" "They suck the life out of you," Rowling said. "They take all happiness and all recollection of anything cheerful in your past out of you so you're just left with despair." Rosie said, "This really got to me because there are people in my adult life who I feel are dementors. There are people who I know who are like that." Me, too, Rosie. Me too. However, I refuse to let my dementors take my soul.

I graduated college in the spring of 2001 with my degree in elementary education. I was a certified teacher and a certified school librarian. It was time to begin shaping lives. I hit the school hiring lottery when I found out that my former middle school, a school just two miles from my home, was hiring a school librarian for the following year. The school librarian was taking a sabbatical, and a temporary hire was needed. I thought with glee,

"Here is my chance!" It was the exact school I wanted to work for, and I immediately applied and was hired.

I spent my first year as the school librarian and I hit the ground running, devising lists of resources for teachers, helping students find books, and learning the ropes as a first-year educator. It wasn't always champagne and roses, but I think I did an okay job for a young kid of twenty-two. Some days were devastating, like the day I found out one of our students had died in an automobile accident. Some days were boring, spent putting books back on the shelves. Some days were surreal, like the day we all dropped what we were doing to watch in horror as the Twin Towers fell. Some days were joyful, like the day I had a student hug me and tell me I was her favorite teacher because I found a good book for her. That first year was a year of growth for me as a person, but also professionally, as I realized that this was indeed the job I was destined to do.

Our librarian came back the next year, so I took a permanent position as an English language arts teacher. I wanted to continue being a school librarian, but I also wanted to stay at my school. I love to teach, I love reading, and I love my school, so it wasn't a hard decision to stay and move to the classroom. I figured I'd teach until our librarian moved on, and I'd apply for that position one day. In our district, school librarians stay in their jobs until they die or retire, and the school librarian positions are few and far between. I could wait it out at my school.

I ended up spending fourteen years as an English language arts teacher at my school. I love being a librarian, but I do miss the years I spent as a classroom teacher. I had so many adventures in the classroom that I wouldn't trade for anything in the world. There were collaborative lessons on the *Titanic* with my friend and coworker Jennifer that I miss, and the funny things that happened after class, like when her phone went off in the middle of a conference to the tune of "Baby Got Back." I miss the wild lessons I had, like the time I thought the kids needed to see if they could start a fire outside with nothing but flint like Brian Robeson in Gary Paulsen's book *The River,* or when the entire class reenacted "The High-wayman," complete with a kid in a yarn wig and a kid pretending to be the wind. There are times when I miss the camaraderie you develop with the other teachers when you teach the same subjects or same grade. Being the only librarian at a school can get lonely.

When you're a classroom teacher, seeing the same kids every day, and eventually the same families over the years, you grow bonds with the children and their families. You get to know kids better by teaching them daily than you do seeing them only a few times a month in the library, and I miss the inside jokes and the closeness that develops. I became friends with some of their parents and still keep up with many of my former students and their parents on social media. There are kids I worry about who are now grown, married, and have their own children, some of whom I teach. There are kids whose lives I've mourned when they passed away and parents of former students whom I sit with at community events to catch up on their kids' lives because I miss them.

I am glad that I taught in the classroom. It gave me a chance to hone my teaching abilities, and I continued my schooling to earn a master's in education and certification as a reading specialist. My experiences as a classroom teacher helped me become a better school librarian and drove home the importance of library programs that collaborate with every teacher in the school. Because I was a classroom teacher, I know what materials and resources can be most beneficial to the teachers. I understand the need to set standards and goals and the value of reteaching when students are not understanding certain concepts. Working in the classroom allowed me to learn more about my community and the people who inhabit it, but working as a librarian allows me to work with all stakeholders in a school.

———

Something else that shaped me and taught me the importance of community was my upbringing in the church. I grew up in Amite Baptist Church, a Southern Baptist church in the heart of our community founded in the early 1840s. We attended every Sunday morning and evening and on Wednesdays. Sunday morning was for Sunday School and "Children's Church," which was a watered-down kids' version in a classroom of what the adults were getting in the main auditorium. We watched sock puppet reenactments of Bible stories about a wee little man named Zacchaeus and practiced reciting Bible verses from memory. When we got older, we were allowed to join the adults in "Big Church," which mostly involved me trying to pay attention while staring up at the swinging lights and wondering if one would fall down on someone's head, and kicking one of my sisters for no apparent reason.

Sunday evenings involved the Children's Choir, where all of us kids with zero musical talent were forced to stand on risers to sing songs off-key about the devil sitting on a tack if he didn't like things or how much Jesus loved the little children. "Red, yellow, black, or white, we are precious in his sight." I never questioned why there were only white children at our church and now realize just how awful some of the lyrics of "Jesus Loves Me" are. After Children's Choir, it was back to Big Church for more time spent trying to stay awake and agitating my sisters, until my mom issued forth what we called the Church Pinch. The Church Pinch involved my mother staring straight ahead at Brother Terry while sneaking her hand over to pinch the leg of whichever kid was closest. It was just the right amount of fingernail to feel like our skin was being pierced. Inevitably, we'd scream, "That hurt. Why did you pinch me, Momma?!" Everyone else in church would pretend they didn't hear anything, and kids across the aisle would sit a little straighter, scared of getting their own Church Pinch.

On Wednesdays, we had Girls in Action, which I look back on now as some form of weird Christian version of the Girl Scouts, which I also participated in after school on Thursdays. Girls in Action, or G.A.'s for short, meant we listened to a lesson and then completed a workbook page on the perils of sin to earn patches for our sashes worn nowhere but at G.A.'s before praying that God wouldn't send another flood to kill us all. Then we'd huddle and gossip about whatever nine-year-olds gossip about. Sometimes we'd dare each other to go down the dark, creepy hallway by ourselves and play Bloody Mary in the bathroom while we waited on our mothers to pick up our younger siblings from the church nursery.

Summers were spent in Vacation Bible School. There we would make crafts out of tissue paper and Popsicle sticks, sing more songs off-key, and memorize the books of the Bible for Bible drills. Bible drills were the perfect game for my competitive spirit. The teacher would call two of us up. We'd approach the front of the room with our Bibles. You were extra cool if you had a Bible cover to put on your Bible, because then it would look like a purse. The Bible would remain closed until the adult called out a Bible verse. Whoever flipped to the verse fastest won and got to stay up front. We'd do this for what seemed like hours until it was time to go, with the final person still standing reigning supreme as master of the Bible drill until the next week.

I tell these stories jokingly, but these are some of my best childhood memories. There was nothing more fun than going to church to see my friends, learn about God, drink watered-down orange punch, eat "church cookies," and roller-skate to hymns in the church gym that smelled like feet. Church cookies were Butter Ring cookies that had a hole in the middle. We would stack them on our fingers like rings and gorge ourselves on them before roller-skating. The person who could stack the most church cookies on their fingers won the game of Church Cookies that day. I still don't know why we had a full-blown roller-skating rink in our church gym, but we did. I chalk it up to the fact that the '80s were a wild ride.

Our church was a church of love, grace, and forgiveness. When someone was in need, the church members provided, whether it was a prayer, a coat during the winter, or a casserole after a death. My mom was on a committee that would provide meals when needed, and I can remember numerous occasions when we sat in the car while she dropped off a dish. Every Corning Ware dish in our house had our family name on the bottom because of this.

I was taught about kindness, about Jesus's work with the underprivileged, and about being a Good Samaritan. Our preacher, Brother Terry, denounced racism and embraced love. We sang old Baptist hymns, and I was taught that God is love and Ephesians 4:32, "Be ye kind one to another."

I often look around my community and see "Christians" who use the Bible and Christianity as weapons. That's not how I was raised, and I'm thankful. I was taught in church that we are all sinners and that it's not up to me to judge others, and this was the same lesson I was taught at home. I think the combined efforts of my parents to raise us in a loving church and to have access to books and libraries, along with my mom and dad's parenting style, all helped me become a kind person with integrity. We were raised to always tell the truth, be thankful for what we had, and look out for one another.

My dad didn't attend church with us, but he did promote a sense of adventure. I always thought he stayed home because he worked long hours and it was the only time when he could enjoy being alone. I've never thought to ask him about it.

When we were growing up, my dad would often load us up in our tan station wagon and announce, "We're going to someplace we have never been before." One day it might have been a new restaurant where we were encouraged to try oysters for the first time. One day it might be a park we had never been to and we'd fly kites. One time it was the landfill, where a seagull pooped on my dad's bald spot. I don't remember the details from all the trips, but there were many of these outings, with the three of us sisters bickering the whole time in the back seat. It was our own sort of *National Lampoon* mini-trips where something always seemed to go wrong, like a flat tire or sibling spat, but the sense of adventure was so right. I credit my dad for instilling in me the notion that we need to try new things and that there are always places out there to explore. He didn't bat an eye when I told him in my twenties that I was going to spend a month traveling in Europe. What could he say? He tried new things so often, I didn't even question when he got me to try a sardine (which, by the way, is disgusting, and I still can't believe he acted like they were delicious treats).

I credit one of my best friends for helping shape who I am in regard to being an ally of the LGBTQIA+ community. Joey Rogers and I went to school together, along with my husband, from first grade to graduation, and are still friends today. We have so many inside jokes, we went on so many traveling adventures, and I practically lived at Joey's house in high school and college. We were two peas in a pod. He was my date at senior prom and later he was an important member of our wedding party. I still don't know how he put up with my high school moodiness, but he always stuck by my side through thick and thin.

Joey came out to me when we were in college, but I think I always knew he was gay. I was relieved when he finally told me. I wanted him to be free to be who he was publicly. He came over one day, sat on my bed, looked at me, and said, "I want you to know I'm gay." I replied, "Duh," and that was that. Well, I did ask if I was the first person he had told and felt like I'd won a prize when he said yes. Nothing changed in our friendship, although it was probably a huge relief for him. We didn't talk about it. It just was what it was. Later, I'd ask him about crushes and worried that he might not find someone in our town.

I was also worried about the repercussions in our community if he decided to come out to everyone else. I didn't want my friend to become another hate crime statistic, and I worried about his safety. It's not that I had ever seen anyone attacked in my community, but I had heard plenty of gay slurs over the years. Calling someone the f-word used to be very commonplace. I was both relieved and devastated when Joey moved away. Relieved because I knew he would flourish, but selfishly sad that I would no longer get to see him daily. I always felt that fear was holding Joey back in our town. After he moved, his whole demeanor changed for the better, and he just seemed lighter and happier, like a weight had been lifted from his shoulders.

As an educator, I have had countless students who were gay or had gay family members. I have had students come out to me the year I taught them, have had moms whisper to me at conferences that they are gay, like it should be a secret, and have plenty of students who are now adults in happy same-sex relationships. I know because they friend me on social media. I've worked with people who are gay but were too afraid to tell anyone else at work. I've heard people I work with making derogatory comments or slurs in front of a co-worker who they don't realize has a gay sibling. When people make negative remarks about these students or their families, it makes my left eye twitch and my blood boil. How dare they? In the earlier days of my career, I tended to keep quiet about the negativity. Now I will not. Now I will shame them if they're an adult. Do I hear less of it now because people know not to speak that way around me, or do I hear less of it because things are getting better? Probably the first one.

The only "gay agenda" I've ever seen is a desire to be included and treated fairly like everyone else. I became a fierce, outspoken defender of LGBTQIA+ rights because I knew from my friendship with Joey that it was the right thing to do, but also because I was tired of seeing people hate on an entire group of people just because they are LGBTQIA+. I often wonder if I'd have different views if my best friend weren't gay or if I hadn't had gay students. I don't know the answer to that, but I hope I'd still be an advocate.

As an educator, I know that it's important to make all students and families feel included. People from outside my community often ask me why I am so open-minded compared with many others in my community. I don't think I'm that different in most ways. Many people in my town are kind and open-minded about most things, but it's as if they have blinders on when it comes to racism or homophobia. And I think that the hateful people, who I truly think are a minority, are just louder. I cannot let them be the loudest voices, and I must speak out for what is right.

The trips to the library, the "We're going to someplace we've never been before," the loving church family, and the friendship from Joey all played a part in the person I have become, and for that I am grateful. I live in a town with two red lights and one middle school. Every child in my community will have me as their middle school librarian. It's important to me that every child and their parents feel safe, loved, and seen in our school, especially in the library. Our school library is for every kid in our school regardless of sexual orientation, race, gender, socioeconomic status, religion, or background. School libraries are for everyone and so are our public libraries.

When I saw what I perceived as an attack on our public library in July 2022 via social media, I knew that it was time to speak out and state my concerns publicly. At the time, I wasn't quite sure what was being attempted, but I knew I couldn't sit on the sidelines. I now know there is a movement to defund our library, an attempt to censor books by marginalized authors and containing marginalized characters, and a so-called culture war against anyone who speaks truth to power. Oh, they will tell you that's not true. They will say, "We don't want to censor books. We just want to relocate them." Their actions say otherwise.

Martin Luther King Jr. once said, "That [blueprint of life] serves as the pattern, as the guide, as the model, for those who are to build the building. And a building is not well erected without a good, sound, and solid blueprint." I was given a solid blueprint for life, and I am trying my hardest to help my child build a solid blueprint for hers. A sound foundation of honesty, integrity, kindness, bravery, and outspokenness in the face of injustice is what I hope she is building.

In MLK Jr.'s famous blueprint speech his second point was "In your life's blueprint you must have as the basic principle the determination to achieve excellence in your various fields of endeavor. You're going to be deciding as the days and the years unfold, what you will do in life—what your life's work will be. And once you discover what it will be, set out to do it, and to do it well." I am a librarian. I strive to be the best librarian I can be. Not for myself, although I do get joy from working hard, but for the community. I have a responsibility to set a good example by being the best I can be. I love my job and I love representing the library world. I want to achieve excellence in my field. To achieve excellence, I must stand up for intellectual freedom against pro-censors who seek to destroy one of the last free public institutions in our community. Sometimes I just sit and reflect on how crazy this world is that libraries and librarians are being targeted for protecting books and stories. How did we come to this as a country? There's an old saying that nothing ventured is nothing gained. Those of us who want to achieve excellence and were raised with solid blueprints have got to speak out and fight back. Is it worth the physical and mental toll this fight has taken? The answer is yes if we want life, liberty, and the ability to pursue happiness.

―――――――

The second week of school this past year, a sweet fifth grader asked me to come over to her by the shelves. She had a question. She feverishly waved her hand for me to bend down so that she could whisper in my ear. I heard the creak of my knees as I squatted down beside her. She said, "My mom said I can trust you and that you're one of the good ones. Can you show me where some books are with gay characters?" I smiled. Having taught the child's mother, I knew they had LGBTQIA+ family members. I was able to reply, "Well, of course. Let me show you some of my favorites." I showed the student some titles and went into the back room, where I proceeded to gasp for air as a single tear rolled down my face because this child trusted me enough to ask that question in a community where asking those types of questions are taboo. This is why I do what I do. This is why I speak out. That one child made every hate-filled comment lodged my way dissolve. Every child in our community deserves to be seen, heard, and have access to age-appropriate books on the shelves of our libraries, books that represent every family in our village.

I didn't realize that one speech at my own public library board meeting would turn me into some sort of national advocate against book banning. I simply went to speak in the parish I grew up in on a topic that's important to me. I'm not happy that I have become a target for white Christian nationalists or the local internet trolls. But as MLK Jr. said in his blueprint speech, "When you discover what you will be in your life, set out to do it as if God Almighty called you at this particular moment in history to do it. Don't just set out to do a good job. Set out to do such a good job that the living, the dead or the unborn couldn't do it any better." That's what I'm trying to accomplish.

So I will gladly embrace this role that has been thrust upon me, and I will do it to the best of my ability. I have been blessed with a solid foundation and blueprint for life. What would Sheila Tubman from *Otherwise*

Known as Sheila the Great do? She'd fake it until she made it, but she wouldn't back down. What would Farley Drexel "Fudge" Hatcher from *Tales of a Fourth Grade Nothing* do? He would jump at the problem head-first. What would Sally J. Freedman do herself? She'd dream of a world that could be better and set out to make it so. What would my hero Judy (Blume) do? She'd speak out, and so will I.

Chapter 5

(Wo)man in the Mirror

We have to confront ourselves. Do we like what we see in the mirror? And, according to our light, according to our understanding, according to our courage, we will have to say yea or nay—and rise!

—Maya Angelou

I have learned so much about myself in the past few years, on this journey to becoming the best librarian I can be for my students and my community. The song "Man in the Mirror" is one I listen to often. The lyrics resonate. I want to make a difference in the world. To make a difference, you have to start with yourself.

Here's where I admit one of my biggest shames: I voted for Donald Trump in 2016. I'm mortified to admit this and dreaded having to write that sentence, but I feel that it's important to be honest. If I could go back in time, knowing then what I know now, I'd change the fact that I voted for that horrid man. At the time, I wasn't paying much attention to the news or the situation in our country. I thought I was voting for the lesser of two evils. My parents voted for him, and all I heard them say was that Hillary was awful. I should have investigated the presidential election more.

I should have forced myself to pay attention. I didn't think I was voting for a good person. I just thought I was voting for the person who was likely to do the least amount of damage. I was so wrong.

I was a different person back then, but that's no excuse. I was interviewed for *Der Spiegel* about extremism and book banning and told the journalist how ashamed I felt about voting for Trump in 2016. I started crying when I confessed this. The journalist said, "But you were just one vote." That doesn't take back the fact that I voted for him or lessen the shame. I think I knew it was wrong at the time, deep down, because I was really upset at hitting that button for him when I voted. I felt sick to my stomach, but I was so unsure of what to do, and I let my "red" community and my family influence that decision too much. I even posted on social media that I threw up a little in my mouth when I placed that vote.

I contributed to one of the biggest evils our country has ever seen and contributed to the current state of extremism in our country. I contributed to the chain reaction of events that allowed hate to become acceptable and normalized in our country. I was a contributing factor in the growing movement of white Christian nationalism. No, my one vote didn't make or break the election, but, collectively, all of us who voted that way did. There are many like me who have been awakened since that election. I guess when some accuse me of catching the "woke disease," it's true. I finally woke up. I find it hard to forgive myself for not doing it sooner and will spend the rest of my life trying to make up for it. One event in my life that helped me wake up was an episode of *The View* in 2018.

In 2018, I clicked on the TV to watch an episode of *The View*. The guest that day was Marley Dias. Little did I know that her ten-minute interview would shake my entire mindset and begin to open my eyes to aspects of my and my students' experiences I'd never thought about. At the time, Marley Dias was only thirteen years old. I watched enthralled as the young teen discussed how in school she was only learning about one person's experience in the books they read. The books they read in class, and the books she saw in the library, seemed to be only about white boys and their dogs. Someone joked and said, "You mean like *Old Yeller*?" She laughed but went on to discuss how she didn't see Black girls like herself being represented or their stories being told, so she founded #1000Black-GirlBooks to collect and donate one thousand books featuring Black girl protagonists.

How could one so young be so wise? I immediately purchased her book *Marley Dias Gets It Done and So Can You*. This thirteen-year-old reminded me that two important aspects of life were educating yourself and finding out what you're passionate about in life. I already knew what my passion in life was and that was libraries, fostering a love of reading, and shaping young minds. At the time, I thought I was an educated individual, but after reading her book, I realized that I had a lot more to learn about life and the things I took for granted.

For starters, I grew up in a majority white school and community. By *majority white school and community*, I mean a sea of alabaster as far as the eye could see, and I never thought twice about it. I graduated with one Black student in my senior class of ninety-six students, and knew only four or five Black people my entire childhood. There was no diversity. Everyone around me seemed to be white, straight, and Christian, or at least that's what I perceived. Anyone different in my community was immediately noticed. For example, everyone knew Freddie, the one Black student in my class. He was an extremely nice person, so everyone wanted to be friends with him, but I also wonder if it was because everyone was quick to prove that they "didn't see color."

I have heard a lot of white people say they don't see color. I used to think that was a good thing, as in we don't consider the color of someone's skin when deciding how we feel about them. But then I started to realize that it's okay to acknowledge our differences. Also, it's a lie. We all see race, and that's fine. If we deny someone's race, we're denying a part of who they are as a person and not acknowledging the person as a whole, and that can slip into dangerous territory. If we ignore someone's race, we're ignoring the different perspectives that they bring. I'm suspicious when I hear people use the phrase to prove that they aren't racist. In my opinion, if you have to prove that you aren't racist, you might need to ask yourself why you feel the need to prove it. Discussions on race can be uncomfortable, but if we only talk about things that make us comfortable, we can never grow.

I started to think about how Freddie's experience must have been much different than mine. When we were in school, I did wonder how his day-to-day life might be different. I wondered if anyone in our town ever hurled slurs his way that I didn't know about. I don't know if anyone else thought about this because it was never discussed. Why didn't we acknowledge that it might have been hard for Freddie or even ask him? After I read Marley's book, I wondered if he, like Marley Dias, ever wished that the books we read in class featured Black protagonists. I wondered if the smile he always had on his face masked discomfort and how difficult it must have been being the only Black student. Maybe it didn't bother him, but I think it would have bothered me.

How would my life have been different if I had been the one white student in school? Would I have changed the way I acted to blend in with my peers? I had taken everything for granted growing up in my community where we all seemed to be the same: same socioeconomic class, same skin color, same religion. Reading this book by Marley Dias had me thinking about how I work at the same school I attended in middle school in the same community, and not much had changed in thirty years. We do have more Black and brown students, but they are few and far between. Were they feeling like Marley? I realized that I'd never asked myself these questions in my first fifteen or so years as an educator, and I was ashamed I hadn't.

We as white people also need to acknowledge that we do indeed have privilege in being white. This is a taboo term in my community. I used to balk at the term *white privilege*, but now I understand what it means. If you bring up the term in Livingston Parish, you will be immediately scoffed at and people will roll their eyes. They'll say that's not a thing. Wrong, because it is. Being born white is indeed a privilege. I am afforded things in society that are not afforded my Black friends. I will never be judged based on the color of my skin. I will never know what it's like to be pulled over by police for being Black. I will never be accused of shoplifting because I was shopping while Black. I will never be seen through a racist lens, and there is a privilege to that. The unfairness of it all weighs me down.

That doesn't mean I am ashamed to be white or that I have white guilt. That's the first thing the Whitey McWhites like to say when the term *white privilege* is brought up. I have no control over the color of the skin I was born with, but I can acknowledge that there is absolute privilege in the fact that I was born white. It's a fact. Face it. And while I don't have control over the skin I was born in, I do have control over how I use the privilege of being born white. I hesitate to say that, because I don't want to give off a white-savior vibe, but I have been afforded privilege and platforms from being white and I should use them for good.

As a teacher, I had tried to introduce stories into my classroom with protagonists of color, but I realized that all the stories and books I had taught for the last fifteen to twenty years were stories revolving around the Civil Rights movement and not just characters who happened to be Black. I think part of it was stupidity and part of it was ignorance—not realizing that I should be teaching or asking more about the Black American experience. I wanted to teach life lessons about what we had (I hope) learned through the historical treatment of Black people in the United States. But I'd forgotten to teach that Black people also live normal everyday lives and that stories about Black joy or stories that just happen to have Black characters exist and should be taught in classrooms and purchased in libraries. I had gradually started to think about this a few years prior, but Marley really had me reflecting. I think more teachers and librarians need to explore this, and I hope that with more books like *Black Boy Joy*, an anthology edited by Kwame Mbalia, being published, that will happen, but we as white people need to make a conscious effort to make sure that we are acknowledging this. I also started thinking about books with LGBTQIA+ characters and other minority groups in the same way.

Adding stories of Black excellence to the collection doesn't take away from white kids. Having my Asian students see a main character who just happens to be Asian doesn't mean I am wiping away the stories with characters who happen to be white. It would be impossible anyway, as most books written for children feature white main characters. Adding stories to the collection with LGBTQIA+ characters doesn't take away from the straight kids. It won't magically turn them gay. It simply gives underrepresented kids books in which they can see themselves. Also, and importantly, these books give the groups of students not historically marginalized ways to learn about other backgrounds. White people feeling oppressed because BIPOC stories are included is ridiculous to me, since books that feature white characters already make up most of the collection.

I knew that I had to start thinking more about the nonwhite and LGBTQIA+ students in my school. While we had more nonwhite students than we had had while I was a student, we were still a majority white school. Every educator at my school at the time was white. In fact, the only Black educator I had ever seen at my school was our beloved former principal Freddie London, not to be confused with the Freddie who was my former classmate. (Until this moment, I never realized that the two most prominent Black people in my life growing up were both named Freddie!) Coach London probably started my initial realization that I needed to do better on including all my students. I wish that I had been paying attention sooner.

Coach London was my middle school PE and social studies teacher, and he became our school's assistant principal the year I was hired. I remember being so nervous in my job interview and wanting to impress him. I think he sensed my nervousness because after the interview he hugged me and was very reassuring about how the interview had gone. I told him at least I didn't throw up from nerves, and he gave a hearty laugh—a laugh that all kids who went to my school can instantly recall.

Coach London was famous in our town. If you ask anyone who attended Live Oak School from the 1980s to 2015 about Coach London, they will light up and have a story to tell. The entire community can tell you how Coach London's hands were so big, he could drop a quarter through his wedding ring. In fact, when my husband realized that he could do the same thing when we got married, we laughed about it and I went to school to tell Coach. Coach London was larger-than-life, and when he passed away in December 2022, it felt like the entire community showed up to celebrate his life. However, not everyone always celebrated him.

Coach London and his brother were the first Black students at our high school after integration. When I was a classroom teacher, I would have Coach come and speak to my students about his experience, and it was eye-opening. He didn't mince words when telling the kids the names he was called by his friends' parents just for existing and attending the high school he deserved to attend. He recounted that his friend's dad yelled, "Go home, monkey," as he walked into school. Coach London was blessed with the gift of storytelling, and he would pause after saying that and stare off into the air with a look of sadness. The kids gasped. The kids would sit slack-jawed and in outrage that anyone would treat Coach London that way. I wondered if the man who had said that still lived in our community. It didn't surprise me to hear Coach London say that, but I was angered nonetheless.

I learned so many lessons myself from his talks and realized just how privileged I was to be born white. And although the experience he related happened in the 1970s, I realized that not much had changed in our community except what was said out loud. Everyone was still quick to say they didn't see color, but I heard what people in our community said about the majority of Black citizens when our community's citizens got a little too comfortable and didn't guard their speech. If a Black kid "acted white," they were deemed okay. People still say that all the time. "Oh, he is a good kid. He acts white." I got angry and wondered what that even meant. I questioned whether any of my behavior, the types of stories I read aloud, made our students of color feel that they had to act or be a certain way. I questioned whether all students in my school saw themselves in the books we have in our library or if all they saw was white boys and their dogs.

Around the time I read Marley Dias's book I was fortunate to be invited to a dinner during the American Library Association's annual conference in New Orleans. The dinner was hosted by We Need Diverse Books, and it was a small gathering of librarians, publishers, and authors. I felt like I'd hit the lottery when I was seated with the authors Lamar Giles, Kody Keplinger, Preeti Chhibber, and the Detroit librarian Karen Lemmons.

I was fascinated to meet Alex Gino, the author of *Melissa*, who was the first person I'd ever met who used they/them pronouns. I had never been around so many people so different from me, but I definitely stood out as the "different" one. Different because I felt like I didn't have the credentials. I was a kid sitting at the grown-up table. I jokingly texted a friend that I felt very country come to town. I was the boring person of the group, and for one reason or another I was embarrassed that that was all I brought to the table. For the first time in my life, I was the one who was not like the others. I was different in that I didn't feel as cool as the people at my table, and also different in that I was blessed with privilege that I was starting to recognize.

I remember vividly the authors and librarians at my table that night discussing the decision by the American Library Association to change the name of the Laura Ingalls Wilder Medal to the Children's Literature Legacy Award due to racial insensitivity. For the life of me I didn't understand what they were talking about, but these were people I respected, so I knew I needed to pay attention.

I was afraid to admit that I didn't know what they were talking about, so I just listened and took it all in. At first, I was a little indignant. I wouldn't look back fondly on the books if they depicted racism. Was there something I had missed? I had read the Little House books from cover to cover at least five or six times and counted them as some of my favorites. What was racially insensitive about the Little House books? It had been years since I had read the series, and I was mentally going through each book in my head, trying to recall the different characters and storylines. I had completed an entire project for a graduate class on the Little House books, and I would never knowingly promote books like that, would I? I saw several life events involving those books flash before my eyes as I tried to remember the books and figure out what they were talking about.

When I returned home, I got out my Little House books and decided to look at them through a new lens. Holy crap—that's what I thought as I spent the next few days rereading and marking the spots that I now realized were not only racially insensitive but openly stereotypical and even dehumanizing. How had I never noticed this in what had been some of my favorite books growing up? I felt embarrassed. I wouldn't want my own child reading these books now, at least not without first discussing the way Laura Ingalls Wilder portrayed Indigenous characters or the racism of Pa wearing blackface. I would want her to read them only to point out how the depictions are wrong and harmful. But then I think, "Do I need her to actually read them to point that out?" No, and I would not want my Black students to pick up the books and see the way Black people were characterized. It would be hurtful.

My realization was a bitter pill to swallow because of how much I loved the books as a child. But the books are not what I thought they were as a child. Strip away my nostalgia, and I knew the books could be harmful. Is it censorship if I take them off the shelf, though? Or is it removing something harmful? I honestly don't know and feel a little lost when thinking about it. I just want to do the right thing, and I admit that I don't always know what that entails. Since I follow my school's collection development policy, and weed out books that haven't been checked out in five years, they have been weeded from our collection. The kids just weren't interested in them anymore, and I needed the shelf space for books that the kids would check out.

So not only was Marley Dias getting me to think about my collection and how it could be leaving some of my students feeling unrepresented, but that fateful dinner left me thinking how some of the books could even be harmful. I went back to my school and spent several weeks going over our library collection. Marley was right. It was a bunch of white boys and their dogs. Yes, that's an exaggeration, but the collection was admittedly not very diverse. We had students who were Indian American, and I couldn't find a single book with an Indian American protagonist. Things had to change.

At some point at the beginning of my time as a librarian, I came across the famous quote by Dr. Rudine Sims Bishop about how books should be windows, mirrors, and sliding glass doors. I knew that I wanted the books in our school library to be that for our students, but it took a while to realize what Dr. Sims Bishop's quote truly means. After reading Marley's book,

I truly reflected upon this quote. I not only wanted our Black and brown students, and our LGBTQIA+ students, to see themselves in the books on our shelves, but I wanted all my students to experience characters that weren't just white, straight, and able-bodied. I wanted to offer books that had protagonists of different races, religions, abilities, and backgrounds. And I knew that Marley was right. I needed to educate myself first.

I began to make a conscious effort to read a variety of news articles, read what I could about diversity in literature, connect with people of all walks of life on Twitter, and pay attention. I wanted to ask so many questions. One of my questions was prompted by a post that said it wasn't the responsibility of Black people or the LGBTQIA+ community to teach me, and that opened my eyes even further. My Black and LGBTQIA+ friends were tired, and I was starting to see why.

A big lesson I learned was about listening, and that really began to sink in in the summer of 2020. The death of George Floyd, the Black Lives Matter movement, and being stuck at home during quarantine with nothing to do but read the news and social media truly influenced the way I began to view the world. I was an observer on Twitter and tried putting myself in others' shoes the way I was raised to do. If I had a question or was curious about anything, I'd look up articles online to learn more. When historical figures were mentioned, I learned about them. I learned to stop talking and listen.

Listen to the pain and the frustrations of people who have been historically oppressed and marginalized. Listen without comment and don't interject. For someone like me who likes to talk, simply listening can be difficult. I learned that if someone voices frustration with something, and it's not directed at you or your actions, you don't need to say, "Well, I don't do that." It's not about you, or maybe it is and you need to listen some more and do a little soul-searching. Not only were my eyes opening, but so was my heart. I started changing the way I viewed news stories. I tried to put myself in the shoes of the protestors and understand why they were protesting. I started to feel a small fraction of their anger and wondered what I would do if I felt oppressed. Of course, I'd be angry.

I also learned about microaggressions. I had never even heard of that word. I attended a webinar on diversity and listened to my friend K.C. Boyd talk about how white women will often touch a Black woman's hair. I am so glad it was a webinar and my friend couldn't see me turn bright red with the realization that I have touched my Black students' hair before. I was mortified. I had so much to learn and I am still learning today, but I will tell you I have not touched a Black child's hair since then. How did I ever think that was appropriate? I guess I thought I was complimenting them and proving I wasn't a racist? But then again, why was I feeling the need to prove that to them? I guess I wanted the kids to know I was trying, but what else was I doing that I shouldn't be doing?

K.C. Boyd, a Washington, D.C., school librarian, has been one of the biggest influences on my adult life, and I thank God she allows me to call her a friend. She makes me want to learn more about myself and be a better person. I have looked up every historical figure and event she has ever posted about on social media. I pick up every book she recommends and have had serious internal reflections because of her posts about the Black experience. I experienced more personal growth from reading her tweets in 2020, and from her continued friendship, than from all other events in my life combined. She taught me that tough questions can be uncomfortable, but we need to step outside our comfort zones.

If I'm doing something I shouldn't be doing, like touching a Black child's hair, even though I am trying to compliment them, I need to address that I've done something wrong. That can be an uncomfortable feeling, but if more people stopped to listen, practiced internal reflection, and actually tried to learn and correct themselves, the world would be a better place. I will continue to explore more of this in my life, because I want to be a better person, an excellent educator, and to set a good example for my child and my community. That doesn't mean it's a fun road to travel and that doesn't mean I'm ashamed of being white. That also doesn't mean I won't continue to get things wrong.

Once your eyes begin to open with one realization, it becomes a domino effect of continual learning. I used to say I didn't see color, but I learned how dumb a statement that really is. We are all different and we should celebrate our differences. I no longer say those words, and when I hear other people say them, I point out the absurdity. As I all too often tell my daughter, it takes all sorts of people to make the world go around. And while I do get uncomfortable discussing racial differences, it's necessary for learning. When the person doing the learning is in the majority, like the white person in a room filled with white people and only one Coach London or Freddie, it is especially necessary to embrace the uncomfortable.

Recently, the author Chris Barton visited our school. I shared with a co-worker a picture of his book *Moving Forward: From Space-Age Rides to Civil Rights Sit-Ins with Airman Alton Yates.* This person winced and sighed and said, "It's a great book, but I'm not sure I like how the white people are portrayed. We're always portrayed like this." He flipped through the book for a few pages to point out depictions of angry white men, and I wasn't sure what he expected me to say. I wanted to say, "Well, duh. That's the whole point. These white people were wrong in their treatment of Black people and the people doing the mistreating were indeed white. It's pointing out the racism while also telling the story of Alton Yates. His life wouldn't be accurately portrayed without it. Can't you see that?" Instead, I diplomatically replied, "Well, it's nonfiction, so it is historically accurate. Do you want them to lie about what really happened?" He replied, "No. I just get tired of it." Well, guess what: so do the Black people who experience it! I try so hard to be aware that some people in my life are further back in their journey than I am. A few years ago someone was probably thinking the same thing about me, so I'm learning to find these teachable moments where I can make my points without losing it. I do know that this particular person is trying and is a good person. That doesn't mean it doesn't still frustrate me. I also recognize that I am a far cry from being done learning as well.

I am so afraid of getting things wrong, but refusing to talk about it is no solution. I want to do justice to these issues and be able to act with sensitivity. I fear causing additional harm by going about things the wrong way, and I experience extreme anxiety in certain situations. I'm afraid to ask questions if I sense that I can find the answers on my own. I am afraid to say the wrong thing and cause someone pain. I think many people have these fears, but we cannot let that hold us back. The solution is to talk about it, but be very careful to do more listening than talking.

Once I had this realization, I became very cognizant of the need to make sure that all my students are represented and made to feel safe, whether they're white, Black, brown, Asian, straight, gay, Christian, Jewish, atheist, and so on. I want all students to feel protected and loved. Every kid deserves to see themselves reflected in my lessons and to see themselves represented in the books on the library shelves. The world is still going to suck, but I want to do my part to make it suck a little less for them. Life is still going to present challenges, but perhaps I can help them a small bit to meet those challenges.

We should listen to the kids. They all want to be included. It hurts nothing to include them. I have lost more former students to suicide than I care to think about, many of whom I suspect died as a direct result of being made to feel excluded in our society. I'll be damned if I'll continue to just watch it happen. There's just no reason for excluding whole sections of society, no matter what your beliefs are. The kids are watching us. They want a safe place to learn, to be included; they need adults to look up to; and we should set positive examples for them.

Listen to the kids. I am blessed to teach close to seven hundred of them a year. They are growing up to be more understanding than my own generation. And check your privilege. I know I am learning to check mine. It has only made me a more empathetic and understanding person, and I owe it all to that uncomfortable dinner hosted by We Need Diverse Books, my friendship with K.C. Boyd, and that catalyst for change, a thirteen-year-old named Marley Dias, whom I saw on *The View* in 2018.

Chapter 6

Hell Hath No Fury Like a Librarian Scorned

Rule number one: Don't fuck with librarians.

—NEIL GAIMAN

Growing up, I looked upon the school and public librarians in my life with reverence. They were the keepers of the books and opened the gates to knowledge. They were there to help me find books and access other worlds, always with a kind smile. As a child, I always thought that librarians were "old," because you tend to think of all adults as old when you're a young child. There's a stereotype that librarians all keep their hair in a bun, wear cardigans, have cats, and walk around shushing people. Maybe that's what we once were, but there's a whole new type of librarian in the world now. While I can't say we don't favor cardigans, librarians are so much more than the stereotype. Little did I know growing up that librarians are secret badasses.

When I stepped into my role as a librarian, I made a concerted effort to befriend any and every librarian I could find, whether locally, across the state, or across the nation. There is strength in numbers, and I wholeheartedly believe that we learn more from one another than from any other place. I networked at conferences and joined conversations on social media. I jokingly tell people that I forced my friendship on other district school librarians in my parish when I emailed them all and formed a group email chain my first year. I am so glad I did, because it can be lonely being the sole librarian at school. Sharing lessons, resources, and best practices makes us stronger and better at what we do.

I discovered pretty quickly that librarians come in all forms and from all backgrounds. At my first national librarian conference, I remember standing in line at registration and smiling when I saw how many had brightly colored hair and a cool fashion sense. I lined up for author signings and overheard conversations in which librarians discussed their tattoos. I sat in on conference sessions that emphasized that librarians are sometimes the only defenders of intellectual freedom and that it was a job to be taken seriously.

I couldn't have imagined that one day I would join the ranks of the FReadom Fighters and step up to defend my town against people set on destroying our public library system. But I knew immediately that I had found my people, and the feeling settled around me like a warm blanket on a freezing day and gave me such comfort and joy. I do have a penchant for cardigans, and you will find me with my hair in a bun when I'm at home, but you will never catch me shushing in the library, just like you will not catch me backing down when I see an attack on a library or librarian.

I am a librarian, damn it. I'm not some weakling. So, after a weekend of crying and hiding for days as I watched my reputation being dragged through the mud, my shock and fear solidified into anger. I was seething. I was pissed. I wanted to karate chop those responsible in the throat. I don't think words can adequately express the burning rage I felt toward these assholes who were posting complete lies about me on social media. All I kept thinking was "How dare they?" I was also livid at some of the comments from people I knew. It was like a who's who parade of people in my town, people who had committed actual misdeeds, who were suddenly judging ME just because I spoke at a public library board meeting.

A fellow educator whom I know only vaguely reached out to me via Facebook Messenger to quiz me about my comments from the public library board meeting. We aren't friends and I don't know her. She kept asking, "What book are you pushing to keep in the library?" I kept repeating to her that I hadn't gone to speak about particular books but about censorship in general. She kept quizzing me like I was a student she was giving some wild pop quiz to. She made comments about "agendas" and things against her religion and kept trying to find some "gotcha" moment with me. It's a good thing this conversation happened through Messenger, because I almost came unglued and wanted to ask her who was she to quiz me about religion, morals, and agendas when she had a very public affair while she was married, to a police officer who was also married, and both of their marriages ended in divorce because of it. I kept thinking that she had a ton of gall.

I also noticed that a woman I'd known for several years, whom I thought was a friend, was openly laughing and participating in some of the online negativity against me. She posted the laughing emoji on posts mocking me. What the hell? I think that if you had peeled off my skin and rubbed salt on me, it wouldn't have hurt as much as those emojis. She and I had laughed together on field trips as parents of kids the same age. I thought she was a truly nice person. It was like a punch in the gut to see her join in the takedown.

Then I saw that her husband was also posting extremely hateful things. This man had had a decades-long affair and secret children behind his wife's back. But there he was online, discussing my morality because I spoke up about library reconsideration policies. That might be the most maddening part of being defamed online—knowing the character of the people throwing the stones while they sit on a moral high horse. Even if you had a problem with me speaking out against censorship, it pales in comparison to cheating on your spouse, in my opinion, but here we are.

I hope that I don't ever see that man in person, because I feel a lot of anger toward him for his comments, and also for how he has treated his wife and kids. I did end up seeing his wife. She comes to my hearings and sits with my defamers. At the last hearing, I tried to smile at her, but she wouldn't make eye contact. I'm attempting to come to terms with forgiving her, but I don't know if that will ever happen. I blocked the entire family on social media, and it saddens me that I won't get to follow the positive things happening to her adult son, whom I still adore. I'll eventually see them again. My child and their youngest will graduate high school together in the same class. I'm dreading it already.

Even though they've hurt me, truth be told I don't wish ill health or harm to anyone. I may have fantasies of kicking them in the crotch with all my might, but I would never do that. Mainly because I don't want to go to jail, but also because kids look up to me. That would surely be the wrong example to set. But sometimes karma has a way of handling people who judge others and don't see their own faults, and that's on them.

For several days after the initial barrage of hateful posts, I went through the first stages of grief: shock, bargaining, and depression. Pretty quickly the pain solidified into the fourth stage: anger. The anger was building up into a mighty storm, and it scared me. It's not a pleasant feeling to walk around with pent-up rage for weeks on end. My blood pressure soared, I had several panic attacks, and I started losing chunks of my hair. My weight was plummeting because I was too upset to eat. My blood sugar was all over the place and I had fainting spells. I didn't know that stress could be so traumatic that you can forget to eat or drink. I wish I hadn't learned it from experience.

Throughout all the pain, I was able to rely on an amazing group of Louisiana school librarians. Tiffany, Kelsye, Kristy, Amanda, Lovie, Tammy, and I were on the executive board of the Louisiana Association of School Librarians during this time. They were truly my rocks. I honestly don't know what I would have done without them. They let me scream. They let me cry. They offered jokes and support and were outraged on my behalf. They stood by me and still do. In truth, they saved me from dropping off the edge into hopelessness during one of the darkest moments of my life. They reassured me that I had in no way brought this upon myself. I'd wake up sad and scared, and there would be a funny GIF or inspirational quote.

I'd voice frustration, and they would let me get it all out and then offer suggestions or support. I don't know how I'll ever repay them.

I don't remember who first suggested that there had to be something that could be done. I lodged a criminal complaint against the two ring-leaders, but the sheriff's department said it was more of a civil matter. That was a huge letdown. Someone in our group suggested I file a lawsuit. My friends were just as enraged and wanted to see justice take place. None of us knew how to do that or how much it would cost, but we talked about it at length. The more we talked, the lighter I felt. In shifting to discussions about getting revenge and filing a suit, the sadness eased a little, and I focused more on what I could do to set the record straight.

I thought about filing a lawsuit for several days. My mind changed every few hours from thinking it was a great idea to thinking it was pointless. I went back and forth, worrying myself silly over all the pros and cons. It seemed impossible at first, because I had no prior experience in court proceedings. I didn't know how to obtain an attorney or have any idea how much the process would cost. I was lucky that I'd never had to deal with the court system, but some knowledge of the law would have come in very handy at that moment.

While I was mulling what to do, I mentioned the idea of a lawsuit to a childhood friend. Turns out, she had been talking about my situation with a friend who is an attorney named Ellyn. She relayed Ellyn's thoughts on what was happening and suggested I contact her. I emailed Ellyn and asked if she thought I had a case. She called me that night, and we discussed the various options. Ellyn was so kind to me and outraged on my behalf. She outlined the costs and the various routes to take. It was a bit overwhelming, but I was grateful that she took the time to walk me through it all. Ellyn ended up giving me free legal advice for a week before I started to seriously think about suing these men.

I brought the idea up to Jason. He just looked at me, sighed, and scratched his head. I know that he wanted the whole thing to just go away. Join the club. He was worried about the money. We do all right, but it's not as if we were rolling in dough. He said, "Where will we come up with the money to afford this?" He said that was his only trepidation about filing a suit. Jason is way more practical than I am. While I'm ready to throw it all in and go down in a blaze of glory, Jason is thinking about mortgage payments. I asked him if he would back me if I could find the funding. I remember he looked at me with wide eyes and asked how I was going to do that, and I said, "We shall see. Do you trust me?" As soon as he gave me his blessing, I asked the group for ideas about raising the funds.

My friend Tiffany said I should set up a GoFundMe. I laughed at first. Who was going to donate money to me, but the group came to the consensus that I should at least try and find out. I was skeptical. I went back to Jason and asked again if he was okay with me moving forward. He said, "Go big or go home, I guess. Let's just not go into debt in the process." I immediately sat down at my desk to make plans for going big.

I called Ellyn again and told her I was interested in hiring her as my attorney. Ellyn said her retainer was $7,500, so I went back to my friend group. They all thought $7,500 was attainable. I was still doubtful but decided to go for it. My friend Tiffany created a GoFundMe, and I announced on social media that I intended to sue the people dragging me through the mud and posted the link. Boy, did it take off! I was shocked when I met my goal within fourteen hours. I knew that I'd eventually need more than $7,500, so Tiffany increased the goal to $15,000.

With the money, there were also many messages of support from all over the country. I texted the group, "I'm trying so hard to focus on the positive love and not those asshats." That can be difficult when one of the asshats, Ryan Thames, donated to my GoFundMe just to taunt me. His message? "Let's goooo!" Hey, if he wants to go, I'll give it all I've got. Let's go, indeed.

Around the same time, I told K.C. Boyd, my friend and school librarian in Washington, D.C., about my plans to sue. K.C. suggested that I talk to John Chrastka and Patrick Sweeney at EveryLibrary, and she made an email introduction. John and Patrick were super supportive and introduced me to Kelly Jensen, a former librarian turned author who writes for Book Riot. Kelly was interested in my story and asked for an interview. I am so glad I said yes.

I realized that I had a lot to say and that sharing my story helped ease my anger. Kelly also asked questions that led to some important internal reflection. For instance, I knew that I wanted to file a lawsuit to stand up for myself, but as I was talking, I also realized that it was important to speak out as a white straight person. If I was going to talk the talk about how libraries are for everyone, I need to walk the walk and defend them, and especially for the librarygoers most affected. I told Kelly, "White people need to speak up and out. Historically marginalized communities shouldn't have to fight this fight because the fight is against them. This is their material and their lives. More white people need to show up, speak out, and do the work."

Of course, they made more memes about that quote and continued to mock me online, but I knew that I was in the right. At that time, I was still looking at their socials, because I hadn't yet made the decision to protect my peace and just not look. The posts made me angry, but they didn't jar my system as much as the initial posts. It's not my fault Ryan Thames and Michael Lunsford didn't get it or simply refused to get it for all the wrong reasons. In my opinion, it is probably a bit of both. These are unthinking people who've been enlisted as foot soldiers in a broader cultural war that has nothing to do with books and everything to do with finding purpose and belonging in a world. However you slice it, it's too bad for them. They're missing out on a lot of the positivity the world has to offer. I feel sorry for them that they don't understand why it's so important for people like us—people who are white and straight—to stand up for LGBTQIA+ and BIPOC communities. If they were truly men of God like they claim, they'd get it. But that's just one of the many ways in which we differ, and I was starting to feel a sense of relief in the knowledge that I was not the same type of person.

I told Kelly about my fears, and she agreed to let me share whatever I was comfortable sharing and even let me look over the article before it was published. I owe a lot to Kelly. Not only did she help me share my story, but she was kind. She gave me a platform to defend myself publicly for the first time. I refused to argue with these people on social media but wanted to get the truth out. I also needed to publicize my GoFundMe, and her article helped propel my fundraiser forward. Even if the article hadn't gone as far and wide as it did, I wouldn't have regretted talking to Kelly. Unlike everyone around me, she was someone on the outside looking in, and her personal encouragement made me feel a little less crazy.

After Kelly's article was published, my GoFundMe really took off, and the emails started rolling in for more interviews. I would text the group, "Hey, there was another donation and we're up to $20,000," or "Someone from *Insider* just contacted me!" It was very overwhelming. Not only was I dealing with my whole community openly talking about me on social media, but the main aggressors were still posting horrible things. I was also now dealing with journalists, and, to top it all off, the new school year was starting.

Having been selected as Co-Librarian of the Year for *School Library Journal* in 2021, I'd had some experience speaking with the press, but I was still nervous. It's not like I'd taken a class in college on media relations. Kara Yorio from *School Library Journal* wanted to interview me, and I immediately said yes because I knew and trusted Kara. However, when I received an email from Tyler Kingkade of NBC, I felt real fear at how far my story was traveling. This was going to be seen outside the library world. Sharing my story was one thing. Knowing that people across the country would read about me was terrifying. I had also seen that once one news agency ran a story, another usually followed, and I was unsure if I was prepared for that. Was I prepared for Fox News picking up my story as one of their culture war talking points and the flood of extremist hate that would surely follow?

Things were getting too public, too quickly. This was at a point where I was still hiding in my room and crying daily yet starting to get angrier and wanting to take charge of my life. I was beset with conflicting emotions and my anxiety was high. I weighed the pros and cons, talked to friends and family, and decided to do the interview for NBC anyway. I formally hired Ellyn as my attorney, and she helped me navigate that interview.

Speaking about what was happening to me, while cathartic in some small way, was also very weird. That a journalist from NBC was interested in what a small-town librarian was facing in my suburban Louisiana community was unfathomable to me, but I guess so was having my reputation smeared by two random men whom I'd never met. I understood why Book Riot and *School Library Journal* were interested. But NBC? It's still hard for me to grasp. At the end of the day, I figured that if they were interested, and it would help spread the word about what's happening to people who stand against censorship, I had a responsibility to speak out.

As someone who checks multiple news apps daily, including NBC, I was shocked the day the article came out and I saw my face in that familiar app. It's not every day you wake up to find an interview you've given wedged between a Donald Trump story and the news of Anne Heche's death. My eyes grew wide. "This is really happening. I'm an actual national news headline," I thought to myself. It was surreal. I didn't think, "Oh, I'm so cool on NBC." I thought, "I hope I don't get further attacks because of this." I read the article quickly and emailed the journalist to thank him. It was very well written and covered everything thoroughly. I sent a screenshot of the headline, along with the link to the story, to my family and friends. Jason called me from work and said, "Wow. That really is you on NBC." I was torn between feelings of pride and wishing the interview hadn't been necessary in the first place.

Tiffany soon texted me to check the GoFundMe. It had jumped by twenty thousand dollars. Holy hell! It became a joke in the friend group text about how high the number would go by the end of the day. We were all refreshing the website and would text every time another five thousand dollars was raised. I hadn't realized how scared I'd been about the cost of my lawsuit, and I finally breathed a sigh of relief. Ryan Thames taunting me on my GoFundMe solidified my conviction that I was doing the right thing by filing suit and standing up to him.

The messages of support started rolling in by the hundreds. People messaged me on social media and emailed. Strangers, former students, friends I hadn't spoken to for ages. I was also messaged by librarians who related how they were dealing with similar situations in their own towns. It was overwhelming, but I tried to answer everyone. With each message the tide of grief and anger receded a bit more. I smiled internally and started to feel validated. I had been harboring tremendous self-doubt.

I wrestled with the fear of the additional hateful posts that might come from the attention, and the thought of losing the lawsuit hung over me. However, I started to realize that I was not alone. So many other librarians contacted me to thank me for speaking out and taking action. Librarians were experiencing similar situations all across the county, and it was so difficult to speak out or fight back. The main thing I realized was that it didn't really matter if I won in court, because I would be winning by telling my truth to journalists. I would defend myself in the court of public opinion against the lies just by filing. And, broadly speaking, I had faith in the public, especially as I received messages of support like the following.

> Thank you for standing up for our children, for readers everywhere. The news is filled everyday with hatred and lies. We have to fight back, take a stand like you. Thank you for being brave and for being an example for us all. Please stay safe.

> Reading all about what you've been through and what you continue to go through in the face of some truly horrible bullshit from some terrible humans. Stay strong sister, we are with you!!!

> I hope that one day our son has a librarian anywhere near as wonderful as you and that he inherits a love of reading and of books. You guys play an incredible role in society and are so appreciated (although I know it may not always feel like it.)

One of my favorite authors, Newbery Award winner Erin Entrada Kelly, tweeted, "This is moxie. Sending my love and support to you, Amanda. I'm so proud you're from my home state. #FReadom." I was so honored by that tweet I got a tattoo of the word *moxie* on my left wrist to remind myself to hold fast in my determination and have courage. That bit of ink gives me strength when I start to doubt myself and reminds me that I am on the right side of history.

They wanted to silence me, which cemented my will to speak my truth. These groups operate by instilling fear so that no one will challenge them, and I knew it was important to take a stand. I knew I had privileges that others did not. It should not be up to the historically marginalized groups most at risk to be the only ones speaking out. I had the platform, the support, the connections, and lower risk to my job that put me in a position to fight back. If not me, then who? In the end, the outcome of the court case didn't matter, but having the courage to file it in the first place did matter. Speaking out matters.

Soon after hiring Ellyn, we filed suit. I filed to stand up for myself and to stand up for other librarians and educators who are tired of being raked over the coals. I filed for those of us who are tired of being defamed by keyboard warriors on social media. I filed to prove a point that they would not silence me. I filed to show others that there is a way to fight back. I filed because I wanted my reputation back. If they could take me down and silence me, they can do it to anyone. Someone needs to stand up to them, or they will continue attempting to silence others. I filed because I had done nothing wrong. Regardless of whether I won or lost the lawsuit, I would win just by taking a stand. And I thought, "Well, if I lose the court case, at least I gave it a shot and that's winning to me." If the haters are reading this book right now, I've won twice. I fought back and I spoke out. I took a crappy hand and did the best I could with it. I've made lemonade out of lemons.

Of course, the haters mocked me for filing a lawsuit and continued to post about me on social media. I made the right decision. Some people are on horses so high, it's going to be excruciatingly painful when they eventually fall off. Mark my words. They will fall off their high horse one day because karma is a bitch. Will I laugh? Will I think justice has been served or get some satisfaction from it? I hope not. I hope that I'm better than them and their hate.

These people set out to destroy me, but they woke something up inside me that I hope never dies. The court labeled me a public figure and their lawyers called me an activist when I was just a school librarian. I figure if people are going to label me an activist, I might as well act like one and show them what I'm made of—grit and perseverance. As my sister Melanie commented, "Those jerks sure did mess with the wrong one." Hell hath no fury like a librarian scorned.

Chapter 7

The Battle Begins: Initial Court Proceedings

It matters not how strait the gate,
How charged with punishments the scroll,
I am the master of my fate,
I am the captain of my soul.

—"Invictus," by William Ernest Henley

The initial few weeks of harassment took a huge toll on me physically and mentally. I became so petrified the posts would incite someone to come after me that I purchased a Taser and pepper spray, and we increased security cameras around our home. Jason was supportive every step of the way and wanted me to practice at the gun range. When he said that, I knew he was worried about my safety as well. Every little noise had me peeking out of the curtains at night and watching the security footage. When I did leave the house, I feared being followed, and I'd take long routes home, watching in my mirror the entire time. I would check under my car for GPS tracking devices. My daughter noticed my behavior and asked why I was doing these things, so I tried to dial it back a bit or be more secretive about it. I never told my daughter about the death threat, and it took me several days before I told my parents. I didn't want my grandmother to find out and be worried.

I didn't leave my house for weeks, and even today I'm hesitant to go out in public. I sleep with a shotgun under my bed. If I travel country roads, I carry a handgun. I installed dashcams on my vehicle and set them to record at all times. Debilitating panic attacks came frequently, and I worried incessantly that some crazed fanatic would harm my child, or my students, to get at me. Care packages arrived from kind strangers—things like books, cards, tokens of appreciation. I was scared to open them, wondering if they contained something toxic or even a bomb. Our school secretary opened the packages for me because she saw how upset I'd get if I didn't recognize the return address. It might sound silly to some people, but I was living in a constant state of terror. I asked my attorney Ellyn if there was anything we could do, because the sheriff's department would not, or could not, do anything to help.

Ellyn filed a temporary restraining order against the men. She seemed to think we could prevent them from posting about me, or at least have them slow down. I didn't know anything about the law and followed her lead. In my mind, it was obvious that I was in danger, and I naively thought a judge would see that and grant the order. I was so hopeful that the posts would finally stop. I anxiously awaited the judge's decision, still thinking the world was fair and that justice would prevail in the court system.

Finally, Ellyn texted me and told me that the order had been granted! I screamed with joy and I texted everyone I knew with the news. I was so relieved. I thought, "Take that!" My prayers had been answered. My daughter, Josie, came running into the room after my joyous yelp, and I told her the bad men had to leave me alone. We smiled at each other. I started crying with happiness. But my joy was short-lived.

I am glad I didn't post on social media that I'd been granted a restraining order, because a friend of mine texted back and said that she had heard otherwise. That's the way it is in a small community where everyone knows everyone and we all share everyone else's business. She had a friend at the courthouse who had heard it was denied. I was confused, so I called Ellyn again. Ellyn didn't pick up, and I waited two hours in agony. What was going on? Why would she tell me the restraining order had been granted if it hadn't been? Paranoia set in again. Were people playing with me? Was there some conspiracy? I'm not saying it was rational, but these were the thoughts going through my head. I kept thinking, "It's fine. Everything is fine." And then it wasn't. Ellyn called back and apologized. The clerk had given her the wrong information and the restraining order had indeed been denied. For the first time in my life, I let out an uncontrollable wail. The sound was weird and unnatural, and I couldn't stop myself.

I lost it. The room started spinning and I gasped for breath. Jason rushed into the bedroom to see what was wrong, and I couldn't get the words out. I have never lost full control over my body like I did after that devastating phone call. To go from such a high to such a low in the span of a few hours was devastating. I was angry at Ellyn for making me believe it was a fore-gone conclusion that the restraining order would be granted. I was angry at the judge for not seeing reason. I was angry at the courthouse clerk who had given Ellyn the wrong information. I was angry at myself for daring to feel hopeful. I was angry at all the people posting about me. I was a seething ball of rage and pure desolation. I felt hopeless that nothing would be done to help me.

I could not stop the massive sobs that shook my entire body to the point that Jason went to distract my daughter so that she wouldn't hear me and be frightened. At one point, I thought that he might even slap me like they do in the movies when people come unglued. I could see the fear in his face and see that he didn't know how to help. I even got angry at that, as if he should have magically known what to do as he watched his wife crumble before his eyes, and I knew that was unfair. Nothing made sense anymore.

In the middle of this, I remembered that within the next hour I was supposed to be in back-to-back Zoom meetings for two American Association of School Librarians committees. There was no way I would be able to attend. That caused me to panic even more. I called my friend Courtney, who was president-elect of AASL. Courtney sat on the phone with me while I sobbed and tried to speak. She stayed on the phone with me for ten minutes listening to me cry. She was truly the perfect person to call, and I am so grateful for her. She didn't try to issue false hope or platitudes and clichés. She was just there for me when I needed her, and she instinctively knew what I most needed then was a friend on the other end of the line. She was a lifeline and offered to contact the AASL leaders for me to tell them I couldn't make it. I crawled into bed and cried for hours.

I was angry at Ellyn and started to doubt everything. I wasn't sure why I was mad or even if I had a right to be. She's a wonderful attorney, and I know she was doing her best. It wasn't her fault that the courthouse gave her incorrect information, but I wondered if she should have double-checked before telling me. I still go back and forth in parsing my feelings toward her and usually conclude that I was just frustrated and looking for someone to blame. My friends and family suggested I hire a different attorney, that the whole situation shouldn't have happened. But I really wanted to stick with Ellyn out of loyalty and kept telling myself that people make mistakes. I tried to give her grace; I really did. I didn't do so well back then, but I hold no ill will toward her, nor do I blame her for anything that happened. I didn't have long to think about it, because Ellyn told me a court date had been set and we would go before the judge. Ellyn thought that when the judge heard the evidence, she might even change her mind. I guess, like me, Ellyn believed in justice.

I was extremely nervous in the weeks leading up to the first hearing. School was starting, and I didn't want to go to work. I couldn't focus. The joy I normally felt at the start of a new year was not there. I usually spend weeks getting ready, making lesson plans and creating displays. I did none of that. I dreaded going back. Going to work meant eyes on me. I wanted to be alone. All I could think about were the falsehoods spreading around town, and I wondered if people at work believed them. We had a few new employees. Would they hate me before getting to know me? Going back to work also meant having to be around an administration that had said nothing publicly in my defense, and I'd have to face those administrators after feeling let down.

Each year, my school hosts an orientation for students before the first day of school so that they can pick up their schedules, meet their teachers, and tour the school. I look forward to it every year and decorate the library. I usually have a green-screen station set up to take commemorative photographs of the students and their families, pass out information on reading challenges, and arrange book displays for checkout. For the first time ever, I closed the library for orientation and asked to be placed at a different station. My principal readily agreed, but I felt like I was disappointing him and the school. Several colleagues asked why the library wasn't open, and I told them I just couldn't face the public in the library by myself.

I didn't want to be in the library hosting parents and community members who'd been reading about me online, some of whom may even have helped spread the falsehoods. I feared comments and even physical harm. I didn't want judgmental looks. I didn't want to talk about the issue, even if I might get expressions of support. It pained me to not open the library. I missed inviting the kids into our space and welcoming them back to school. Instead, I helped the PE teachers pass out gym uniforms, with my hair hanging in my face, hoping that nobody spoke to me. I asked our administration to make sure that the school resource officer was on campus because I was petrified. I felt like I was a bother just for asking but didn't want to attend the event if he wasn't there.

Orientation ended up being okay. I did feel like I got a lot of dirty looks and stares, but two separate people realized who I was and were supportive. One parent of a returning student said, "I've been reading what's been happening to you. My family knows it's a bunch of shit and we support you." I held back tears and told her thank you. Another parent said, "You have my support. Don't let them get you down." I looked around quickly hoping nobody else heard or noticed. I didn't want any attention thrown my way, even though I was grateful.

My co-workers didn't really say anything to me, which was a relief, but also a disappointment. A few people hugged me and told me they supported me. I tried to speak to my administration about it, but they didn't seem to want to talk about it. For people who claim we are one big family, I didn't feel like the heads of my school family were very supportive. It is what it is, I guess. I've come to the realization that maybe it's not that they were trying to be unsupportive, but perhaps they didn't know what to say. At least, that's what I tell myself when I get sad or angry about it. However, it was obvious to all my co-workers that I was not myself at the beginning of the school year. One co-worker even reached out to one of my sisters out of concern because she noticed that I was in the depths of despair.

A few weeks after school started, I had my first court hearing. I felt very unprepared and didn't really know what to expect. I was depressed and didn't trust anyone. I don't think Ellyn realized how scared I was. I'd email her my concerns and get short replies that answered my questions but didn't ease my mind. All I knew about court was what I had seen on television shows like *Law & Order.* I should have at least visited the courtroom to get the lay of the land. I met with Ellyn for an hour beforehand, and she gave me a rundown, but I was still nervous. She seemed to think it would be cut-and-dry. We had witnesses ready to testify if the judge needed to hear about my emotional stability and the repercussions of the social media posts. We went over what Ellyn thought would happen but didn't discuss the possible outcomes that might lie ahead. She seemed to think it was a sure thing that we would win, so that's what I thought would happen.

On the day of the first hearing, I rode to court with my mom and sisters. I told Jason to go to work as usual in case he needed to get our daughter after school. My grandmother looked at me with tears in her eyes and wished me luck. We prayed together before getting in the car. I fought back tears the entire ride there, which was almost the exact same route I had taken to get to the public library board meeting a few months prior. I thought back on my speech that night as we drove down the winding country roads and asked myself if I regretted speaking out. I did not. I still don't.

I started to panic halfway there and reached for my anxiety medication. I had been prescribed medication a few weeks prior because I was struggling to cope. Nobody really said anything on the ride there, and I practiced taking deep breaths. I stared out the window, looking but not seeing as we drove the twenty-five minutes to the courthouse. I was hanging on by a thread and afraid I would lose control again.

My family and I slowly exited the vehicle, and I reminded them that they couldn't bring their phones into the courthouse. Several friends were waiting, and we all walked in together. I felt like I was dragging my feet and didn't want to go in. I didn't want to see those two men and their smug faces ever again, but I sucked it up and kept walking. As we entered, I realized that we had to go through metal detectors, which I found odd. The deputies thought we were all attorneys, I guess because we were all dressed up. I saw members of the press, recognizing one from the public library board meeting, and one I already knew. Our local news reporter nodded at me and smiled, and I remembered thinking, "Well, at least one of them will report fairly."

My friends had come to support and sit with me. But instead of sitting on the defendants' side behind his attorney, Michael Lunsford made a point of sitting directly behind me and my attorney, in what in my opinion was an act of intimidation. He sat where my family should have sat and I couldn't look back for reassurance without him smirking at me. I was cut off from even my mother's comfort. I was engulfed with hatred toward him.

I tried not to look around the room, but I noticed that the opposition's side was packed. I knew it would be that way; they had posted on social media that they wanted as many people as possible to show up. Someone told me that one of their churches held a prayer vigil for one of the men the night before. That angered me. What were they doing? Praying he would get away with defaming a local educator? That didn't sound very Christlike to me.

My friend Rachelle, whom I have known all my life, drove two hours to sit with me, and my friend Kelsye drove an hour and a half from Lafayette. My friend Tiffany was there waiting for me in the parking lot when I got there. My friends gave me strength that day simply from their presence.

The first hearing was much ado about nothing because it ended up with the defense asking for a postponement. They claimed that they hadn't received the court paperwork in time, and the judge granted them a continuance. They all cheered like they had won, and I couldn't stop rolling my eyes. I was disappointed because I wanted to get it over with. Michael Lunsford took a selfie of himself in front of the courthouse and haters posted that the hearing was postponed because my attorney was incompetent. I knew that they were just trying to rile me up. Ellyn had told me to expect a postponement, so I wasn't that surprised.

After the judge granted the postponement, the other side all went and stood in a cluster at the back of the courtroom. At first, I don't think they necessarily did it on purpose, but they were all standing there hugging and staring at me, and I was starting to get a bit scared. They wouldn't leave the room, and it started to feel like a mob scene. What were they waiting for? I didn't want to have to squeeze through the wall of people to leave. I saw the bailiff eyeing them as well, and he glanced at me with pity.

When they didn't leave, Ellyn asked the bailiff if he could disperse them and he did. They regrouped in the hall. That's when I started to wonder if they were purposely trying to intimidate me. The bailiff seemed agitated, and he went outside and told them to disperse again. I finally got the courage to walk out of the courtroom with my friends and family shielding me from anyone who might approach.

We hung back and waited for everyone to leave. When they finally went downstairs, so did we. When we were about to leave the building, we noticed they were still all mobbed, milling about just outside the courthouse doors. I asked several deputies to escort me to my car and thank goodness they did, because I didn't feel safe.

When I got back in the vehicle, I gasped a sigh of relief and released the sobs I had been holding inside. I sat back on the ride home as my sister Colleen trash-talked the two men, hoping to make me feel better. I gave a little smile at her effort, but nothing anyone could have said would have helped. The hearing had been postponed for a few weeks, and I realized at that moment that everything had gotten to be too much, and I was worried I wouldn't be able to handle all that was coming at me. My sister Melanie, a licensed therapist, told me that I should really get some counseling to help myself.

I did end up starting therapy. What was supposed to be my initial one-hour session lasted almost two hours because the therapist just let me keep talking. Therapy has been a huge help along the way, and I encourage everyone who faces difficulties to seek help. I'm very glad I sought therapy when I did. Before my next hearing was to take place, the opposition filed to have my court case dismissed. My doctor helped me prepare for all possible outcomes and gave me some valuable coping strategies.

Every week, I'd call Ellyn looking for reassurance. Ellyn seemed to think that it would be impossible for the judge to dismiss my case. The evidence was clear that lies had been posted about me online and that I had been targeted after speaking out at the public library board meeting. I wanted to believe her, but I still spent days praying for God to give me strength regardless of the outcome of the hearing. I prayed for the ability to keep my cool, prayed for my heart to not hold so much hatred, prayed to forgive these men, prayed that I wouldn't gloat if I won, and prayed that justice would prevail. I prayed morning, noon, and night for guidance.

The night before the hearing, I couldn't sleep and paced around the house. I normally go to bed around 10 P.M., but it was almost 1 A.M. before I lay down. I stared at the ceiling for an hour before deciding to take Benadryl. I sat in the dark in the living room and finally went back to bed at 3 A.M. I tossed and turned all night and woke up several times in a sweat. Every time I woke, I'd start crying. When the alarm finally went off, I resigned myself to facing the day.

Again I walked next door to my parents' house when it was time to go and rode with my family down that winding road to Livingston that was becoming all too familiar. Again I had to take anxiety medication to head off a full-on panic attack in court. My grandmother hugged me again like the previous time, and we prayed. She tried to say more, but she choked up and started crying. That broke my heart, and I had to rush out the door. I think Ryan Thames should have to look my ninety-six-year-old grandmother in the eye and see the pain he has caused our family, although I doubt it would make a difference to his cold heart. Maybe his wife should also have to look my grandmother in the eye. Would she feel guilty about all the ridiculousness she has posted about me, making me out to be the devil and her husband a saint.

This time when we arrived at the courthouse, I at least knew the procedures for entering the building. Three friends from Lafayette were there, as well as several local friends. My friend Rachelle once again drove two hours to support me. As instructed by my therapist, I went into the bathroom to practice deep breathing and do what she called the Superman pose: standing straight up like Superman with hands on hips and shoulders back for two whole minutes. It's probably all in my head, but Superman combined with a prescription for Xanax did help me calmly walk into the courtroom. This time when Michael Lunsford sat in the row behind me, my mom wasn't putting up with it. I tried so hard not to laugh when she sat down practically on top of him and attorney Joseph Long until they got uncomfortable and moved to the other side. Score one for team Jones. I think that was the only point we got that day.

The other side again had a large turnout, and I noticed the library board member Erin Sandefur sitting with them. This time, I brought a binder with me that contained printouts of the messages of support I had received over the weeks and focused on those to calm my nerves. My therapist was there in support and gave me a bracelet with a Bible verse reminding me to be strong. I thought my attorney presented the facts clearly, and things seemed to be going well. Then Joseph Long, the attorney for Ryan Thames, got up to speak.

Joseph Long is very reminiscent of the Looney Tunes character Foghorn Leghorn. He was like every stereotypical southern old white lawyer from the movies all rolled into one, and my first instinct was to roll my eyes. He railed, he waved his hands around, and he paced. Every time he said my name, he said it an octave higher like he was speaking in all caps. AMANDA JONES. He painted me out to be some attention-seeking far-left liberal who wanted to stifle a poor, innocent parent's freedom of speech. That was news to me. I just wanted them to not post lies about me. No, I do not advocate teaching eleven-year-olds about anal sex. No, I do not give erotica to six-year-olds. The man was so comical and performative, I thought surely the judge wouldn't take him seriously. Michael Lunsford's attorney didn't add much, but I noticed that he looked like he was embarrassed to even be there representing his client.

The first thing the judge did right out of the gate was classify me as a public figure, which makes it harder to prove defamation because of the extra step of proving malice. I had repeatedly asked Ellyn if she thought the judge would say that I was a public figure and Ellyn kept assuring me that it most likely would not happen, that it would be outrageous if it did, and that she had previous court cases to cite to refute it. Well, the judge sure did classify me as a public figure, stating, "A limited purpose public figure is an individual who voluntarily injects himself into a particular public controversy. This was a particular public controversy, and such as by inviting attention and comment thereby she became a public figure in connection with that."

Then the judge said, "It's not up to this Court to determine whether those books are appropriate or inappropriate. There is a procedure in place, and that's not before me today." I wondered why she was talking about books. We were not even there to discuss books. We were there to discuss horrible lies being posted about me online. She continued, "But there is no definition for what constitutes erotica or pornography. Courts can't agree on that. Adults disagree on that. That is in the eye of the beholder." I started to see red, and I could tell which way the wind was going to blow.

The whole time the judge was talking, I stared at the binder in front of me. At one point, I closed my eyes and tuned her out, just focusing on breathing. I clasped my hands together under the table so nobody would see my hands shaking and bent my head forward so that my hair would obscure my face from anyone but the court officials in front of me.

To me, it was pretty cut-and-dry. The facts are that I went and spoke at a public meeting. My speech was well-documented, and there was audio of the entire meeting. I did not say anything about any particular title, did not advocate for pornography, and did not talk about anal sex. I was then singled out and attacked online. I was the only one who spoke that night, out of almost thirty people, who was singled out by these men. Ellyn argued, "This was a speech about policy. It was a speech about a blanket restriction that the Library Control Board was asked to consider, which circumvented the existing policy in place for addressing that. And so Mrs. Jones' comments in that regard, there's nothing in there—because there's nothing in there about content, because she's not advocating for any book. To say then that she's advocating for erotic material to be provided to children is a false statement of fact, and there are damages—that is actually defamatory per se because it either states that she's guilty of a crime, or strongly implies that she's guilty of a crime; but it also . . . causes great damage to her reputation. She's charged with caring for children."

Joseph Long brought up the list of books that library board member Erin Sandefur had brought to the meeting. The judge asked me if the list was the correct list. I had no idea, and I was confused, because what did that have to do with me or any of the issues at hand? I didn't go to speak about a particular book and never mentioned any specific books. Erin Sandefur was even speaking out to the attorneys from her seat several rows back while my attorney was speaking to the judge, and talking about "these books" and how I wanted them in the library, and the judge never stopped her from shouting out in open court.

Joseph Long said, "It doesn't say that my client is accusing Amanda Jones of teaching children to have anal sex, which would be a crime. Advocating teaching anal sex is what these books are doing, and I have a copy of that. A photograph of—not a photograph, but a drawing. It's pretty explicit, Your Honor. That's a picture of two males having oral sex with each other." He was then allowed to show a picture of a book that not only was not discussed at the public library meeting, nor was on any list provided that night but also insinuated I said that book specifically should be in the children's section of the library. The judge didn't stop him, even when Ellyn said, "Objection, Your Honor. That book was not on the list of books that was presented by the Library Control Board member that presented this issue to—" She wasn't even allowed to finish her statement.

Joseph Long said, "Your Honor, Amanda Jones' position is that all the books in the library should neither be removed nor reclassified, that if you don't like the book, don't read it. And so by saying such—I will read exactly what she said, Your Honor . . . She says, if we remove or relocate books with LBGTQ or sexual health content, what message is that sending to the community members? Why is your belief system any more important than others? What will be next if you accomplish your mission? Parents have a personal responsibility to monitor their own children's reading and nobody else's. That's in her speech. And so she's telling us all the books in the library should stay where they are, all right, including these books here." He only read that snippet of my speech. Ellyn asked the judge if she could read the speech in its entirety, and the judge said no. If she would have allowed Ellyn to finish the speech, she would have heard where twice I referenced policies that were in place for parents and community members to object to books and that we needed to allow the library to follow procedures already in place.

Joseph Long conveniently left out the next part of my speech where I stated, "If an individual is concerned about a children's or young adult's resource or its location in the library, that individual has the right to go through the library's reconsideration policy that is already in place." I then reiterated and said again, "There is already a book challenge process if a community member does not like a particular book or location of a book in the library." All I did at that public meeting was ask that library policy be followed. I never once said that books should never be relocated or removed. All I could think about right there in the courtroom was the unfairness of how the judge wouldn't allow my attorney to read aloud the entire speech for the record to prove it.

Ellyn did try, I'll give her that, but the judge seemed to have made up her mind about things before we even got there. Ellyn pointed out, "Again, Your Honor, I'm objecting to the relevance to any of this because it wasn't books that Mrs. Jones spoke to. These books (on a list brought to the meeting) were not even made available to the public, the titles or the content, prior to the meeting, and the speech was not about these books or their content. In fact, if Mrs. Jones testifies, she will testify that she was in support of one of the books that was on the list being moved out of the young adult section. That's not the issue before the Court, and it's not relevant." It was extremely difficult to not show emotion.

It seemed lost on the judge that this was a defamation trial and not a trial about where books go in a library. It was as if I were the one on trial. The judge kept looking at me with disdain, and I knew before her ruling how things were going to go. So even though my speech had nothing to do with anal sex or giving erotica to children, the judge ruled that the defendants were allowed to express their opinion and to post those things online about me. The judge gave some half-assed semi-apologetic speech about how the posts were unfortunate but not against the law. I remember hearing my mom make a slight noise of protest behind me, and I heard the same from my friend Rachelle. I looked up at the judge only once, and she didn't seem to want to make eye contact, so I put my head back down. Case dismissed.

The other side started celebrating, and Ryan's wife made a huge deal about crying and hugging him. I often wonder about that celebration. Did she realize she was celebrating her husband completely smearing a woman's reputation online by posting lies and mistruths? Is that a cause to celebrate? Hooray, my husband can be a jerk online! Maybe she was celebrating the fact that her husband's dumb mouth wasn't going to hurt them financially? I try to believe that was why she was celebrating and not taking joy in her husband getting away with being an online bully. I wonder if she has ever, through any of this, thought about what her husband has done to me, a woman he doesn't even know. If she thinks it's okay, then she is just as bad as him, and I feel sorry for their children that they have parents teaching them such warped morals. If she doesn't think it's okay, I wonder why she doesn't speak out against his behavior or make him stop. I pray for her a lot.

The hugging and celebration got to me. I've thought about what I would do if the roles were reversed, and it was my husband that had done that to anyone. I don't think I'd be celebrating. I'd be telling him he should be thanking his lucky stars that the court ruled in his favor. I don't think I would have even gone with him to court. He'd have to sit there by himself in all his shame. However, my husband would never do that to someone, which is one of the reasons I married him. And Ryan Thames didn't seem to express any shame, which is another big difference in the type of men she and I married.

I'd have divorced Jason if he cost us financially because he felt like targeting a random woman online that he had never met just for shits and giggles. I don't think my husband would ever put us in that position, but I believe in my heart that I would have made my husband take down the posts the minute I saw them, and if he didn't, I think I would have left him. I'd like to think if I were in her shoes, I would go up to that other woman and apologize to her and assure her that Jason would no longer be bothering her if he wanted to stay married to me. There's no way I'd stay with someone who gets pleasure out of bullying and belittling people online, but there she was, acting like he was some innocent man who was saved from the evil librarian.

When the judge left the courtroom, I turned and looked at my friend Rachelle. She had a smile on her face and mumbled, "Don't let them see you cry. Keep smiling." I repeated that over and over in my head as I pretended to laugh like she had said something funny. My mom and sisters did the same thing as if we had an unspoken pact to not show any disappointment. This time, the group didn't congregate in the back like they had at the previous hearing. They were too busy celebrating, so my family and friends and I quietly walked out of the courtroom with our heads held high. I could feel the hysteria bubbling up and thought that I just needed to get to the car and I would be okay. A reporter stopped me to ask me questions, and I said I didn't want to be interviewed. She followed me for several steps until I had to rudely ask her to leave me alone.

I was aware that I was being filmed by a local news agency, and I kept the grin on my face the whole time. My mom tried to talk about it once we were in the car, and I asked her to wait because I felt like I was about to break down. The minute the car pulled away from the courthouse, the dam broke and I lost it. My mom and sister were indignant on my behalf, and I won't repeat the things that were said on the way home. I've never seen my mom so mad. I just kept thinking about how unfair it all seemed.

Of course, the haters posted triumphantly that they had slain the dragon and stood up for the children, continuing to pretend it wasn't a defamation lawsuit and that it was about keeping sexually explicit material out of libraries. I was devastated and basically shut down the rest of the day. Joseph Long felt the need to post a press release and threw in a jab about how I needed to grow a thicker skin. How thick does one's skin have to grow to not care about being lied about and having one's reputation ruined? I called in sick to work the next day because I didn't want to face anyone. Not only was the lawsuit dismissed, but the judge determined I was responsible for the opposition's court costs and attorneys' fees. In my mind that was the icing on top of a big shit cake.

I really thought long and hard about what I was going to do. Should I appeal? Should I drop it? I agonized for days and didn't know what to do. I was so tired and frustrated, but also incensed at the injustice of it all. I wanted justice yet wanted the whole debacle to go away. I wanted to take a stand but also wanted my life to go back to as normal as possible. I asked my friends and family what they thought. Some people in my family thought that I should just walk away, because that would be best for my health. Some of my friends and family wanted me to continue the fight, but only if I felt up to it.

Did I have the mental bandwidth or monetary means to continue to fight this? I didn't know. I wasn't as concerned about the money as I was about my health. I don't think anyone who has not experienced something like this realizes the huge emotional toll it takes. This had been all I'd thought about for months. It was draining and traumatic. My heart races now as I write about it, having to relive this time in my life.

I spoke to a political adviser, and he told me that people like Michael Lunsford feed off of drama and that, by appealing, I would be giving in to him. That made sense to me, and I listened to what he said, but I wasn't so sure. He seemed to be missing the point. That was frustrating. I didn't want to base my decision on what Michael or Ryan wanted or cared about. This was about me, my limits, what I could tolerate, and how I wanted to live my life. I wanted to make the best decision for myself. I wanted to set a good example for my child. I made a list of pros and cons and told Ellyn to give me a week or two to come to a decision. She was ready to appeal. I wasn't so sure.

A week after the hearing, I was driving to work and thinking about everything. It's all I ever seemed to do. I started to pray, and I decided to finally turn it over to God. Quietly crying as I drove, I asked for a sign to be given to help guide me. Right then, the song "Hold On," by Wilson Phillips, came on the radio. I perked up and wiped the tears from my face. The beginning of the song says, "No one can change your life except for you / Don't ever let anyone step all over you." I wondered if this was the sign. And then I heard, "Don't you know things can change? / Things'll go your way / If you hold on for one more day." I realized THAT was the message. I don't know how to explain it, but I just knew I was being told to hold on for one more day. Some people might scoff, but I got chills in that moment and just knew I should be paying attention. I can't put it into words—it was clear as day that I needed to hold on because something was coming. I didn't know who, what, when, or how, but I knew something was coming.

A few days earlier, I had spoken to Katie Schwartzmann and Andrew Perry from the Tulane First Amendment Law Clinic. They were kind enough to let me ask their opinions on the matter. I told them that while I really liked my attorney, I didn't think she seemed to have the time, resources, and expertise I needed for my case. I should have originally found someone whose main practice was First Amendment law, but I didn't know any better, and hindsight is 20/20. Ellyn had done a good job, but I wanted an expert, and I was starting to feel like I needed to consider options. They put me in touch with the law firm Amond and Mills, and I had scheduled a Zoom meeting that just so happened to be the same day I heard the Wilson Phillips song in the car.

On my Zoom meeting I met with Alysson Mills and Kristen Amond. After five minutes, I knew that they were what I was holding on for. It wasn't like they said anything super special, even though what they said was supportive. They were honest and listed all the factors I needed to think about: my health, money, different options I could pursue, and how it was my decision. But for some reason, talking to them and listening to their answers to my many questions caused a huge weight to be lifted from my shoulders. Imagine a bookshelf has fallen on you, and you're just lying there in awful pain, slowly dying and hoping help is coming. Then someone comes along and pulls the shelf off you. Think about that sense of relief. That's what I felt talking to Alysson and Kristen. I just knew I needed to hire them and that, by hiring them, I would eventually be okay. It would be tough, and not always fun, but I would come out the other end in one piece.

I couldn't pinpoint why I felt so sure, but I did, so I decided to trust my gut. I made the tough decision to break away from Ellyn, and I formally hired Alysson and Kristen. I felt bad for letting Ellyn go. She was in my corner from the get-go and hadn't done anything wrong. I wrote her a heartfelt email, telling her of the decision I had made and why, and hoped she wouldn't be upset. I didn't want to hurt her feelings. I just felt like God was telling me to go in a different direction. Luckily, she understood. I was relieved and ready to move forward.

I met with Alysson and Kristen many times over what had happened initially, why I had filed suit, and what had happened at the last hearing. They told me I had two options if I wanted to go forward. I could file an appeal, or I could ask the judge to reconsider her first opinion. By asking the judge to reconsider, we would be able to get more evidence and case law into the courtroom. Alysson also wanted to include more about my stellar reputation as an educator and what I had lost by the actions of these men. My original sixteen-page court document turned into a ninety-four-page document of pure amazingness.

They warned me that the judge would most likely reject my case again. She would have to admit that she was wrong the first time, and they said that rarely happens. I'd have to once again go and subject myself to sitting in a room with these men, not win, and walk back out of court with a loss. They'd turn to social media again to crow about it and they'd declare victory, but we'd have so much more to bring with us to the appellate court. I said let's do it. I was at peace with suffering another loss if that meant we could appeal with more already on the record. I was at peace because I didn't give up on the first go-round and was continuing to stick up for myself. Like Wilson Phillips says, "No one can change your life except for you / Don't ever let anyone step all over you." I wasn't going to stop trying.

Knowing the outcome before it happened helped me for that third hearing. I was resigned that I would not be victorious, but I understood the long-term strategy. They say the third time's the charm, and I was much calmer before the third hearing. I still didn't trust myself to drive and again rode with my family. I still had to take anxiety medication. However, this time I walked in with a little more confidence because I was going in with Alysson and Kristen. This time, only my friends and family attempted to sit behind me, and I sat with my head held high. This time I was not afraid to look around the courtroom.

The judge took a very long time to come into the courtroom and when she came in, she didn't look happy to be hearing my case again. Gone was the pretend look of pity she had from the previous hearing. The attorneys from the opposition seemed to phone it in too. Joseph Long wasn't as show-boaty and didn't yell my name quite so loudly, but he did make sure to say the words *anal sex* repeatedly. There was a woman sitting on the other side who had brought her two young children. She seemed determined to cause a scene and make the hearing a circus.

Every time the anal sex meme was mentioned, she quickly ushered her children out the door, only to reappear moments later. The commotion was such that the bailiff looked considerably irritated. My sister said that another court official asked her to stop it, but I didn't see that happen. How someone could so obviously use her children as a tool of hate is beyond me. I know I could never, but some people have no shame. Alysson and Kristen had written a very solid court document that clearly laid out all the facts, along with precedent and case law, proving that we could meet the four factors of defamation. I am happy that it's public record. My hands no longer shook, and I didn't have to close my eyes this time. I brought my binder of positive

messages, which was twice the size it had been at the previous hearing due to the influx of wonderful people who had reached out to me in support, and it was a comfort. I knew what was coming. So inevitably the case was once again dismissed. This time I didn't hang my head. This time I would show my true thoughts about the injustice of the entire situation. This time I would outwardly show that I disagreed with the judge's decision and came prepared. Without saying a word, I took out my Ruth Bader Ginsburg lace collar, placed it around my neck while looking at the defendants, and walked out of the courtroom without looking back. I wanted everyone to know that I didn't agree with the judge's decision and dissented. And this time, I didn't look online to see what the haters posted. I decided that I no longer cared. I had already won.

Chapter 8

Are You There Michelle? It's Me, Amanda: It's Hard to Go High When the Haters Go So Low

I'm going to take the high road because the low road is so crowded.

—MIA FARROW

Have you ever just wanted to punch someone in the face with all your might? Maybe someone has said something awful to you, and the thought crossed your mind that a good ass whipping would wipe the smirk off their face and teach them a lesson. I don't advocate violence, but I have thought about how good it would feel to knee my haters in the groin. However, violence is never the answer, and neither is yelling or screaming at someone or attacking someone online. If you want to really get the best of someone, you must rise above it. Yeah, yeah, I know what you're thinking. That's no fun. Taking an eye for an eye sounds better than turning the other cheek. But you know what's better? Besides forgoing assault charges, winning and having the last laugh by playing it smarter than your adversaries is the better feeling in the long run. Trust me.

At the 2016 Democratic National Convention, former first lady Michelle Obama famously said, "When they go low, we go high." In an interview with Oprah Winfrey, she said, "My purpose in life doesn't revolve around taking care of my own little ego, but instead to ensure that I am a positive role model for the next generation and I am creating positive change. There is a bigger purpose for me out there. So when I respond to something, I have to think about that." I think her motto is something we should all aspire to. It's admirable, but something I struggle with. It's especially important when you're an educator who is looked up to by the children in your community. I want to set a good example, but it isn't necessarily what I wanted to do when I was being smeared on the internet.

To be honest, I wanted to go lower than them. I wanted to launch a full-scale attack in retaliation.

I wanted to let the public know things I was privy to about these two men, and things I knew about other people making horrible comments about me. It seems a lot of people in my community have been tormented online by these two and their friends, and many people were sharing screenshots and stories with me. I was not the only one. I wanted to make my own memes and call them names, because the ones I made in my head were funnier and smarter. But what would that solve? It would make me feel better for about two seconds until they wrote more vitriol, and the back-and-forth would continue.

That's not to say I always get it right, and that I don't have occasional lapses in judgment. Even writing this book, I have wrestled with how much is too much when describing these people and the hatred I've felt, and sometimes still feel, about them. I don't want to say or do things I wish I could take back. Have I gone too low in this book? I don't know the answer to that. I hope not. If you knew the things I really wanted to say, you'd probably be shocked. It's a struggle, one that I am continually engaged in, but I do try. I have said some things I'm not proud of, and I can't take them back.

I rewatch Michelle Obama's speech to remind myself it will do no good to go any lower than I have, and I should try harder to be kind.

A few things have stopped me when it has crossed my mind to unleash some fury online. If you are going to talk the talk, you must walk the walk. If I tell students and my own child that it's not okay to bully someone online, and I teach them lessons on reporting, ignoring, and taking the high road, then I have to do the same. The easy thing to do is be petty online. The hard thing to do is ignore it. My adversaries are setting a horrible example for children in doing what they do online. They say they do it because they are protecting children. The irony is that they're teaching children horrible lessons on ways to bully others. These men are fathers. What kind of example are they setting for their own children? I wonder what their reactions would be if someone attacked their daughters online the way they attacked me. I am sure they wouldn't appreciate it.

Besides, it solves nothing to engage in a back-and-forth with anyone on social media. It's giving food to parasitic behavior. It's exactly what they want. No reaction is the best reaction. I wanted so badly to strike back publicly that it was physically painful not to, but I refused to give them the attention they were so desperately seeking. Make no mistake: their behavior was desperate and says more about their own low self-esteem and discontented lives than it says about mine. You have to be a very miserable person to attack someone online simply because you didn't like a speech she gave at a public library board meeting.

Instead of engaging with my haters, I channeled my energy into gathering as much documentation as I could. I took screenshots and copied URLs for every single negative post about me. I created files on each player with evidence of their misdeeds. Every tip or screenshot that was sent to me, I filed away and kept a record, even when they deleted posts. I cross-referenced the players and their connections to each other and their connections to other organizations. In the process, I began to see huge patterns, like the donations that flowed from some commentators to politicians when those politicians posted on social media about libraries. I began to see connections to donors, legislators, and local politicians. I found connections between some of the players and known extremist groups documented by the Southern Poverty Law Center, local churches, and connections to accused child abusers. I saved these files in multiple clouds and on multiple devices, and I made sure friends and family had access to everything in case anything happened to me. Librarians excel at curation. It's one of the things we do best. Running your mouth on social media is weak, but collecting knowledge is power.

Eventually I realized that I needed to take a step back. Actually, it was my therapist who told me I needed to step back. I was becoming obsessed, and it was consuming my life. If I let it consume me, the haters would win. So, after promising my therapist I would no longer look at their posts, I asked someone else to continue collecting information for me, relieving me of the role. It was one of the best decisions I ever made. It was very freeing, knowing that someone else was documenting for me and that I would be spared the hate. To this day, I have all of them blocked and still do not look at their posts. People occasionally send me screenshots, but now I just laugh. They have been posting furiously for a year, not realizing that I don't read any of their posts. True power is the ability to live rent-free in someone else's head when you don't think about them at all.

It was odd when the haters initially called me an activist. Before they decided to bother me, I was just living my little librarian life in my little hometown. Yes, I had won some awards and spoken at national conferences as a guest speaker, but I spoke about all sorts of library issues. I mostly talked about virtual field trips and building a professional learning network. I had spoken about censorship on a few webinars and panels, but suddenly the requests for speaking gigs increased. I leaned into it. I figured if they wanted to call me an activist, and I was being given a platform on a national stage, I might as well pick up the gauntlet. Again, while I don't have to go low, I also don't have to be silent.

The requests from reporters for interviews came from all directions. I didn't want to be on television, but I thought long and hard about accepting those requests. I spoke to several friends and family members to weigh the pros and cons. My earlier experience with the media had been positive on the whole. I was not going to fight back on social media, but a big pro for speaking with reporters is that I could tell my side of the story; however, I was very careful about whom I spoke with. I didn't want to speak with anybody and everybody—just professional journalists with track records for unbiased reporting. I was also very careful to make sure that my school or school system was completely off-limits and could not be named in any articles.

I am extremely lucky that I connected with an organization called Campaign for Our Shared Future. Through an introduction from Kathy Ishizuka, editor in chief of *School Library Journal*, I met Eliza Byard, the former executive director of GLSEN: Gay, Lesbian, and Straight Education Network and a cofounder and senior adviser of Campaign for Our Shared Future. COSF is a nonpartisan nonprofit organization working to keep politics out of schools, and they were taking an interest in the book banning movement happening across the United States. Eliza gave me some sound advice on dealing with the press and connected me with other leaders like Heather Harding, COSF's executive director, and the COSF communications team. Campaign for Our Shared Future helped me vet journalists and organizations seeking interviews, and they taught me about the importance of messaging. Rachel at COSF would help me craft statements and guide me through interviews.

I also had to weigh how speaking with journalists would affect my upcoming court case. Winning in court would not be guaranteed, but one thing that speaking with the press could guarantee was that I could share my story on my own terms. I made the decision early on that if I lost in court because of speaking out publicly, it just was what it was. At least by lodging a court case, I got evidence of their misdeeds in the public record, and at least by speaking to journalists I could share my story. My attorneys agreed and supported me in this decision.

I continued to speak with journalists and started compiling the articles on my website in a section titled "Speaking Out." I made sure that every person I spoke with was a journalist, and COSF helped me check into each journalist who requested an interview. A local newscaster repeatedly

emailed wanting a comment and interview, but I declined. I didn't want to be on a video, because I often get choked up when I tell my story. Print articles are just easier. He was very persistent to the point that I started to feel harassed by him, but I stood my ground, as I did not want to be on local television or video of any kind.

I was asked for interviews with *USA Today*, the *Washington Post*, *Insider*, *Education Week*, and the *Los Angeles Times*, among others. Seeing myself on the cover of *USA Today* was a very odd feeling. My friend Becky Calzada was on the same cover, and I remember messaging her to see if it was just as strange to her and it was. I was invited to be a guest on the *New York Times First Person* podcast with Lulu Garcia-Navarro, again trying to hold it together while talking about one of the most painful experiences of my life. With each interview, I shared my story and told the truth and tried not to stoop to name-calling. It was draining. Reliving the worst event in your life over and over every single day is not an enjoyable way to spend the evening after a long day of teaching.

I was working all day with students and coming home to spend hours each day being interviewed or working on building a library alliance in my community because the censorship crowd was still plotting and scheming. I was not present for my husband and child during those months. I've repeatedly seen associates of the two men I was suing say that I was seeking fame and fortune. It's very weird to me that they thought I was seeking fame. Who wants to be famous for being defamed? Nobody says when they grow up that they hope they can be in the news for being bullied online. What I was doing was important to me, standing up for myself, speaking out against censorship, and working to protect our public library, but it came at a great personal cost physically, mentally, and emotionally. I didn't seek out interviews but was asked, and I was never paid for any of them.

I cannot get back the time I was so preoccupied and not focused on my family. I hope that one day my husband and daughter realize that those six to eight months of nonstop anxiety, interviews, and work were to give our daughter and our community a brighter future, but I don't begrudge them if they don't see it that way. They have been very understanding so far. I was not a present parent during that time, and it took a while for me to realize it through therapy, prayer, and medication. After about eight months, I started being more selective in interviews and saying no if it interfered with family time.

With each interview, I weighed my words carefully. There wasn't a single interview I did in the fall of 2022 where I did not cry, but it was cathartic in some small way to talk about the pain.

I agreed to an interview with John Burnett from NPR, who was covering censorship in Louisiana, and I think I cried in 50 percent of that interview. I was embarrassed and had to stop several times to compose myself. Maybe it was my imagination, but even his eyes seemed a little damp after our conversation. I've gone back to listen to myself in that interview several times, and you can hear the pain in my voice. Little did I know how far that segment would be heard.

Not long after it aired, I was contacted by a former student now living halfway across the country. He wrote, "Hi there! I don't know if you remember me but you taught me in 7th grade around 2009 I believe. I was a bit of an awkward kid and you were always very kind to me. I wanted to let you know I currently reside on the border of Minnesota and Wisconsin.

I live right on the shore of Lake Superior and work as an aircraft mechanic. This morning on my drive to work I heard your story come on Minnesota Public Radio. I heard your familiar voice and I was shocked to hear a story so close to home. I'm so glad to have known and been taught by you. I'm so sorry for what you are facing, but also so proud of you for standing up for what's right." Bless that kid who is now a grown man. I'm tearing up just remembering receiving that message.

Not only did I remember him, but I can tell you what hour I taught him and where he sat. I can also tell you where his older brother sat when I taught him a few years prior and can tell you his mother's name. I can tell you how smart both he and his brother are, and how I always thought both were kind. I don't remember him as being awkward but remember him as being a deep thinker and way more mature than a lot of the other kids. Once a student is "my kid," they are always "my kid," and I remember each and every one of them. Shawn, if you are reading this, thank you for sending me that message. It was a bad day, and I needed it more than you know.

So many former students who are now in their twenties and early thirties contacted me to show support. Many of them were posting positive comments online too. A former student named Travis, who also worked with me for a few years, posted about me, "The best former teacher and coworker you could ask for." I choked up reading that. A former student named Amanda messaged me and said, "I don't understand Livingston Parish, but people like you are the shining gems of the place. Keep doing what you're doing. You rock." A student named Monica wrote me and said, "I love you to the moon and back," and one named Wayne messaged, "Wahoo you are hard to find online. So grateful that I was blessed to have the head banging rock and roll English teacher my 7th grade year! Giving 100% support." There were so many of these, it was overwhelming in a good way.

At one of the lowest moments of my life, I also felt extraordinarily loved and realized just how truly blessed I was in life. How many people can say that they have positively affected hundreds, if not thousands, of children's lives and made a difference to them? People who go low, spewing nothing but hate to others, cannot say they have changed lives for the better like I have. That's not to say I think I was the world's greatest teacher. I'm sure there are kids out there who didn't like having me as their teacher, and there were days when I was probably pretty grumpy. But I love all my students, and they felt loved, as evidenced by all those who contacted me with support. Nobody can ever take that away from me.

So while what I was going through seemed like a nightmare caused by these two men, my reaction to what they did to me led me to my own kind of *It's a Wonderful Life* moment as the messages from former students rolled in. I have saved them all. By choosing to go high when they went low, I was reminded of my purpose in life. Those men tried to ruin me, but I was being reminded that my life has had meaning and has helped make the world a better place. They cannot say the same.

With each new story, the haters would again post online that I was fame hungry, and they would go crazy. Then it became a game of sorts to me. The more interviews I did, the madder they got, and that was funny to me. Nobody was asking to interview them except whackadoo alt-right bloggers. I was being interviewed by legitimate journalists. There was satisfaction in that. If the haters were more self-aware, they'd have realized that most sane people in our community were starting to realize what jerks they were, but they just kept posting and doubling down. Perhaps they didn't care and were just stuck being hateful because they didn't want to admit they were wrong. I guess I will never know, but I don't really care anymore.

The fact of the matter is that I wouldn't have been given any attention if they'd stayed in their lane and left me alone, so I was a monster of their own making. They thought they'd trash me online and I'd slink away. They messed with the wrong one if that's what they wanted. If they wanted me to be silent, I was going to do the exact opposite.

And while I did get a little satisfaction in making them angrier with each interview, it eventually grew beyond me and them, and I didn't think about them anymore. There was a larger movement of censorship taking place across our country, and I wanted to do whatever I could to warn others about what was happening. If I could give courage to another librarian in

another part of the country facing the same bullshit, I'd do my best to be strong. If a queer kid read that I was speaking out against efforts across the U.S. to keep LGBTQIA+ books in libraries, maybe they'd know that there were people out there fighting for them. That's all that matters to me: that I'm giving hope or strength to someone. Who cares if people know my name? It's not about fame. It's about speaking out for what is right.

The articles did help me raise money to fight back and helped my GoFundMe donations increase, but there was always a corresponding increase in online hate. The support I received helped me keep holding my head up high. I received a handwritten note, delivered to my local bookstore with five one-dollar bills. It said, "Can you see to it that this gets to Ms. Jones? I saw what she is dealing with, and I wanted to send her a little something to help her fight the good fight. A fight we cannot lose. I know the enclosed is not a lot but use it as you need to use it." I framed the note and five dollars to remind me that there are good people in the world. I would like to meet that man one day and thank him. That letter, and those five dollars, are worth their weight in gold.

A former student from Livingston Parish named Stacy Wayne Durham, who is now an author, retweeted one of the articles and wrote, "Not a librarian in my hometown where I never felt safe as a queer kid, making national news fighting tooth and nail to make space for queer kids and the authors they grew up to be . . . I hope she knows she's saving lives. I hope she knows nothing but good fortune for the remainder of her days." I was humbled. In that moment I again felt that I had already won, regardless of the court's decision.

I started to see from the outpouring of love and support sent my way that Michelle Obama was right, and I began to understand why it's so important to go high when they go low. You become the bigger person, able to push out the hate and focus on the positives. I wanted to pay forward the support that had been given to me, so I found ways to help other educators and librarians. I started monitoring discussions about libraries and schools across Louisiana that were being posted on social media. Any time I saw something negative about a librarian or educator, I would skip over all the hate and look for the positive comments. If I saw a former student or patron of that person, I'd private-message these total strangers and encourage them to send an email to that person telling them how much they meant to them. I'd drop a link from one of my articles and tell them the messages of support saved me, and maybe they could help save someone else.

When you're given a platform, whether intentional or not, you should use that platform for good. It's very important to me for everyone to understand that I was not alone during this time. I had the power of hundreds of librarians behind me, hundreds of people across the country who read about me and reached out, support from friends and family, and the knowledge that I had made a difference as an educator. That was a mighty realization. It would have all been wasted if I had gotten into the mud-slinging business to seek revenge. The world was watching, and I did my best to navigate to the top. I will never regret that decision.

Are you there Michelle? It's me, Amanda. It's excruciatingly tough to go high when the bottom-feeders go so low that they're scraping the bottom of the barrel. It's especially hard when you see the same thing happening to hundreds of librarians across the country, many of whom are your friends. However, you are so right. We can be positive role models for the next generation and create positive change. I'd rather walk with lightness than darkness. Thank you for that lesson.

Chapter 9

The Mob Song

What are a handful of reasonable men against a crowd with stones in their hands?

—George Eliot

I love Florida, particularly Santa Rosa Beach, where we often take family vacations. It's within easy driving distance, and we pack our swim goggles, beach chairs, and sunscreen for a few days of blissful relaxation. Actually, if I'm being honest, it is mostly fighting the beach equipment through the sand and getting sunburned, but we love our days there even if we all scream at each other in an epic meltdown at least once. We fly kites on the beach, and my daughter and I coax sand crabs out from their hiding places with breadcrumbs. Peanut butter and jelly sandwiches hit differently at a picnic on the beach. Sometimes we travel a little farther to Cape San Blas with our entire extended family to fish, snorkel, and cook scallops we catch ourselves. Sadly, those trips are now only memories. Now when I think of Florida, I don't think about it as a vacation spot but as a state that likes to terrorize educators and librarians.

These days, you won't catch me spending money in Florida unless I have to or it's in support of Florida school librarians. In October 2023, the national conference for the American Association of School Librarians was in Tampa, Florida. There were many librarians who didn't want to go to a national conference in Florida, because of the current climate of librarian hate and the pro-censorship policies of the DeSantis government and Moms for Liberty headquarters. But there was no way I wasn't attending AASL23. It's the only national conference specifically for school librarians, and it happens only every two years. I was one of the national conference co-chairs, so I had to attend. I also understood that conference locations are planned far in advance, and it would have been near impossible to pivot to a new location.

The main reason, though, was that I wanted to show solidarity with the Florida school librarians. I know dozens of them and was fortunate to keynote their conference in 2022. I spoke to so many school librarians at that conference who were petrified of losing their jobs and worried about the hate being lobbed their way not just from members of groups like Moms for Liberty but from governing institutions and school boards. The school librarians in Florida are fighting tooth and nail for their students, and I was not going to turn my back on them. I also wanted to meet the amazing members of the Florida Freedom to Read Project, a grassroots organization of parents that is setting the bar very high for tracking book bans and hate in their state.

The librarians of Florida have been facing a lot of hateful rhetoric, and I've even had school librarian friends lose their jobs or be reassigned because they dared to speak out. Another friend of mine even had Ron DeSantis show up for a press conference at her school two weeks after she posted concern on social media. Was it a coincidence that he randomly selected her school from which to give his big press conference? Maybe. I'm sure it didn't feel that way to her.

Back in early August 2022, right at the very beginning of my ordeal, I was asked to speak to school librarians in Santa Rosa and Escambia Counties on collection development and several other topics. They were wonderful, and we talked about all sorts of topics related to school librarianship, but I remember warning them to make sure that they had strong policies in place because of what I was afraid was coming for them. Even with the strongest of policies, it couldn't have prepared them for what was to come. I'm not sure anything could have.

A few months later, Escambia County made headlines when a high school teacher challenged 116 books, claiming that the books had sexually explicit content, graphic language, and political pushes. According to NPR, others filed challenges, and the total number of challenged books rose to 197 titles. I spoke with several school librarians in Escambia who didn't want to speak out for fear of reprisal, scared that they would be punished and even fired. Every book decision they make can be taken out of context, misconstrued, or used against them. Even a nonfiction children's picture book like *And Tango Makes Three*, based on a true story of two male penguins who formed a bond at the Central Park Zoo, could put a school librarian in the sights of someone who wanted to go on the attack. Order the wrong book, and there are cries echoing Gaston's cry of "I say we kill the Beast!" in the classic Disney movie *Beauty and the Beast*.

One of my favorite movies happens to be *Beauty and the Beast*. Most people think my affection stems from the massive library in the Beast's castle. Don't get me wrong, the library is pretty iconic, but what I actually love most about this movie is how truly intelligent the character of Belle is. She possesses the ability to look past appearances. She is independent. She's not waiting around for true love's kiss or a male to save the day. One of the film's most memorable scenes is when Gaston, who's seriously jealous of Belle and the Beast, throws out some fiery language and a slew of lies about the Beast, which enrages the villagers. Gaston goes from group to group riling people up, overexaggerating the threat of the monster in the castle. As the hysteria spreads, Belle tries to tell everyone the truth, but Gaston proclaims, "If you're not with us, you're against us!" Gaston locks Belle up, and she cries to her father, "I have to warn the Beast!"

This is pretty darn close to what is happening in our country's libraries. One person falsely posting on social media that libraries contain pornography or critical race theory can turn into a witch hunt. In the United States, our libraries are the Beast and the castle. The Gastons of the world, like Tucker Carlson, Libs of TikTok, and Moms for Liberty, go from platform to platform on the internet, furthering the hysteria and stoking fear about the hypothetical boogeyman. The librarians are Belle, trying to warn everyone, but we are often no match for the mighty hate machines of Fox News and social media. Meanwhile, the enchanted objects in the castle are the books, authors, librarians, and marginalized community members being hurt in the process. Can you imagine the movie ending differently, with Gaston and the villagers eradicating the Beast and destroying the castle and everything in it? That will happen to our libraries if more people do not start speaking out.

———

There's no school librarian I know who's had more "Kill the Beast" cries hurled her way than New Jersey school librarian Martha Hickson. Martha has been stoically fighting the good fight for years now and is a profile in courage. She has been described as a sex offender at school board meetings and is often targeted on social media for defending intellectual freedom at her high school. When several books were challenged in her district, Martha did something about it—she spoke out, reported it, and refused to back down. She was supported by many community members and students, but she still suffered. She wrote in the *School Library Journal*, "I felt overwhelmed. The school nurse found that my blood pressure had skyrocketed. With that, in addition to the sleeplessness, appetite loss, digestive distress, and anxiety that had plagued me since the September board meeting, I had reached the breaking point. When my blood pressure remained dangerously high the next day, my physician ordered me to stop work, prescribed medication for anxiety, and referred me to a therapist for help managing stress. Defeated and at an all-time low, professionally and personally, I wept." I am thankful for Martha's honesty about the toll these personal attacks can take. For the past few years, she has worked tirelessly to create support systems and tool kits for other librarians facing similar issues. To me she is a hero, and I strive to be as stoic as Martha.

Another New Jersey school librarian I admire is Elissa Malespina. Elissa is known for her positive rapport with both students and educators alike and is a leader in the field of school librarianship. However, after twenty-three years as an educator, Elissa was let go from her school. Her final evaluation from the school accused her displays as being too diverse, stating, "Mrs. Malespina does a nice job with creating collections for display about equity, specifically regarding the themes of race and LGBTQIA+. However, the selections never seem to go beyond those two topics. It is recommended that there is a reflection on what the space is for and how it can be better utilized to serve the student and broader community." Luckily for Elissa, she found a job at a new school that appreciates her, but she told the *School Library Journal*, "I start to question—how balanced do I need to make these displays?" she says. "I'm always in my head now, questioning my thoughts and how I do things, realizing that if I put up that sign, I can face backlash because of it." I can relate. Even at my own job, I'm filled with anxiety as I overthink even the simplest of tasks, like creating a book display. One false move in the eyes of the angry mob and I will be defamed online all over again.

So many of my school librarian friends have essentially gone into hiding after being targeted. Educators who were once the face of the most popular sessions at librarian conferences have disappeared for their own safety or the security of their families. I miss seeing their faces and learning from them. Some have even completely left social media, so librarians I messaged and kept up with through those avenues are gone from my life. I think of them often and wonder if they are okay. I do not fault them and understand completely. Their safety and mental health should be their focus, and they need to do what they need to do. A few of us have even formed our own support group online on a private Facebook group page to help offer moral support and suggestions for coping through the stress of it all. What kind of world are we living in that has some of our most devoted community servants living so terrified?

A high school librarian in South Carolina (who wishes to not be named) has been the subject of numerous FOIA intimidation attempts, but one family in particular made her their special project. At the direction of the parents, a child began taking photos in the school library of books with LGBTQIA+ characters. Apparently, the idea was to initiate a confrontation, which would then be recorded. The librarian did not engage and requested a meeting with the parents, which resulted in a barrage of insults. Over the next few weeks, the librarian found the student hiding in the library before she arrived. Or he would simply pace back and forth in front of the building, throwing sullen looks her way. The child continued to bait the librarian by blocking her path in the hallway and hovering to eavesdrop when she spoke to other educators. When she told me this, I was incredulous and wondered what I would do in this situation. Nobody should have to face these conditions, and she confided that she was unsure of returning to work the following year. She explained, "In my decades-long education career, one of the things I am most proud of is my ability to connect with students from a wide variety of backgrounds and life experiences, but this situation has shaken me. Now I feel uncomfortable and suspicious because I do not know if a student was directed by their parents to search for something they can use to fuel their attack on libraries."

A school librarian in Idaho, (let's call her Megan) told me, "I no longer have the drive to do anything extra outside of school hours. My school was my whole life and now I get sick to my stomach on Sunday evenings thinking about going back the next day." Megan was the focus of her community's harassment after she spoke up about school library policies at a school board meeting. I stumbled on a series of TikTok videos created to mock her and reached out to make sure that she was okay. Multiple people who do not even live in her district, nor even have school-age children, have called her names in person and online and booed her in public. She finds solace in writing, meditation, and reading but is struggling to focus on anything for longer than ten minutes. "It's all-consuming. I start hyperventilating thinking about the people I've known for years who are now posting that me and other school librarians are groomers. What did I ever do wrong? I'm the same loving educator I have always been. I love their kids and the kids love me. It's parents in our community who have gotten involved in the local "parental rights" groups who now think I am doing something I am not. I can't stay in this profession much longer. It's too heart-breaking."

This is happening all across the country, even places known for inclusivity like the Seattle, Washington, area. In 2021, a school librarian named Gavin, who works in a district with a strong LGBTQIA+ community, decided to focus on including more books for his LGBTQIA+ students. Gavin gave serious thought to the titles and carefully vetted the books. Two months after a few of the books went on the shelves, Gavin's principal irately confronted him with one of the books and told him she could remove whatever books she wanted. Gavin insisted that she should follow the policies in place for challenges, but she said she didn't have to and told Gavin nobody would support him. She intimated that his librarian credentials could be jeopardized and even removed a book from his latest book order. The story was reported to Kelly Jensen of Book Riot and was picked up by the *Seattle Times* and retweeted by the author Neil Gaiman. Suddenly the books were quietly placed back on the shelves. But it didn't stop there.

The principal sent pages of the removed book, out of context, to other teachers at the school, which were read aloud in a departmental meeting. The staff turned on Gavin, who was iced out and shunned. The school district hired an independent investigator, who discovered an email the principal had written claiming that Gavin was "victimizing" students. The union stepped in and requested a change of building. Gavin began waking up in cold sweats, unable to go back to sleep. This level of emotional distress is something I've heard from over a dozen school librarians. Gavin received threatening emails, and one mentioned his wife by name.

Gavin found overwhelming support from the library community, found an ally on the school board, and was approached by parents who praised him. But school life was painful. Gavin admitted, "I would feel my pulse race and a panic attack threaten to set in when I got to the school building. I spent as much time as I could locked in my office with the blinds closed." Gavin switched schools the next year, after using up his sick days at his old school. He still will occasionally wake up in a panic but can go back to sleep when he remembers he no longer has to return to his old school. He joined the Washington Library Association's intellectual freedom section and serves as vice chair to help others. He is trying to move on from the trauma he experienced. I say good riddance to the adults at that school, who lost a kick-ass, thoughtful librarian who wanted the library's book collection to reflect the student body. Shame on them. Gavin will quickly tell you that he loves his new school, faculty members, and students, but "this event completely transformed my life."

I think that's something that those of us who experience this all-consuming harassment and hatred find hard to explain to others. It is difficult to admit how depressed and angry we can get. The physical symptoms are easier to describe, but the mental anguish is embarrassing and hard to put into words. Part of the trouble is wondering what others think of you even when you know you've done nothing wrong. Lies become truth on the internet, and my inner demons won't go away. My mind feels like the blades of a helicopter, constantly whirling and stirring up dust. Knowing how it feels to become a target, I do my best to support other targeted librarians, but there are so many that it can become overwhelming. I am in constant fear that I will lose a friend to the strain of pressure or the actions of a fanatic. The destruction that lies in the wake of their hate doesn't seem to matter to the white Christian nationalists.

Sometimes I think it's what they want. They want educators and librarians to be so worn down that it becomes difficult to fight back. They don't care if they destroy good people for the sake of their cause. The whole point is to defund libraries and public schools through any means necessary. We are just collateral damage to them in their quest, and so are the students who do not fit into the mold of what they deem acceptable, which is white, straight Christians. I pray for the hate, lies, and attacks to end for the sake of our profession, my friends, and our marginalized community members, but the haters just keep spewing their hate.

———————

My prayers have been answered because it gets harder for me to care each day about the personal attacks. I have become desensitized to the lies being spread about me. I know that they're not true, and so do rational human beings. I hope others' prayers are answered soon and that they, too, will be able to brush the hate aside. It's very difficult, as I know all too well, and it took me a long time to get to this point. If it's become easier for me, I still get angry on behalf of friends who land in the angry mob's sights.

Citizens for a New Louisiana recently posted a blog with the subject heading "Miscreants and Malcontents" and referred to my friends Lynette and Melanie as "known associates of Amanda Jones." We're thinking of getting matching tattoos or creating a T-shirt line of Lunsford's dumbest quotes. Things like that make us laugh so much, and we find the humor in the absurdity of it all. Michael Lunsford and Ryan Thames are trying to stay relevant, but the posts and blogs get wackier with each passing week. I wish they knew about the large gaggle of Louisiana librarians who share and mock their most nonsensical comments in a closed group. We have a list of the greatest hits. It's like watching animals backed into a corner begin gnawing their own legs off. They are obviously spiraling downward. Lynette told me, "Fascism is hungry. So hungry it eventually eats itself. We are just trying to keep it from completely swallowing the library in the process."

I saw a post from the Moms for Liberty national Twitter account referencing an article about me on CodaStory.com titled "America's Culture War Targets Librarians." They tweeted, "You want to groom our children and we're supposed to give you love? She should be crying in bed for days. If she had any conscience at all, her own shame should have her inconsolable. Cry more." If I had seen this a year ago, I would have gone into a tailspin. These days, I take it in stride.

I feel sorry for whoever posted that. I worry about their own children and their households. They are part of a misguided social movement whose leaders know only divide and conquer and the quest for power. The followers understand none of this. The hate they spew creates a compelling group identity. It is emotional, not rational. It gives their lives meaning and a sense that they matter. There are better ways to find meaning, more constructive, positive ways. Ways that build things and people up. The haters only tear things down and hurt good people.

I doubt people like that will ever know the joy I experienced when a former student called me to interview me for her library science class and asked if I could mentor her for her practicum. She raved about the programs she's seen me post about on our library's Instagram, and I was thrilled to answer her questions about cataloging and the process of finding the right books for kids. She's currently student teaching, and I am so damn proud of her and how hard she's worked. I am honored that I was the one she called.

They'll never know the feeling of pride I felt when I ran into a former student turned co-worker in the teachers' workroom who told me how she had found the courage to voice her concern to a district supervisor about an issue our teachers are having with curriculum materials. I have hundreds of former students whose lives I have touched and who in turn will be touching the lives of their own students. The love I have for my students, whether they are current students or students in their thirties, is everything and trumps all the hate.

It's easier to disregard the hateful comments coming from random people I don't know than comments from people in my own community. That, I have to tell you, still stings. There's nothing quite like the twisted knife of a backhanded post or vindictive comment

Moms for Liberty ✓
@Moms4Liberty

You want to groom our children and we're supposed to give you love?

She should be crying in bed for days. If she had any conscience at all, her own shame should have her inconsolable. Cry more.

"America's culture war targets librarians"

codastory.com

7:34 AM · 1/3/23 · **12K** Views

38 Reposts **10** Quotes **182** Likes **5** Bookmarks

from someone whose child you love and have helped, or someone you directly know. From someone you can't for the life of you understand why they would say something so personally hurtful when you can't think of what you could have done to them. From someone who has taught your own child or lives in your neighborhood. From someone you've called a friend and you've shared authentic smiles with. From a relative you've hugged. There's nothing quite like it. And, really, it's only explicable if you consider how far and wide extremist views have spread and how passionately held they are, even in your own community. Apparently, the tenets of the MAGA, White Christian Nationalist Right are so compelling that they trump your own personal experience with people you know, who have taught and nurtured your own children. Whichever way you understand it, it hurts. But as a co-worker told me, "They are beneath you. Even if you thought they were your friend, their remarks say otherwise. It sucks, but at least you know now who they are and you have plenty of others who know you and think you're good people." Yes, indeed.

There are more and more librarians having to go high when the haters go low. So many take the high road each day as continuous conspiracies of "porn in the library" and cries of "Groomer!" spread like a stomach virus across our country, making me want to vomit. At least once a week, a librarian will email me asking for advice on what to do, because they, too, have been maligned in their community, falsely accused of exposing children to sexually explicit material or pushing hidden agendas. Each one of these librarians' stories has a familiar ring to it, whether it takes place in the North or the South, the East or the West, blue states or red states, and in small villages or large cities. It's a contagion, but it's a contagion that is well organized and fueled by fear and the mistaken notion that turning back the clock will fill the void in people's lives.

There is a small faction in our society who have clambered into the trenches of our ongoing and nonsensical cultural wars and refuse to give quarter. That libraries, and librarians, are their latest targets only shows how crazy things have become. Libraries, for God's sake. These foot soldiers and their puppet masters have decided that libraries are not needed or that they should belong only to a select few. These people decry government overreach as they try to use the government to dictate what citizens can and cannot read. They have decided that libraries are somehow evil and that librarians must be "put in their place." This is insane. We are your mothers and fathers, daughters and sons, friends and neighbors, cousins and members of your congregation. We implore you to listen to common sense. Before it's too late, stand up against those who are slinging lies and hate as they pick up torches and march to kill the Beast.

Chapter 10

Some People Are Ride or Die. Some People Aren't.

If you come across a bear, never push a slower friend down . . .
even if you feel the friendship has run its course.

—National Park Service on Twitter/X,
February 23, 2023

I am very open about how I was diagnosed with depression in my twenties. After the birth of my child, I went through a period where I simply couldn't get out of bed. I had zero energy, and even the smallest of tasks sent me into a panic. Pregnancy took a toll on my body, and after several visits with specialists, I realized that I had developed sleep apnea, that my thyroid had essentially stopped working, and that I suffered from major postpartum depression. Through therapy, I discovered that I'd probably had undiagnosed depression for most of my life.

The symptoms I experience with depression usually manifest as anger rather than sadness and are controlled through medication and therapy. Growing up probably would have been a lot easier if I had known then what I know now, which is that it's okay to admit you have emotions you need help controlling. I was angry too often and gave my parents hell over the smallest issues. Back then, I could suddenly fly off the handle, but now I'm medicated, older, and wiser. I'm better at walking away, counting to ten, and taking a day or two before responding to someone. At least I hope so.

I have been reflecting on how anger manifested in my teenage years and my reactions to several events in life. One of my biggest flaws is my tendency to hold grudges. I promise I'm working on that, but it's hard, especially when there are so many online products devoted to revenge. Did you know you can send anonymous poop-grams to people you don't like? There's an actual website where you can even choose the type of animal poop. I'm not saying I've ever done that, but I'm not NOT saying it either. I'm kidding, because I would never do that. One of my favorite things to say to people when they tell me a story of someone being mean to them is to say, "I hope someone sends them a poop-gram." There's a big online business devoted to petty, and the possibilities are endless.

When I was younger, I might yell at someone. Like I said, I'm older and wiser now. Yelling solves nothing. Poop-grams don't, either, but it is funny to think about.

I can be petty on someone else's behalf if I feel that a friend has been wronged. I have a huge sense of loyalty and will go to bat for friends at the drop of a hat. There were several instances in high school that almost got me in trouble. When you live in a small town, there's not much to do on a Friday night. As teenagers, we used to hang out at the gravel pits. It's exactly what it sounds like: a secluded site on the Amite River where gravel was quarried. Nothing says small town Friday night like standing around in a pile of gravel in the middle of nowhere. Eventually, the sheriff would come and tell us to scatter, so we'd all drive to another spot to hang out. Nothing much happened but talking and drinking disgusting lukewarm beer, but there were occasional fights. Another aspect of small-town life are the rivalries that develop between neighboring towns, which usually revolve around sports or turf battles involving hangout spots.

I remember a time when a few girls from the rival town of Denham Springs showed up and started talking smack about my friend Christin.

They stood in a cluster and loudly called her a slut and a bitch. I remember my eyes narrowed, my blood began to boil, and my hands clenched into fists. The smack wasn't directed at me, but nobody was going to call my friend names. I started getting in their faces. Of course, there were no actual blows, but it was an epic screaming match.

Another popular hangout was the Denham Springs McDonald's. We didn't have a McDonald's in Watson, so we'd venture into rival territory to get our fix of greasy French fries. That meant encroaching on Denham's hangout spot. I remember that we were in line once and a girl accidentally/on purpose bumped into my friend Allye and said, "Watch it, bitch." Allye got behind me to smack-talk back, probably because she knew that I would defend her. I laugh now about how I started taking out my earrings and asking the girl if she wanted to go outside. What was I even thinking? I'm no longer so hotheaded thanks to my medication, but I will always defend my friends in any way I can short of resorting to violence. After all, I'm now a grown-up and must set a good example for my students. I also wouldn't look good in jailhouse stripes.

I will not go looking for a fight but do feel a huge sense of responsibility to be a good and loyal friend. If you're friends with me, I will be at your side. You need help, just ask. Most of the time you won't even have to ask. I'm not saying that I'm the best of friends, because I do have major flaws, but I am loyal. I just assumed that everyone was like me—willing to go to bat for their friends regardless of the personal cost. Imagine the hurt I felt when it was time for friends to step up for me and some didn't.

When I started facing online abuse within my community, some people did indeed step up, but most did not. Many former students reached out to me. My family supported me. But it opened my eyes to several of my local friendships that weren't as solid as I'd believed them to be. I have walked away from a number of these over the past year. I look at my job and my co-workers differently now. The sense of betrayal I felt toward friends who didn't speak out publicly was huge. It's something I'm still coming to terms with. The support I received from across the state and across the country was loud and clear. From many of my hometown friends, all I heard was crickets.

At the time, the lack of support felt almost as bad as the attacks. I kept waiting for my school "family" to step in and say something publicly. Nobody did. That's not to say I didn't receive support from some people I work with. Many reached out over the summer and then came to talk to me in person when we returned to school. They sympathized with me and said they were angry on my behalf. But if they were so sad and angry, why hadn't they said anything publicly? I've asked myself this countless times, and it has affected my interactions at school. I understand that they didn't want to be attacked themselves, but it still hurt.

Not only was I saddened by the lack of support from people whom I'd been friends with my whole life, I was surprised at some of my friends' comments on social media pages I guess they thought I wouldn't see. One person I'd been friends with for decades wrote "I guess you can never tell about people" on a page where someone called me a groomer. I was taken aback. Why was my supposed friend surprised I spoke out against censorship, and why did that seemingly make me a groomer in her eyes?

A woman whose children I taught wrote that kids needed to be protected from me and the books in our school library. She worked for the education association I was a member of and had taken me out to dinner the previous year for winning librarian of the year. I got so upset that I withdrew my membership from the organization. I had been an active member for twenty years and had presented at conferences for them.

Random people dropped into my friends' and family's pages to write awful comments. Most of them defended me, but some did not. One woman I don't even know sent a friend the message, "Why do you support Amanda's perversion? Explain. I wanna understand. She's not who people think she is. My kids attended the same school as she's at. Something in the tides turned. She's just part of the indoctrination agenda in schools." A local proud Christian woman wrote on my sister's page, "It would be nice if she told the truth instead of fabricating it out of desperation for media attention. Attention seeking isn't an attractive quality."

I learned two lessons. One is that I thought the world was one way, and realized it wasn't. I thought when people said they were your friends or family, they were, and would stick by you through thick and through thin. When they don't stand up for you because they don't really care, or even turn on you, you realize that they were never who they said they were. I took them at face value, because I try not to do or say things I don't mean. Then there are those who are your friends, but they are lacking something inside that prevents them from sticking up for you publicly. These people ARE your friends, they just don't have the backbone to show it publicly when it matters, and that can be just as hurtful. You want them to make a public display of solidarity, but they don't. Those are the people I try to give grace. I really do try.

Nobody owes me anything. My friends shouldn't be forced to defend me, but it would have been nice if they had tried. I would have done that and so much more if the tables had been turned. Early on, when my attorney thought that we could get a temporary restraining order on one of my harassers, she asked if there was anyone at work who would testify on my behalf about the anguish I was experiencing. I constantly worried someone would show up at school and harm a child in an effort to get at me. I did try to ask someone I work with if he would speak in court for me.

I remember trying to build up the courage all day to talk to him. I walked by him several times and chickened out. I wasn't worried about him. I was concerned that I would start blubbering so hard. I'd make myself hyperventilate. I was in a constant state of anxiety, and my emotions were all over the place. Finally, I got up the nerve and approached him with my head down. I could feel my hands trembling. Normally, I walk everywhere around school pretty fast and greet everyone I pass. Those days I tiptoed and tried to stay hidden from prying eyes. I guess it wouldn't have mattered how I went in.

I couldn't even get the full request out of my mouth. I started, "Hey, so you know how those people keep posting about me?" He looked up surprised, like he hadn't realized I had walked in. I continued, "My attorney says she thinks maybe I can get a restraining order, but she says people I work with need to testify about how scared I've been and . . ." Then, before I could even finish, he yelled, "Absolutely not." At that moment, I felt as if I had been slapped in the face. I turned bright red, and my lip started quivering. I don't think I could have replied to that if I had wanted to because of the lump suddenly lodged in my throat. All I could do was walk back the way I had come, trying to hold it together, and thinking, "Well, that was awful." I retreated to the library and hid in the supply room, unable to see through the tears streaming from my eyes. That was the moment I started peeling the cuticles away from my fingernails. I was always a nail biter, but I started to chew my nails down to bloody nubs. I know now, from intensive therapy, that is how some people physically react to trauma.

I was hurt and angry and devastated all at once. Later that same evening, he texted an apology and said he was sorry for raising his voice. He said some nonsense about how we had different political beliefs. Since we had never really discussed politics before, my assumption was that he was referring to my open support of the LGBTQIA+ community. I'm not implying that he is anti-LGBTQIA+. I think he is welcoming to everyone, but in my community one doesn't tend to advertise empathy or you will face backlash from very vocal alt-right citizens. Politics trumps empathy here in Livingston Parish.

I happen to see my support of marginalized groups as an issue of morality and basic human empathy and not as a political matter. On another level, I was simply asking for support from a colleague whom I'd worked with for over two decades and whom I considered a friend. This was the other moral dimension here. If the roles had been reversed, you wouldn't have been able to stop me from helping him. In fact, I had defended him against rumors within the school and our community for years. I've always stood up for him and I will continue to do so, even if he wouldn't for me. But the realization that the loyalty wasn't going to be returned was a little shocking. When politics and image are more important than standing up for colleagues and friends, we are in a world of trouble.

Both he and I were respected members of the community, with a history of hard work and dedication to our students. If he had posted on his personal social media some sort of positive statement on my behalf, it would have helped me so much within the community, as well as personally and emotionally. He didn't do that. Most people didn't, but he's a community leader, and I still wished he could have stepped up to the plate. If he had had the courage to stand up for me, others would have followed. I try not to be bitter about it. In all honesty, I don't feel anger as much as a kind of sadness. I realize that he owes me nothing. It's not about owing anyone something, though. To me, it's what friends do. Friends should stand up for each other, even if they hold different political beliefs. The political part of the equation took a while to really sink it, and when it finally did, it only brought more sadness.

That whole episode was a huge disappointment to me. The damage was done, and to this day I don't think of him the same way. I just can't. I thought we were a team and that I had helped him make our school something we could be proud of. It didn't seem to matter. I had thought wrong. That was the moment I realized that for all that talk that we are a school family, we are in fact just co-workers.

Any illusions I had were shattered that day. I felt like a kid who discovers that Santa Claus isn't real. I will never again allow myself to feel close to him, to protect myself from another great loss. I have learned to deal with the fact that for twenty-two years, things were not as I thought they were. In talking to a friend about it, she said, "Well, at least you know now that the sentiments you had for some people weren't returned." I would have rather not known. I would have rather gone ten more years with my head buried in the sand and retired still thinking we were all one big family. I guess ignorance is in fact bliss. Some things I'm glad I know, but this isn't one of them. It's hurtful when you think one thing for decades only to realize you were not looking close enough or willfully ignoring the telltale signs that were probably there all along. Sometimes we want to see the best in other people. I read an article in *Psychology Today* that said, "The human mind is shockingly good at filling in the gaps of perception." I guess I get an A-plus-plus.

Another huge disappointment to me was a local elected official whom I had thought was a friend. I will call her Katie, although people in my community will know the person I am talking about. I'm not bringing her up to settle a score—at least, I hope I'm not. I'm including her so that you know the whole story. Maybe in the future it will protect the peace of another educator, someone going through something similar.

I taught Katie's daughter years ago, and Katie had always been very supportive of our school and me. She volunteered for a social studies program I created and came on field trips when I taught her daughter. She was very supportive when I became our school's librarian. I would ask her to come read to the kids for World Read Aloud Day and invited her to an awards banquet when I won an award for having the top middle school library program in the state. She is a former newscaster for a Baton Rouge television station but was born and raised in our town. Katie was instrumental in getting us new flooring in the library and is a real asset to our community. You will find her at most local high school sporting events and programs. She and I will both tell you that we bleed blue and gold, our school's colors, and we both love our alma mater. In that way, along with the fact that we both have only daughters, we are very much alike.

In 2021, when I found out that I was named a *School Library Journal* Librarian of the Year, she was one of the first people I texted after telling my family. I was so proud to tell her, not because I had won an award, but because I was making a name for our school system and that our school library would be in a journal. A few months later, she honored me at a school board meeting for winning that award. She read a letter to me with tears in her eyes, and I fought hard not to cry as well as she told the people in attendance what a valuable employee I was for our school system. She said my community was lucky to have me. She gave me a pair of earrings that I would wear and tell people, "These are my Katie earrings." She had the governor of our state issue me a proclamation. It was one of the best moments of my career.

Fast-forward a year, and she was being very silent. When the attacks on my reputation first happened, I sent her the screenshots. I tried to tell her that all I did was speak out against censorship at the public library board meeting. I hadn't mentioned our school system. I certainly hadn't advocated for the teaching of anal sex to children or said I wanted to give erotica to children. She assured me that she knew I wouldn't do anything like that and said she was sorry this was happening to me. I never asked her to speak publicly for me. I didn't feel it was my place to ask, but I did wonder why she wasn't saying anything. She knew that the things being posted about me were false. She could have quieted it down with a single post on social media. She is very much beloved in our town, and people would have listened. I was very hurt that she didn't, but I made excuses for her. But a few weeks into the school year, the hurt turned to bitterness.

One day she finally made a post about the situation, and I really got my hopes up that this would be the post I had been waiting for, the post that would stop the lies, but it wasn't what I had hoped for. Someone told me she had posted and I grabbed my phone in anticipation, just knowing that she was going to put it all to rest once and for all. My friend was going to help me! The cavalry had finally arrived. My heart started beating faster as I opened social media to see the wonderful things she had to say about me and I was filled with gratitude. Once again, I was let down by someone I admired and had thought of as a friend.

She posted to say, "We do not have inappropriate books in the library at ——— school," and I thought, "You're damn right we don't. I can't wait to see the wonderful things she writes about me next!" But she didn't write anything positive about me at all. Her post continued and said, "The school system, principals, nor myself would ever allow this." Well, of course they wouldn't; that was obvious. However, neither would I, but she didn't say that. I wondered when she was going to say that and add nice things about me. I kept reading. She didn't include my name or say the school librarian would never do that, and she could have. I wanted her to add that. In my mind, I think she should have. Still, I tried to give her the benefit of the doubt. In the moment, I thought maybe she didn't realize she needed to make a stronger statement. Maybe it was unintentional? One year later, I don't think it was unintentional, and I've thought about it a lot more than is healthy.

I saw in her post that a lady made a derogatory statement about me. I just assumed Katie would correct that person, because that's what friends do. That's what leaders do. I waited impatiently for a solid day, and she didn't correct the lady. That hurt. Against my better judgment, and for the first time since the online bullying started, I responded to that lady. I explained what had actually happened—that I spoke as a resident about our public library at a public meeting and the issue had nothing to do with my school library. I immediately got a scolding text from Katie saying she didn't appreciate me doing that and she deleted my comment.

I felt like a child being admonished by my mother for doing something wrong when I hadn't. I started to have doubts about myself and about her. Why was she angry at me? I wondered if she was mad at me for defending our public library or defending marginalized communities. Then I started to wonder if that was the case, and if she was mad about the people I was defending, was she even a good person? I apologized to her for defending myself on her social media. I regret that now, because I had nothing to apologize for. I told her it was just so hard to not defend myself when people were posting obvious lies about me. She didn't say anything in return.

Then Ryan Thames took Katie's comments and ran with them. He posted, "It's good to have people of integrity looking out for our children. It is not only your right, but your obligation to protect children from harmful content and from people that might cause them harm with that content. Thank you!" I couldn't believe it. He was using my friend against me. Looking back, I guess she was no longer my friend at that point, and maybe she never really was. At the time, I still had hope and still naively thought that she was going to stick up for me and set him straight. I took a screenshot of his post and sent it to her. She texted back, "Maybe we should come up with a statement." I was instantly relieved. She was going to finally help me! I waited with my phone in hand for days. My relief was short-lived. She never made a statement, and that was the last she texted me, until she texted me to do some victim blaming a few months later.

She had the chance to reply on his social media, or make a statement on her own, that I would never harm kids or have inappropriate content in our school library, but she didn't. Not once. The community started praising her, saying she would be there to protect our students from that evil librarian Amanda Jones, and she seemed to lean into those comments. In fact, someone shared that post on Katie's Facebook page and commented, "Thank you, Katie, for being a person willing to stand in the gap for our kids. My mind is blown, and my heart is broken at the number of people and parents who are hell bent to sexualize our kids. We love you." It seemed that Katie would rather act like the community savior, from someone she knew would never do the things they were accusing me of, than to dispel the rumors. Maybe she thought that I was guilty of the things people were accusing me of, but I don't think so. If that was the case, wouldn't she have investigated? She didn't comment, but she also didn't delete it. That hurt big-time. That was the day I unfriended her on social media.

Around the same time, election campaigning was happening. She ran unopposed for our local election, so I knew that her silence wasn't because she was scared to speak out due to the elections. I did not realize at the time that she was getting ready to run in a much larger election the following year. However, I did notice that she was heavily promoting a friend of hers for another office. I noticed that same friend of hers was very vocal on social media about me and school libraries. He said things would be different in schools if he was elected. He would be looking into the situation, insinuating that I was someone who needed to be investigated, maybe? She never corrected him, either, at least not on social media. I started to get very angry with her. It's one thing to sit silently. It's another to promote someone who was trash-talking me online. I felt very betrayed. The day he lost his school board election, I cheered.

Not long after he lost his election, I made a comment about it at school. Almost every morning before the students get to school, I go to my friend's classroom to visit, as do many others. As the school librarian, I'm usually far away from the rest of the staff, in the library, so I look forward to a cup of coffee and a chat with my colleagues before the kids arrive on campus each day. One day, I mentioned that I was glad that man had not won his election, because he seemed to have a lot of fringe ideas and often posted derogatory comments about school employees and the school system. I should have stopped it right there, but I said, "I can't believe Katie would align herself with someone like that." I was in what I thought was a safe space with friends. I continued, "One day, I'm going to have a heart-to-heart with Katie on my thoughts about that man and his comments about me. I'm really upset with her about all of that. Serves both of them right that he didn't win his election. Too bad for them."

I knew that a relative of hers was in the room when I said it. I have no regrets about saying what I said. I didn't care that she had heard me, but it was obviously relayed in a way that stretched the truth of my comments into something uglier than they were, because I got a text later that night. In fact, I got it in the middle of another public library board meeting that I was attending. So as I'm watching another attempt by pro-censors to destroy our public library, the whole reason I spoke out in the first place, I got a text message that seemed to blame me for the whole ordeal.

"Amanda, I was told I cannot have any communication with you once you got an attorney and filed the lawsuit. It's against school board policy. Mr. —— also confirmed this. So please quit saying ugly things about me, when I have no control over this." I wondered what ugly things she thought I was saying. I even asked her, "Ugly things? I've only said you have not shown me public support, which is true. And that people shared things on your social media and you did not delete them and that hurt my feelings." It didn't stop there. No, she had to put the final nail in the coffin and closed our friendship.

"I've been told it's been ugly things. I do know people whom you don't like, and perhaps don't like you." I couldn't believe what I was reading. Why didn't she just ask me what I said? I'd tell her the truth. No, she was just going to believe whatever she had been told and then throw gasoline on the fire by telling me people don't like me. Okay. I wrote back and told her maybe we should no longer communicate if she was told not to. She continued, "We had a discussion on your court case in executive session and I was told I cannot have any communication. Mr. —— should have told you this months ago."

Hold up. I was discussed in an executive session at a school board meeting? I knew for a fact that I am supposed to be notified and allowed attendance if I was being discussed in an executive session. I pushed back on that and said, "Just to clarify for legal reasons, you're saying that I, as an employee, was discussed in an executive session without my knowledge? I need to know this before I ask my union representative and my personal lawyer for clarification on these laws." She immediately backtracked her statement. She said it wasn't me they were discussing but communication in general once people hire attorneys. I wondered if she thought I was born yesterday. Still, she didn't stop there.

"Many teachers have reached out to me very upset with you for putting our schools in a bad light." Wow, I thought. Way to victim blame. Was it supposed to be my own fault for people making up lies about me on social media? If other people were reaching out to her about me, she should have told them the truth of the situation. That's all it would have taken. Tell the truth. Amanda spoke at a public library board meeting about censorship and people are trying to ruin her reputation. Amanda works very hard at her job and did nothing wrong.

I sent my sisters the text messages and asked them if I was being irrational for getting so upset over the text messages. One of them made several graphics breaking down the text messages to show me that, no, my feelings were valid. She wanted to email them to Katie. I asked her not to. It wasn't worth it. It wasn't going to make Katie see reason, since she already had her mind made up.

I also wondered: If Katie was not to communicate with me, why was she texting me? Did she text just to make accusations? Was she just trying to make me feel bad? I could promise her I was already feeling pretty crappy. There was no need to make me feel worse. I wasn't sure what she was hoping to accomplish. Did she feel guilty and she was trying to justify not defending me publicly? I struggled to pay attention that night at the library board meeting and not run out crying in the middle of that meeting. There were people at the meeting taking pictures of me and recording. I didn't want them to see me looking dismayed, even if they wouldn't have known what I was upset about.

What Katie didn't know when she texted me was that Mr. ——— was at that same public library board meeting. When it was over, I showed him the texts. He looked at me sadly and told me none of that had ever happened and she had never been told that she could not communicate with me. He didn't call her a liar—he is too kind for that—but simply said what she was saying was not true. My heart broke a little, even though I already knew what she'd said about communication was untrue. She didn't work for our school system. They couldn't tell her she could not communicate with her friend.

I didn't make a big deal about it. I just quietly removed her number from my phone contacts and tried not to come unglued on the way home that night. I showed one of my co-workers the next day at school. He seemed a little confused by her comments, too, but didn't say much. He asked why I believed Mr. ——— over Katie. Mr. ——— had stood by me since day one, often reaching out to check on me and make sure I was okay. He had always been honest with me, even if it was something I didn't want to hear. He's a truth teller. He wouldn't say Katie's texts were untrue if they weren't, I told my co-worker. I no longer wanted Katie anywhere near me or to pay a visit to our school. I found out not too long after that that Katie was running for a legislative office. I noticed pictures of her being posted on social media with some of the same people who had been spreading the rumors about me. I was no longer uncertain about her intentions.

Someone asked me if she actually had done something to me, or had done something for herself that had just negatively affected me. I think her inaction to help me when I needed it was the opposite of what a friend would do. To me, her inaction was an action. She made a conscious decision not to help when she could have. It was cowardly, but I also think she thought of her own interests first. That's the exact opposite of the servant leader she claims to be, so I no longer want to hear about what an advocate for educators she is.

I guess I have a sense of pride in thinking that I would never treat anyone the way so many of my so-called friends have treated me over the past year. It still hurts when not only do people whom you think are friends not stand up for you but they lie to you and then hang out with people who have knowingly hurt you. So, yeah, I can smile and say I took the higher road, but the higher road is pretty lonely when you discover you've lost friends you never really had in the first place.

Throughout this whole ordeal, I have felt that there was an attempt to silence me. Whether that was because they just didn't want to deal with the issue because of their own fears or anger at me personally, I will never know unless I ask, and I'm not going to ask. There was a movement to silence me through the posts of these two men and then an attempt to silence me from people I thought were friends. There is a massive amount of political pressure in our community from the Far Right and our citizens and leaders let their fear of becoming targets, and their cowardice, affect their decisions. It takes bravery to speak out. I guess it is courage many do not have.

After all of this went down between Katie and me, I spoke to one of my sisters, who admitted that she had emailed Katie on my behalf pretty early on and I had no idea. My sister wrote Katie to say, "I've seen my sister cry more during this time than I have in my entire life. It wasn't at all shocking to hear, considering the circumstances surrounding her, when she informed me she's considering taking leave. BUT it broke my heart tremendously because I know how much she LOVES what she does. It deeply saddens me that she is in this position. I know in the past she has turned down job offers with higher paid salaries because she tells me, 'I already have a job I love.' I write . . . to respectfully ask that you consider a way to show Amanda some form of public support by a statement about her reputation. It would mean so much." Melanie never received a reply from Katie. I found out that Melanie also sent similar emails to my principal and superintendents. They also did not reply.

I told a friend about my sister emailing Katie with no response, and she told me that she, too, had emailed Katie and gotten no response. That was the case for several people I spoke with. It touches my heart that I do have friends and family who were willing to step up for me, even if it was in a subdued way. I try to hold on to that. Hold on to the ones who did do something. Anything. I need to give them more credit and grace, because maybe there are actions many of them took that I don't even know about. Maybe helping silently was the best they could do. I try not to be too disappointed with those like Katie and focus more on those who did help. It seems to be human nature to focus on the negative, so I am working hard on the positive.

For several weeks, I was receiving a text message every one to two hours from librarians across the United States, friends who were checking on me. Just when I would be falling back into despair, a message would pop up like the text from my friend Andrea, who sent me a link to the poem "Invictus," or a text like the one from my friend Karina saying, "Thinking of you today." My friend Courtney sent me the cutest pictures of her cats, and I'd share one back with a smile. There were a few people at work who regularly stopped by the library. Jennifer would stop and see if I was okay, or I'd find a treat on my desk like the time Brooke left me a pack of Starbursts with the message, "Sorry you 'burst' into tears yesterday. I hope things get better." One day I found a notecard in my school mailbox from my friend Heather. I keep it in my binder to remind myself that I do have friends who care. I don't want my friends to feel unseen amid all my negativity. I value them more than I can express.

I used to blame the two men for ruining my friendships with people. They made it impossible for people to speak out. They used continuous posts and their friends and family to keep up the tactics on social media. Essentially, what they had hoped to accomplish was successful for a brief moment. I was scared. My friends and family were scared or perhaps didn't know what to do. I also used to blame my friends, because I thought they should have said something. Through much therapy, I have tried to walk away from the blame game. There's no point in it. They, just like me, were faced with a situation they didn't ask to be in. They have their own lives to lead and their own families to worry about.

Some people are strong; some people aren't. Some people act in small ways and some people make bigger splashes. I have to learn to be okay with the knowledge that not everyone is like me or as loyal or outspoken. It doesn't necessarily make them a bad friend or me a better friend. It just makes us different. My therapist said that the actions of the people who turned on me are on them and doesn't say anything about me. If everyone I worked with, and all my friends in the community, had stood up for me publicly, I'd be telling a different story, but they didn't. I understand now that I'm not owed anything by them just because we are friends or coworkers. I understand now that some people couldn't. We live in such a small town, and the fear of repercussions is real. There is a huge amount of pressure in these polarized times to not stand out. It doesn't stop the hurt, but it is getting easier.

One thing that helped me accept what was happening was a letter I received from a man I do not know. One day I'd like to tell this man in person just how much his letter came at just the right time in my life. It said:

Dear Ms. Jones,

I'm 63 and a veteran, so I've known and met a lot of very tough people in my time who've served our nation with courage and distinction in wars and various military skirmishes going all the way back to WWII. I'm talking about men (mostly) but also women who've put everything on the line to defend our democratic principles; and I have to tell you I'm hard pressed to think of anyone I admire more than you.

We call our veterans and first responders heroes—it sort of rolls off our tongues with alacrity—but the older I get the more I've come to realize that educators and teachers like you are just as much heroes as the tough veterans (some of them my relatives) I've known and loved who, in a few instances, even fought hand-to-hand with the enemy in faraway places like Iwo Jima and the Middle East. That may sound like hyperbole to some but it's just flat out true. That reality was reinforced over the past several years when Covid lurched across the nation and hit our schools hard. Teachers were suddenly thrust into the trenches in a way that wasn't entirely dissimilar to the hand-to-hand combat those in the military have endured throughout history. Teachers' lives were literally on the line and a lot of them succumbed just because they refused to let the pandemic keep them from their duty to the children and communities they serve.

Now, I know you didn't choose to be a hero—and that's one of the odd things about heroes: the vast majority don't go out in their day looking for an opportunity to be a hero, the situation just sort of happens upon them, often at times when they least expect it, and they were suddenly thrust into a decision point. They find themselves at a fork in the road where they have to decide, the way you did, who they are and what they stand for, and then they make a bold decision to go forward against seemingly untenable odds. It is frequently a decision made in a millisecond, or it may take a few minutes or even days to muster the courage that propels them forward, but they do indeed go forward. I'm sure you've heard the aphorism about courage not being defined as the absence of fear, but rather, feeling fearful and going forward despite it. Some of the bravest people I've known readily admit they were literally shaking in their boots when they jumped out of a plane or flew a bomber over Germany in WWII.

When I think of the heroes I've met, a lot of them are like you, often humble people that I refer to as an "accidental hero." But that doesn't detract from their heroic actions. I know you didn't wake up one day and say you're going to get dressed and go do battle with angry people who want to force their sectarian agenda down your throat and the throats of the people and children you love and support. But there you are fighting what I and millions of your admirers would call the good fight. You're on the right side of humanity. You're on the decent side. You, like so many of the soldiers who've defended our nation's values over the past 245 years, are standing up for all of us—not just in Louisiana, but all across this land and everywhere that small minded bigots seek to impose their narrow views on anyone who doesn't think like them or march in lockstep to their un-American goals.

The last thing I want to say about being a hero is that it can be awfully lonely. Most people (even some of your friends and family) will sit idly on the sidelines keeping score from a distance. Even if they wholeheartedly agree with you, they don't want to risk the condemnation you've suffered. They're not as strong as you and they can't muster the courage to fight this battle. It doesn't make them bad people, necessarily, it just means their fear is strong and they don't have what it takes to stand up for themselves, let alone others. Not everyone does.

It must be heartrending when someone you thought you knew or loved turns their back simply because you stood up for decency. That hurts! And it's a hurt that may never completely go away. The downside of being a hero is that no one else can fully understand what you're going through, and that's what makes it kind of lonely. The best thing you can do, in my opinion, is remember (especially when you're feeling low and wondering whether it's all worth it) that you know yourself better than anyone on this planet, and you trust yourself and believe in yourself and recognize that you are where you are because you can handle this moment. This is where you're meant to be. It hasn't been easy and there probably isn't a lot of easy coming anytime soon, but you are the right person in the right place at the right time in history and, intentionally or not, you have become a hero and role model to millions of people. More important, a hell of a lot of children need people like you to help them find the hero within themselves so they can grow up to be bold and brave like you. You have touched the lives of more people than you will ever comprehend.

I congratulate you on your efforts and on behalf of our great nation wish you the best!

With gratitude and immense admiration,
Bill (New York)

This letter helped me come to some realizations about people in general and about my expectations. Some people are ride or die. Some people aren't. That can be a bitter pill to swallow. Thank you, Bill.

Chapter 11

The Longevity of Hate

Haters are like crickets . . . they make a lot of noise, you can hear them, but you can't see them . . . when you walk right by them, they suddenly get quiet.

—ORIGIN UNKNOWN

When I was maybe nine or ten, we had a tan station wagon. At the time it seemed massive, but looking back it probably only seemed that way because we were small. The back compartment opened up for two additional seats that faced each other. My sisters and I would fight over who got to sit there, wedged into the two bucket seats squished next to the spare tire. Nobody wanted to sit in the middle seat closest to my parents, because when the sister arguments started you might get swatted from the front seat when my mom had finally had enough. And even though I'd mastered the art of building a travel pillow fort in the middle seat, which would act as a force field for wayward smacks, I still preferred sitting in the very back.

My sisters and I all played competitive softball, and we often loaded up the car to travel to nearby towns for softball tournaments. Thinking back, I don't see how our family of five fit into that station wagon along with all our luggage and softball equipment. My dad usually made us listen to Riders in the Sky or Marty Robbins if we weren't being forced to listen to Paul Harvey on conservative talk radio. Usually, one of us would start complaining about the radio station or the volume, or ask repeatedly if we were there yet. It was a domino effect that led to my mom screaming at us to calm down, my dad twitching his eye and threatening to pull over, the arm swat to whichever kid could be reached in the back seat, and then my sisters and I melting into hysterics like wailing cats.

I remember one particular trip, my sisters and I all crammed into the back seat with our luggage pushed against the spare tire. After we'd been traveling for about an hour, we started whining and the arguments began. But this time, before we got to peak meltdown, there was a loud explosion. My dad jerked and swerved the car, everyone screamed, and we were suddenly covered in fuzz. It was reminiscent of those movie scenes of people having pillow fights and feathers flying everywhere. The spare tire had exploded. It was an explosion of epic proportions, raining down insulation over us like a cotton candy snowstorm, and causing us to go completely silent (after the initial scream) as my dad pulled the car over. It scared the living daylights out of us because it came with no warning, and it took a very long time to stop hearing the pounding of my heart in my ears.

The feeling I had after that tire explosion is not unlike the feeling I now have when receiving text messages and comments on social media. I am always on edge and waiting for the boom, and the barbs rain down on me like that itchy insulation, covering me while I try to shake them off. I will have been simply trying to live life and heal, and then *bam*. Another post out of nowhere. I attend my daughter's high school games and wonder if something will be whispered. I enter a drive-thru, and when the person at the window asks me if I am Amanda Jones, I wonder if my food will be spit in. For a long while, I was constantly on edge, waiting for that scare, and the stress from it all was debilitating.

At first, it was extremely hard not to check posts and social media accounts multiple times a day. Once I lodged a lawsuit, they stopped using my name, but their repeated posts about "that librarian" and the people who attend library board meetings were obviously about me, my friends, and others who spoke out on behalf of libraries. It was funny that they no longer had the bravitas to use my actual name, but it was also concerning that they continued to be obsessed with putting me down. Even after a year, they still post about libraries and allude to me. Remember, these are people whom I have never interacted with in person or on social media. It blows my mind that two random people and their friends would latch onto me and continue to post just because I spoke at a public library board meeting about censorship. It's as if they were angry at me for sticking up for myself and not taking their abuse lying down. But I know it's more complicated than that. They are hyperfocused on me because it gives them some sort of power

within the alt-right crowd of conspiracy theorists and the hateful. It's a schoolyard bullying tactic that most people grow out of after grade school when they mature into adults. These people haven't gotten the memo.

I rarely post about them, and when I do, it isn't really about them but something vague about rising above foolishness or updates on my case. I did post on social media one time specifically about Ryan Thames, although I didn't name him. At one of our public library board meetings, when something didn't go the way he wanted, he yelled at the library board that they were pieces of shit and told them they had no testicular fortitude. "God's warrior," the man "protecting children," showed some very alarming behavior that night when he yelled at the library board and made a scene

Amanda M Jones

Nov 22, 2022 ·

The biggest flex you can make to people who defame you is to thrive in spite of them and do it with kindness. If they were thriving, they wouldn't have to try and tear down others. If they were kind they wouldn't want to. They are jealous of what they will never be. That's on them and not you. You just keep on livin', man.

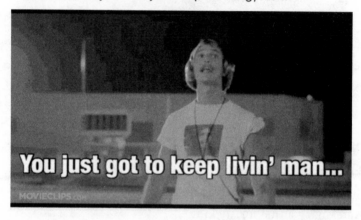

storming out. It was a display of true colors and an appalling example to set for the children in the audience and watching online. Not to mention for his own children, who will one day grow up and learn about his behavior. Someone was standing beside me recording, and I said, "Stay classy," knowing it would be heard on the video they were live-streaming. I also posted the following statement on Facebook and Twitter: "Never thought I'd hear a grown man scream about testicles at a public meeting, but here we are." There are times when I should think before I speak. Posting things like that make me no better than them and I regret it, even if it did make me laugh that night.

I think about the hate these people direct toward me and wonder what their spouses think. I wonder about how they treat their wives and children, and I worry about the example they set and the harmful influence of their actions. Maybe they're kind to their families, but I wonder about the vibe inside their homes. It can't be healthy to hold so much hatred or be conducive to a loving household. I hope their children are completely clueless about how their parents treat others. Surely these people would not want anyone to treat their children the way they have treated me, right? I wonder if their children will grow up with the same hatred. Will their children ask questions of their parents when they get older about why their parents thought it was acceptable to treat someone the way they have treated me, or will they grow up to be the same way? This behavior is not protecting children. It is hurting them. I hope that the cycle will be broken.

My own child is not clueless. She knows how these men have treated me. She's a teenager in the age of social media and internet access. I know that she googles my name. I know she sees the online vitriol. I try to shield her from it by not bringing it up or talking about it, but it's an uphill battle. There are lessons she can learn from seeing people attack her mother online, lessons that can help her see the right and wrong ways to treat people. My husband and I have tried to raise a loving child who is accepting of people from all walks of life. We have raised her to love God and to think before she speaks, and we have exposed her to as many cultures and points of view as we can. I think we have done a good job. Time will tell. That is all parents can do, but if you're setting an example of hatred and bigotry, you're harming your child and setting them up for failure.

One time, I did see a message she posted to a friend: "My mom is a fighter." It was in reference to a conversation that several of her friends were having about an online petition circulating at our local high school. According to a student, several teachers were mocking their decision not to use *he/him* pronouns and go by a different name. My daughter had talked to me about it, and I had given some advice on how the teens could navigate the situation without being disrespectful. My advice included letting that child's parents get involved, ways to have conversations with administration, and what not to do on social media. I was happy to see her reiterate all of this advice to her friend, who replied, "Your mom is a badass." My daughter replied, "I know." I think I'm doing okay in the parent department.

My daughter also sees my successes and can see my reaction to the way I have been treated online and in person. I have tried to set an example of rising above it, seeking help when needed, and taking a stand through proper channels. While the haters post mistruths and insinuations, journalists write accurate reports of the real story. It comforts me to know that she sees that I chose to fight back with legitimate journalists and speak the truth rather than launch a counter smear on Facebook. That would have accomplished absolutely nothing.

In a sense, the haters are why I continue to say yes to interviews and the reason I'm writing this book. If they would leave me alone, I'd have nothing to talk about and wouldn't need to defend myself. I laugh when people post things like "She's seeking her 15 minutes of fame" or "That evil woman is media hungry." I'd actually like the whole business to go away, but as long as I continue to be targeted, I will speak out. And it's no longer just about me. Early on, I felt a larger responsibility. If librarians, authors, and marginalized communities continue to be harassed, and books continue to be banned, I will give interviews when asked.

Continuing to speak out and give interviews isn't doing my lawsuit any favors. My attorney Alysson and I have discussed this at length—it's more important for me to speak the truth about what's happening to myself and others across the country than it is to win my own lawsuit. She agrees. I have a platform, and I would be doing a disservice to my profession if I didn't use that platform to shine light on injustices, not just to myself, but to others.

When I first became Louisiana School Librarian of the Year in 2020, and then a *School Library Journal* Co-Librarian of the Year in 2021, I knew that eyes would be on me from that day forward. I knew I had to learn to think before I speak and make wise choices. I needed to be a leader whether I wanted to or not. I saw the platform that my awards and actions have given me as an honor, but also an obligation. I have always advocated for school librarians within the school system, but now it was time to advocate for all librarians across the country. If someone was willing to hand me the mic, I should be prepared to speak. There was no way I was not going to speak out about what was happening to me and other librarians. That would be a waste of a platform. The downside was that I was maligned not only in my own community but also in the United States at large by factions of the Far Right, most notably white Christian nationalists. The pros were worth the cons, even if they cost me my lawsuit. The issue is so much bigger than me and my town.

And the hate keeps coming. Over the course of a year, the number of people commenting has died down, and now it's just the usual four or five people. The hysteria stopped, but the damage was spread far and wide and deeply. Anytime I have any semblance of success, the posts will start up for a little while, and I'll have to gird myself against the craziness. When I was awarded the 2023 Intellectual Freedom Award from the American Association of School Librarians, it was reported in the Baton Rouge *Advocate*. The Louisiana Family Forum, a nonprofit that claims to be a "Christian advocacy group who actively works to advance the Kingdom of God here in Louisiana," retweeted the article and posted, "Livingston librarian given 'Intellectual Dishonesty Award!'" The only thing dishonest was that tweet.

The award came with one thousand dollars for my school library, and my school system posted to congratulate me. A woman I don't know wrote in the local rants page, "The fact that they publicly congratulated her is a huge issue for me. We are really starting to see what's going on." I'm not sure what she thought was going on, but what actually happened was that a local educator was being nationally recognized in her profession. Who gets mad about a school getting free money for the school library to the benefit of all the students at that school? Apparently this woman named Jill does. The same woman went on my school system's social media page to write, "Further proof [the school system] is going woke." She took time out of her day to comment about me on several pages. This is a woman I don't know and have never spoken to in my life. Haters gonna hate, I guess. Imagine what they could do if they channeled that energy into something positive. This is consistent with many conspiracy theorists in my community, and across the country, who think there's always some hidden agenda in the school system. The only hidden agenda here isn't so hidden. These folks want to gut the public school system and privatize education so they can further exclude groups already marginalized.

A Denham Springs city councilman got so angry about me winning an award that he created a whole post about me. I don't know him either. He wrote, "This is logically inconsistent with one whose first concern is the welfare of children." The post didn't make a lick of sense and was just a bizarre word salad. I was alerted to it because a former student was distraught over the post and wanted to protect me. He is a leader in our local church. Maybe that church should protect the children from HIM. He is not a good steward of God's word.

Winning the award caused all sorts of people to lose their minds. The St. Tammany Parish Library Accountability Project, a group that initiated over two hundred book challenges from just a handful of individuals in St. Tammany Parish, also went on my school system's congratulatory post and wrote, "Isn't this the woman who fought to continue exposing children to sexually explicit material in the libraries? Including materials showing pictures of adults giving each other oral sex, children masturbating, and encouraging children to eat each other's poop and pee on one another for sexual arousal?"

The feces and urine imagery in that post were new to me, but again not surprising after I'd seen some of the things they wrote about their own parish's library director. They posted the following about her: "Your time is near," "Your perversion is hurting children," and "We are coming for you." One woman named Connie, the de facto leader who started the group, sends emails taunting the director. At the last St. Tammany Parish council meeting, it was even noted by council members that they had received similar messaging. People feel very brave behind computer screens, especially when they post from "anonymous" groups. They are emboldened when nobody calls them out for their hate. Connie is even on video snatching a phone out of someone's hand at the same meeting and saying, "You don't want to f**k with me. You don't know who I am." When I saw what they posted about me, I simply added a screenshot to my file on the group for further evidence. It's my hope that one day I can help the library director in that parish in a lawsuit against these people once my own case is resolved.

I feel sorry for people who spend their time posting things like that, because the hate will eat them up inside and must make them miserable. I also get angry, but not necessarily at the easily led. I get angry at the people who create the original hysteria and the politicians and leaders who could make the world a better place but choose not to. When Donald Trump was president, he did a lot of damage to our country because of what he posted on social media. As the leader of our country, he could have chosen words of hope, wisdom, and inspiration. Instead, he posted hate, lies, and bigotry, which sadly resonated with a significant swath of the American public. Many other leaders took note. And here we are again.

America these days is far from realizing its more perfect union. There are problems aplenty and reasons for all political stripes to be grouchy or downright angry. I have my own list of issues and I'm sure you do as well. What I want to see are people working hard to address what ails us, and doing so in a constructive way. Currently, this is not what is happening, particularly on the right. The right has identified the unease and weaponized it into an us-versus-them culture war that is only intensifying. This is not constructive. But for politicians like Trump and his cronies, it can mean power. And for many others it can mean belonging and a way to feel better about themselves.

The rise of social media has only supercharged our culture wars. In my opinion, too many people are easily swayed by what they see on social media. People mistake what shows up on their screens for reality, and it's easy to lean into the hate and distrust, especially when you're unhappy in your own life. If they can find someone else to blame for their own problems, it makes life more tolerable. Others have a natural distrust for authority or a need to confirm their own biases. They find like-minded people spouting hate, and they think it's okay for them to do so as well.

Elected officials could counteract some of this by setting a good example. Politicians often post online, and they have an opportunity to do good things in the world and lead, knowing that people are reading and believing what they post. Mostly, they choose not to. For instance, my state representative, Valarie Hodges, could have chosen to get to the bottom of the library hysteria when it first started in my parish. She visited my school when I won an award in 2021 and issued me a commendation from the Louisiana House of Representatives. I am her constituent. She could have called me and offered help or at the very least asked questions. She could have called our library director to ask about books in the library and library policy. She could have read my lawsuit, which was readily available online, to see that it was a defamation suit and not about the location of books in the public library. She could have seen that it wasn't about silencing parents who were concerned about children but about stopping people from posting lies about me. Instead, she chose to post online and perpetuate the problem. But then again, I suspect that she was instrumental in inviting that anti-library group into our parish in the first place, as they have spoken together at similar events and run in the same hateful circles.

When my court case was dismissed by the local judge, she posted online, "Great win for free speech yesterday. But sexual content should NOT be in children's libraries. We have work to do!" How am I supposed to combat lies being told about me in my community when my own state representative celebrates the online smearing of an award-winning educator in her own community and perpetuates the myth that there is sexual content in children's sections of the library? If she had a moral compass, she would feel shame. She is not protecting children. She is hurting a beloved school librarian in her community who is devoted to children. It's an uphill battle to get out the truth, so I don't know how the haters can criticize me for speaking to journalists and telling the facts. The facts are that nobody is trying to put sexually explicit content in children's sections of our libraries. Any politician who perpetuates that myth, especially without asking questions and seeking knowledge of what is in the library, is either seriously misguided or doing so for their own political gain. I expect better of our supposed leaders, including my gal pal Val. After using the library to pander for votes in the last election, she is now a state senator.

It seemed to me that the judge who dismissed my case set a very bad precedent. The ruling simply opened the door for more people to tarnish the reputations of educators and librarians. To label me, a small-town school librarian, as a public figure was very odd and not what I feel the law intended, but that's what was done. To say that people who posted that I advocate anal sex to eleven-year-olds were merely expressing an opinion, when I have never done or said anything close to that, is dangerous. In my opinion, the ruling gives license to others to continue posting falsehoods about people and to incite violence and more hate.

It's also more than a little frustrating that the judge in my case publicly allied herself with my tormenters. There are postings of photo ops with her and the representative who took shots at me, and with the library board member who started the whole nonsense in our parish, the parish president who also promoted the lies, and various members of far-right groups. I went into my lawsuit with the naivete that the court system was just, but I no longer feel that way. It's something my eyes should have been opened to a long time ago, and I am far more cynical now. Local judges, after all, are elected officials who must worry about elections and the people who vote them into office. When the members of the community who vote them into office are posting lies online, one does begin to wonder how much that plays into decisions.

An attorney friend of mine said that the judge's decision to dismiss my case was due to two factors: she doesn't know that particular type of law very well and she was being cowardly. I don't know what to think. When I see her hobnobbing with people who have spread lies or mocked me online, I think it's only natural to be suspicious. I want to believe in the good of people, but hate is contagious, and there is that old saying, "Birds of a feather flock together." I have seen firsthand in our Louisiana legislature just how influential the combination of hate and money (in the form of donors) can be.

In nearby St. Tammany Parish, journalist Sara Pagones reported that Laura Dinapolis got tired of seeing the librarians in her parish, many of whom are her friends, being called names like *groomer* and *pedophile*, so she purchased a billboard for $6,600. It simply read SUPPORT YOUR LOCAL LIBRARY. Another resident posted a picture of the sign on social media but changed the picture to say SUPPORT YOUR LOCAL GROOMER, and encouraged other community members to call the billboard company and complain. It wasn't up very long before the billboard supporting the library was removed, and Laura was refunded her money.

Meanwhile, elsewhere in St. Tammany Parish, another billboard was erected, but this one said, SEXUALLY EXPLICIT BOOKS, ST. TAMMANY PARISH LIBRARY, PARISH COUNCIL: FIX IT OR WE'LL VOTE YOU OUT. The billboard pictured a child looking at a book in shock with the word *pornography* above his head. To my knowledge, that billboard was never taken down. In response, Laura placed another billboard up in a different location and this one stayed.

Others have tried taking librarians to court. In Louisville, Kentucky, the school librarian Kristen Heckel was taken to small claims court by a man who objected to the library's purchase of *All Boys Aren't Blue*, by George M. Johnson, along with several other books. According to the American Library Association, *All Boys Aren't Blue* has been banned in twenty-one states as of March 2022. The man claimed that these titles were intended for grooming minors for sexual exploitation and that Kristen owed him $2,300 in damages for her book selections. I personally am curious as to how he knows the authors' intentions when it seems apparent that he hadn't actually read the books. After the judge told the man he had to have incurred actual costs to recoup money in small claims court, Louisville Public Media reported she dismissed the case and told Kristen, "I just want to say I'm so sorry you have to deal with this. I admire your courage . . . I wish you had been my librarian when I was a kid."

Gone are the days of using silly words like *snowflake* and *triggered*. Those words have been replaced with *grooming* and *indoctrination*. I have seen *groomer* thrown around an awful lot over the past two years in reference to anyone who speaks out on behalf of the LGBTQIA+ community or anyone who opposes anti-LGBTQIA+ legislation. Having taught children who have been molested and groomed, many by family members, it sickens me to see the word thrown around so loosely. There are some sick people in this world who prey on vulnerable children and abuse them sexually. NPR's Melissa Block reported that Tucker Carlson, Laura Ingraham, and a whole list of politicians have used the words *groomer* and *indoctrinator* to describe teachers and librarians in general. To weaponize that word, and water it down to use against librarians and educators who are anticensorship, is incendiary and harms children who are being abused by real predators.

Words have power, and people with platforms either in the media or in elected office have a responsibility to tell the truth and avoid inflammatory language that furthers lies and spreads misinformation. Pundits and politicians use words as weapons to inflict pain, instill fear, and further their own agendas. Sticking to the truth and away from provocation would be best not only for children but for our country at large. Instead of being true patriots, they only worry about themselves, their own power, and the almighty dollar.

The word *indoctrination* is also used pretty broadly by alt-right extremists. Everywhere I turn, I hear people claiming that a teacher or school is indoctrinating children with critical race theory, the "gay agenda," and social emotional learning. God forbid that teachers want to help out children and their emotional well-being by teaching empathy and respect for others. It's not indoctrination to acknowledge that historically certain groups have had less power and were systematically persecuted over decades and centuries. It is called historical fact. I would love to invite the people who so flippantly declare that teachers are indoctrinators to substitute teach at any school and see for themselves. They would truly learn what "protecting the children" really means and could take notes.

If I had the ability to indoctrinate children, I would indoctrinate them to be kind to one another, return their library books on time, and stop putting their chicken nuggets from the cafeteria in the book return box. I can assure everyone that teachers don't have the time to indoctrinate children with personal agendas even if we wanted to, and we are watched like hawks by our administration, not to mention, these days, by every right-leaning person with a social media account. There would be proof splashed over all of creation if any teachers or librarians were indoctrinating children in our community. There is none because it's not happening. I have even had this argument with my own parents and am often left frustrated. Our community is extremely conservative and that includes the educators, so who do they think is doing the indoctrinating? If there were a rogue indoctrinator, other teachers would report it.

When it comes to my parents, I want to ask them this question: Who exactly is the big bad wolf, or is it a mythical creature created in their own heads based on what Tucker told them on Fox? I know that they don't think it's their own child. Who exactly is it? Because I consider myself a moderate, and I know very few other educators in our community who are not hard-core Republicans. My mother is a former educator, and I expect her to know better than to believe lies that are told about educators. But I get it. The lies are just so convincing when they come from people who are supposed to be trustworthy. Add in the constant barrage of fearmongering that comes from TV and social media, and the hate and panic becomes all-consuming. Would I believe them if I weren't an educator? I question whether I'd believe lies about librarians if I weren't a librarian who experienced it firsthand.

I'm not proud of it, but the frustration I've felt toward my parents can sometimes be too much to handle. I have left their house many times, sometimes by choice and sometimes after being asked, because it was just too much and the conversation devolved into mutual yelling. To tell your parents that something they saw on Fox News is not actually happening and is being twisted just to bump up ratings, and then have them not believe their own child, is gut-wrenching. Fox will show snippets of videos, and I will say, "That's not how that happened. I saw the original video and they didn't play it all," but I won't be believed. I remember watching some congressional meeting when our Louisiana representative talked down to a Black woman and called her "boo." I was embarrassed for our state that this was the type of person representing us. I told my parents, and they laughed and said it didn't happen. I showed them the video, and they still acted unconvinced and said there must have been more to it. There wasn't.

If what has happened to me had happened to someone else in the community, would they have jumped on the bandwagon against that educator or librarian? Would they have believed nasty rumors about another innocent person? Believing what you see on social media is one thing, but it's hard not to believe when you're being spoon-fed nonsense by talk show hosts and politicians. I don't understand how people close to me can see it happen to me, someone they love, and not think to themselves, "I wonder if the rest of what I'm seeing and hearing is also false."

Conservative politicians also love to use the words *groomer* and *indoctrinator* when referring to rival politicians, and they seem to do so unabashedly. In 2022, Michigan state senator Lana Theis sent an email to supporters seeking campaign donations that referred to Michigan state senator Mallory McMorrow as a groomer, stating, "These are the people we are up against. Progressive social media trolls like Senator Mallory McMorrow (D-Snowflake) who are outraged they can't groom and sexualize kindergarteners." Senator McMorrow spoke about the email on the Senate floor and said, "I am a straight, white, Christian, married, suburban mom. I know that hate will only win if people like me stand by and let it happen." I completely agree with her. Staying silent is akin to compliance, and we must not be complicit. We must speak up and call out people who say these things.

My friend SarahJane Guidry, executive director of the Louisiana Forum for Equality, told journalist Alex Woodward, "Legislators never sit down with youth, never sit down with LGBTQ people, never sit down with the libraries. Those conversations never happen and there's a reason they push legislation faster and harder and quicker." I know the reason. Inflammatory words sell, and politicians have learned how to push hate rhetoric for votes and funding. She went on to say, "These attacks are on our children, and it comes to a point where you keep seeing these conversations [with] constituents saying, 'You are killing us by filing this, by speaking on this.' It comes to a point where you have to ask, do they even care?" I don't think that these politicians do. Power and influence matter more to them than the actual welfare of human beings.

Our society is devolving into one of hatred and intolerance, and politicians and talk show hosts posing as news anchors are dividing our country. I have a relative whose kid's entire birthday theme was "Let's Go, Brandon." Imagine someone putting that phrase, an underhanded way to say "Fuck Joe Biden," on a ten-year-old's birthday cake. I have a relative who posted a meme saying, "They say we are alt-right, but I say we are right-so-far." She has LGBTQIA+ relatives whom alt-right politicians literally want to exclude from society and call subhuman. Another relative wrote, "Totally agree." I almost threw my phone across the room in anger, because she has a gay granddaughter. When did we decide as a society that full displays of hate were okay? When did they become the acceptable norm?

Last fall, I was invited to speak to a group that included many trans women. As I was listing my woes of being called names online, I had a huge epiphany. Here I was crying to these women over something that at most will cause me turmoil for a few years. Meanwhile, they will face harassment forever. What a horrible thought—that what I'm feeling for a few months or years is someone's entire life? Because I have diarrhea of the mouth and sometimes just let my newfound thoughts ooze out of my mouth with no thought, I said this out loud. They clapped and snapped for me. That's when I realized that we all face difficult situations each in our own way. Some situations are worse than others and some last longer than others. Our pain is our own and it sucks. It doesn't mean I'm belittling my experience or saying it's not painful. It's just different. I've faced this hate because of what I said (and didn't actually say), but they face it because of who they are. Nobody should ever be made to feel less-than for who they are. This constant barrage of hate toward the LGBTQIA+ community is not normal behavior.

Homophobic and racist people try to justify their hate, but it boils down to their fear of anyone who looks and thinks differently from them. What used to be whispered is now a very outward display of hate. Or maybe I just noticed it for the first time? I guess that makes me woke. Woke. Ha. That's another word that's thrown around a lot. I'd rather be accused of being woke than be accused of being a hateful bigot. The kids in my town are paying attention. I want them to know that not everyone in our town hates the LGBTQIA+ community. I want them to see that there are adults in the world who truly want to protect children and not just mock and malign people. Not everyone is actively racist. I must think of the children in our community and set a good example.

Chapter 12

Think of the Children

I am the biggest threat to your hollow, hateful scheme because you can't claim that you are targeting marginalized kids in the name of—quote—"parental rights" if another parent is standing up to say *no*.

—MICHIGAN STATE SENATOR MALLORY MCMORROW TO
MICHIGAN STATE SENATOR LANA THEIS, APRIL 19, 2022

Y ou've heard the names some people call them: Klanned Karenhood, Minivan Taliban, Assholes with Casseroles, and QAmoms. I have seen others reference those self-professed joyful warriors known as Moms for Liberty with these names and more. A person who hasn't been following their antics might look at their mission, which states, "Moms for Liberty is dedicated to fighting for the survival of America by unifying, educating and empowering parents to defend their parental rights at all levels of government," and think that doesn't sound so bad. These are just a bunch of moms who love their kids, right? You'd be wrong, according to the Southern Poverty Law Center, which classified them as an extremist group in 2023, writing, "Moms for Liberty and its nationwide chapters combat what they consider the 'woke indoctrination' of children by advocating for book bans in school libraries and endorsing candidates for public office that align with the group's views. They also use their multiple social media platforms to target teachers and school officials, advocate for the abolition of the Department of Education, advance conspiracy propaganda, and spread hateful imagery and rhetoric against the LGBTQ community."

Here are some of their greatest hits:

- "Gender dysphoria is a mental health disorder that is being normalized by predators across the USA." Moms for Liberty, July 25, 2022, tweet regarding California SB 107
- "Twitter and Reddit are censoring the word groomer to describe adults who talk to children about gender switching and sexuality. What else are we supposed to call them?" Allie Beth Stuckey, video, Moms for Liberty website
- "He alone who OWNS the youth, GAINS the future." Moms for Liberty, Indiana chapter, quoting Adolf Hitler in their newsletter
- "I'm telling you, if I had any mental issues, they would all be plowed down by a freaking gun right now." Missy Bosch, Arkansas member of Moms for Liberty, discussing a school librarian

With all the hate they push, it's not surprising that people make up names associating Moms for Liberty with other extremist groups. Basically, they are for the rights of some parents and some children as long as you're not associated with the LGBTQIA+ community. Our local chapter recently held a meeting in Baton Rouge and brought up gender ideology. The group's members asked our state superintendent, who chose to align himself with this group and attend their meeting, how he planned to combat gender ideology in schools. After stating that he didn't know what that was, he then said that he didn't think teachers should be teaching any kind of gender ideology. He didn't even know what gender ideology was, but this was his considered opinion. Okay. Please make it make sense.

I've seen the term *gender ideology* crop up anytime there are reforms benefiting the LGBTQIA+ community. Depending on which extremist group you ask, it might be in reference to transgenderism or the use of pronouns or any number of other topics. Much like critical race theory, if you ask the people who use the term to define it, they usually cannot. But that doesn't mean they won't swear that it's taking over our schools. It's like the mythical creature Baba Yaga. They've never seen her, but they just know that she's there lurking in the shadows, waiting to get their kids. What they're really saying is that the LGBTQIA+ community shouldn't be given equal rights or even be acknowledged. They can't just leave queer people alone. No, they want to take away their rights and "other" them. Alt-right conspiracy theorists fixate on the idea that teachers and librarians are all in a plot to turn their children gay. It's ludicrous, and I wish they would take off the tinfoil hats before our country no longer has any educators or librarians. But perhaps that is the idea.

Groups like Moms for Liberty are popping up like zits all over the country. Mothers calling themselves "mama bears" and other parents' groups are screaming from coast to coast as if they've suddenly had all their rights taken away. These people are harming public education and they're harming our public library systems. Nobody has ever threatened their parental rights, just like nobody is putting sexually explicit material in children's sections of libraries.

As a parent myself, I understand wanting what is best for my child and the desire to raise her the way I see fit, but that doesn't give me the right to force my views on other people's children. If I don't want my own child to see a certain book, I monitor her at the library. If I don't want her to check out a certain book, I don't let her. I have never once thought it was the responsibility of librarians in public libraries to police what my children are reading and looking at. That is *my* responsibility as a parent, so why can't these joyful warriors be responsible for their own children and let me worry about mine? The answer is that they are for parental rights as long as they get to dictate what those rights encompass, and that includes what books are available. If they don't like a book, they want it removed, regardless of whether other parents want their children to have access to the title or not.

Nobody loves to talk about parental rights more than people running for office like my local elected official Valarie Hodges. My gal pal Val loves to talk about keeping children safe in libraries, but she's the kind of hypocrite who goes silent when it's time to find solutions to school shootings and gives an AR-15 as a door prize at campaign fundraisers. (I secretly hope that gun companies will start painting AR-15s in rainbow colors and she'll decide guns are woke.) She recently posted on Facebook, "Protecting children and parent's [*sic*] rights has always been a top priority of mine. My record shows that! Kids should just be able to be kids, but the left is injecting a sexual agenda, and gender ideology into places it has no business." The post was complete with little stick-figure children to drive home how truly focused on children she is. (Insert eye roll.) Kind of like how she pushes for religion to be in places it has no business to be, like our education system, but she doesn't see the irony. Her platform touts that she is a mother and grandmother. She has said, "It is my business to protect children and

Valarie Hodges for Louisiana State Senate - District 13 · Follow

Jul 1 · 🌐

Protecting children and parent's rights has always been a top priority of mine. My record shows that! Kids should just be able to be kids, but the left is injecting a sexual agenda, and gender ideology into places it has no business.

As a legislator, mother and grandmother, it is my business to protect children and parents rights from a radical, leftist, evil agenda.

We must have a veto override Session to restore the three bills that protect children and parents rights from sexualization. Please call your state senator or representative and tell them you want them to call for a veto override session to protect our children's future.

👍 3

parents rights [*sic*] from a radical, leftist, evil agenda." I emailed her to ask what the radical agenda entailed, and to ask who exactly was pushing it, but I didn't get a reply.

Another Louisiana politician who likes to shout about parental rights, saving the children from the fictitious woke disease and sexually explicit material allegedly in libraries, is Louisiana attorney general Jeff Landry. Jeff decided that he was going to run for governor of Louisiana, so what better way to launch his campaign than by announcing his librarian tip line? The tip line, aka the snitch line, is a website where anyone can write in to post lies about porn in the children's section of libraries. When he announced it, Nola.com reported he said, "Librarians and teachers are neither empowering nor liberating our children by connecting them with books that contain extremely graphic sexual content that is far from age appropriate for young audiences. If this type of taxpayer-subsidized sexualization of children has impacted you or your family, tell us about it." There was not a single example or piece of evidence to back up this claim that librarians and teachers are giving children extremely graphic sexual content, but who needs evidence?

It was plain to me that he was just pandering to the Far Right, but I couldn't fathom why most of the community didn't see this. I was at a school librarian conference in Florida when I heard the news of his tattletale hotline and just stared at my phone with a sneer. I messaged a librarian friend about how ridiculous the whole thing was getting. I thought about the harm his tip line would cause teachers and educators by insinuating there was pornography in the library, and I feared more librarians would become targets of harassment. Here was a chance for someone in power to make a real positive change in our state, but he selfishly chose to raise a whopper of a false flag to empower himself and his own interests. The American Civil Liberties Union of Louisiana criticized his actions and stated, "Children are not being exposed to obscene content in libraries, and it is troubling that anyone would suggest that LGBTQ-related content is in any way harmful to children." I wish librarians, community members, and parents would pay attention to the news and were more outraged by his antics.

I was asked by several journalists my thoughts on the snitch line and didn't mince words. I compared his hotline to the Red Scare. My friend Lynette Mejia, founder of Louisiana Citizens Against Censorship, was also outraged. She told me and several news organizations, "The idea that library officials are exposing our children to sexual content is frankly ridiculous. A policy that turns neighbors into Stasi-era informants should terrify everyone. Our education professionals and librarians work incredibly hard to ensure the safety of our kids. It is just shameless and insulting on his part. I think it is just some sort of scare tactic in his run for governor next year." Good ol' boy Jeff was just jumping on the latest right-wing conspiracy, behind a long line of conspiracies that include election interference, vaccines, and indoctrination in schools. "We must think of the children!" (Insert eye roll.)

Some in our state enjoyed a laugh when Landry's snitch line didn't get the results he was hoping for and instead made him look just plain dumb. The Louisiana Illuminator's Piper Hutchinson revealed that a public records request turned up 5,500 pages of complaints made within the first seven days, and they were mostly spam. Several people submitted the *Bee Movie* script and the Bible, while others submitted comments calling Jeff Landry a bozo and telling him off. Someone submitted the list of Catholic churches and clergy who had been accused of sexual assault, and another person wrote, "In 2018, the Louisiana attorney general stated that he couldn't set up a tip line for people to report clergy sexual abuse because he didn't have the authority to prosecute them . . . Clearly the Church has an established history of child sexual abuse, but you have decided to waste funds on a

AG Jeff Landry ✔ ···
@AGJeffLandry

Our legislation aimed to help protect the innocence of Louisiana children has become law! #lagov #lalege

6:28 PM · Jun 29, 2023 · **3,272** Views

9 Retweets **1** Quote **30** Likes **1** Bookmark

dead-ended search for abuse in libraries rather than where it really exists." I wondered the same thing. If Jeff Landry really wanted to protect children, he would protect them from actual harm. Books and librarians are not harming children. Books provide comfort and libraries provide safe spaces. If anyone says otherwise, I'd ask them when they'd last visited a library or spoke to a librarian.

A few months later, Jeff Landry released his "Protecting Innocence" report, a fifty-four-page guide on a solution to a problem that didn't exist. It wasn't enough to create a pandering tip line; he had to add insult to injury and create a report about it, full of pictures of books in adult sections of libraries. This farce of a report gave instructions on how to write your legislator and included sample letters and resolutions on how you, too, could contact your public library and push this nonsense about sexually explicit material in children's sections. At this point, I just had to sigh and wonder what else this man would do to push his own political agenda at the expense of librarians and our state's libraries. The report didn't hold back on melodrama: "Sometimes, when you are traveling through darkness, you must be the light," and "Like Pandora opening her box, some things are better not faced too soon, because you can never unlearn something once you have witnessed it." Give me a break with the grandstanding! Parish governing boards ran with it, like the good puppets they are. Suddenly, it seemed that every Republican in Louisiana running for office decided there was porn in dem thar liberries and that the liberal wokeism disease was harming children.

I don't have a problem with library oversight or wanting to help parents understand how libraries work; however, I take issue with Jeff Landry's obvious ulterior motive. Libraries are public entities, and the community has every right to ask questions about budgets, collection development, and other policies. I implore parents to take an active role in their children's reading habits and make decisions that are right for their own families. This was not the point of this supposed "protecting innocence" report. The point was to instill fear in our state and further conspiracy theories about libraries, which in turn would help advance certain agendas and politicians. It worked. Jeff Landry is now our governor.

My parish councilman Garry Talbert jumped on the bandwagon, as reported by journalist Piper Hutchinson. Is it a coincidence that he was also running for office? Is it ironic that he didn't even have a library card? I'll let you be the judge of that. He used Jeff Landry's "book report project" to justify dismissing the only person on our Livingston Parish Library Board of Control who had a library science degree, for the crime of not returning a phone call fast enough. Seriously, he publicly admitted that the tardiness of the return call was the last straw. That little comment was repeated in our legislature the next session and helped us successfully kill a bill that would have been harmful, so thanks, I guess.

Garry then invited our library director to a parish council meeting under the guise of reporting about the library and ambushed him with the news that he'd hired a private investigator to infiltrate the library's computer system by "backdoor methods." The supposed objective was to prove that pornography could be accessed through the library computers. In breaking news, water is wet. Of course, if you circumvent library computer policy via "backdoor" methods, it's reasonable to assume you could figure out how to get on pornographic websites. Especially if you have the skills of a private investigator. Kids couldn't or wouldn't access material on library computers this way. The library has a reasonable amount of security in place on its computer systems so that the average curious child or adult would not be able to access porn. What's laughable is the thought that kids who have full access to the internet in the palm of their hand are going to the library, signing in with their library cards, and then trying to use backdoor means to enter websites, looking for porn.

The parish councilman played right into the hands of the pro-censors in our parish—the same people whom he will publicly state he can't stand. These people smear him online almost as much as they smear me, which makes his actions even more frustrating. He could have been a voice of reason or a library ally.

People running for office around here seem willing to go as low as possible to promote themselves, and they jump into it headfirst without thinking of the repercussions. The scene that played out that night at the council meeting was embarrassing to our parish. Our award-winning longtime library director, Giovanni Tairov, had brought our library system into the twenty-first century and was named the Louisiana Library Association's Public Library Director of the Year in 2019. After springing the news on Giovanni about the investigation, Garry aggressively grilled him, treating him like a common criminal. Giovanni was openly disrespected when he should have been thanked, all for some votes and grandstanding. Giovanni resigned not long after that shit show, and then, a few weeks later, so did our assistant library director. In the same meeting, Garry also decried "rainbow books" and said that they didn't belong in our library. For people who say they're all about protecting children and not about censorship or marginalizing the LGBTQIA+ community, their actions suggest otherwise. Pretty soon, Garry was backpedaling and insisting that he loves libraries, but it was too little, too late. The damage had been done. Our award-winning director left, we lost a valued member of the board, and the notion that there is sexually explicit material in our libraries spread further. Garry's reputation in the community also suffered for it, so it was lose-lose.

Meanwhile, over in St. Tammany Parish, the pro-censors were working overtime spreading moral panic. One of the deluded leaders of the local library accountability group, a group that has bogged the St. Tammany library down with over two hundred frivolous challenges aimed at the LGBTQIA+ and BIPOC communities, put on her tinfoil hat to inundate the librarian snitch line with the notion that "pornography is pervasive in libraries." According to the Illuminator's Piper Hutchinson, Connie Phillips wrote "the [library directors] are hostile and on a mission to keep the material in the children's section of the libraries. The (American Library Association) President is a self-described Marxist so it is no surprise that this happening [sic] all across the country as she has millions of taxpayer

ST. TAMMANY PARISH LIBRARY
STOP PEDDLING PORN TO OUR KIDS!!!
MEETING:
LET YOUR OPPOSITION BE KNOWN!
11/28 6:00PM
SLIDELL CITY COUNCIL
2045 2ND ST
SLIDELL,LA 70458

LALA_Boratory @Laborat25867370 · Apr 1   ...
Connie Phillips recruiting people to file book challenges

> **Connie Nichols Phillips**   •••
> Nov 20, 2022
>
> We are looking for volunteers who will fill out a Statement of Concern objecting to certain books containing pornography etc. We must document our objections yo create a record. If you are interested in filling out a couple , please message me and I can send you the form and a link w the books we are opposing. That way you can make sure these books are books of your choosing.
>
> 👍❤️ 6
>
> 👍 6   💬 16   📨

dollars that she uses to advance her social justice agenda and thousands of indoctrinated foot solidiers [*sic*] who are disguised as librarians. Please help us put and [*sic*] end to this madness and protect our children." Is the madness in the libraries, or is it in the accountability group? The people in this group attend library board meetings to yell at the librarians and the board, and they post on social media that librarians are groomers. It isn't hard to see which party is hostile, and it's not the people against censorship.

While I giggle at the whole "foot solidiers of the ALA" nonsense, it blows my mind how many people buy it. Don't get me wrong: most people don't fall for it, but the loudmouths are loud enough to make it seem like they're in the majority. Librarians go into the field of library science because they love literature and libraries and want to serve their communities. We certainly don't become librarians for fame and fortune, regardless of what my haters think, and we certainly don't want to see harm come to any child. Librarians join the American Library Association to access information on the latest books, to network with other librarians, and to learn about new technologies and services. The fact that far-right activists wage war on a group of people devoted to community service and children still puzzles me. The fact that they malign our professional organization is mind-blowing to me. Think of the children? Librarians love children, but we love all of them and not just a select few like the pro-censors want us to do.

The pro-censors and "think of the children" crowd use social media and cyberbullying as a weapon, emboldened by the example set by Donald Trump. Name-calling is acceptable in their eyes, unless they're on the receiving end. They shout slurs, hurl profanity, and issue veiled threats at public events like children throwing temper tantrums. Their behavior sets exactly the wrong kind of example. What kind of message is this sending to our children? One of our roles as school librarians is to teach digital citizenship. We teach kids about their digital footprint, ways to stay safe online, and how to report and prevent cyberbullying. While school librarians are teaching these skills, their parents and grandparents offer up real-world examples of how NOT to act online. Children emulate those they trust and care for, and that's often their parents, family members, or trusted adults. The kids are watching, and I can only hope that they see the hate for what it is and choose to be better. I have faith that the kids see through the lies and twisting of facts.

When the haters found out that my friend Tiffany had started a GoFundMe to help with legal fees, a GoFundMe for Ryan Thames was created as well. I didn't begrudge him wanting to gather his own relief for legal fees, but I take issue with the messaging posted on his account. It stated, "Should prepubescent children have unrestricted access to books which contain overly graphic and explicit sexual content? Some librarians in Livingston Parish have decided that they should and, now, a concerned father in the community is being sued for taking a stance against the government." I laughed so hard at that, because he is absolutely not being sued for taking a brave stance against the big, bad government. He is being sued for defamation. On social media he told people, "If you want to protect children, please consider donating." That's a pretty large jump in logic to say that by helping fund the defamation suit he brought upon himself from online bullying, a person will somehow be helping children. Many people messaged me to ask me if he was for real. Was he twisting things on purpose, or did he actually believed his own foolishness? It's hard to tell because it can be a slippery slope, from lies to believing. I posted the court documents for anyone interested in the truth. Ryan comes off as rather unhinged, post by post, so it's not hard for them to see. His continued obsession with me has shown his true colors, and the tide is slowly starting to shift. I can tell this because more people are reaching out to me and pushing back online.

But it didn't stop there, and the post got even more ridiculous. It went on to say, "This GoFundMe campaign is raising defense funds for Ryan Thames, the father who spoke out about the location of certain books in the Livingston Parish Library system. Thames was subsequently verbally attacked and threatened by members of extreme leftist groups, and he has recently become the target of a lawsuit." I was at the meeting, and the whole thing was recorded. He never stood up and spoke. He sat with his arms crossed, scowling, and never had the courage to speak. Instead, he sent a text to a female in attendance about masturbation. He's a coward who hides behind a keyboard, so he waited to "speak out" from his computer when he wanted to suck up to Michael Lunsford like a sycophant. Textbook keyboard warrior, only "speaking" online and never in a public forum. I wish that he had the wherewithal to be embarrassed by his behavior and how people are starting to talk about him.

At that public library board meeting over two dozen others did speak up and out. These people were thinking of children—all the children in our community—and they spoke about the importance of inclusion, the dangers of censoring books by and about the LGBTQIA+ community, and the necessity of following library policies. People who speak out on behalf of all children are the real MVPs who want to save children's lives. I have never met someone who died from reading a book, but I have met more people than I want to think about who took their own lives because they were treated as less-than in Livingston Parish. Our priorities in this parish are so skewed.

Our library board members have also been treated as less-than by our community simply for standing up against censorship and seeing reason. When Ryan yelled at them, it was the only time he's ever spoken at a public library board meeting. I guess he thinks that counts as standing up against the government? I call it despicable behavior. The board members were abusively name-called for not creating an additional committee to probe the alleged deviant books that board member Erin Sandefur insisted were in the library. They used common sense and reminded her that there were already policies in place, and anyone including Erin could submit a challenge form. For that, they publicly got called pieces of shit and ridiculed online.

Four of the library board members were also targeted by Michael Lunsford and Citizens for a New Louisiana after that November meeting. An entire blog post was written claiming that four board members were "standing in the way" of protecting children and insisted that the four board members had voted to block efforts by Livingston Parish Library staff to review existing content for erotic and pornographic materials. The truth is that they stood with the library staff and against blatant attempts to censor library materials by people with ulterior motives. They voted to uphold the current policies that already reviewed materials and offered residents ways to challenge books. These people don't think about the children and grand-children of our well-respected library board members. The four members targeted included an attorney and three retired educators, one of whom has volunteered on our library board for thirty-eight years without getting a single dime. A person who doesn't live in our parish thought it acceptable to go online and malign public servants because he didn't get his way.

At each public library board meeting, community members have spoken up for our library system, but not as many as there could be. People don't want to be targeted for speaking up after they've seen how the "protect the children" crowd so easily spews hatred online. Many anti-censors in Livingston Parish have their own children to think about, and several people have quietly admitted to me that they don't think they could handle the online hate. One friend texted me, "I wish I could go speak, but I don't have the mental bandwidth to be around these assholes or to become their next target." I understand, but it is frustrating.

Most people see what is happening, yet they don't do or say anything to stop it. Nobody wants the haters zeroing in on them, so people are hesi-tant to speak. They have good reasons, and fear is one of them. The alt-right ideologues are loud and quick to hurl insults. People with small businesses won't speak out for fear that their businesses could be targeted. Politicians either won't say anything or join the screamers because they don't want their words twisted—and, believe me, any show of support will be twisted. Parents don't want to stand up because they're fearful of their children being bullied. I get it, but what I don't understand is why this silent majority doesn't see their potential strength in numbers and come out swinging.

Rational people take it all with a grain of salt because the antics of the pro-censors are so over-the-top. But staying silent is a kind of complicity, and when people don't push back, censorship efforts gain traction, and one day I'm afraid it will be too late. What the general public needs to know is that these people won't just stop at censoring books or ruining libraries. They will continue to wreak havoc on our public education system until it is irreversibly broken. White Christian nationalists want to decide for everyone what is allowed. They claim their parental rights are being taken away, but they're taking away the rights of other parents. As a movement, their ultimate goal is to do away with democracy and institute forms of governance and institutions that take their cue from the Bible as they interpret it. Libraries, books, and our public school system are steps along the way. Instead of simply walking by a Pride display, ignoring songs they don't like, or monitoring their own children in libraries, they want to dictate to others what displays are allowed, what songs can be sung, what books are good, and what books are bad. Instead of having their children put a book back on the shelf, they openly trash librarians and push to defund libraries. Who will suffer the most? Our children.

———

There is actual harm taking place in our country, but it's not coming from librarians or books. The National Children's Alliance website indicates that there are over 600,000 children abused in the United States each year, and an estimated 618,000 children were victims in 2020. The Centers for Disease Control and Prevention report that 1 out of 7 children experienced child abuse and neglect in the past year, and the rates of child abuse and neglect are five times higher for children in families with low socioeconomic status. With all the cries about protecting the children, why aren't more people talking about these statistics? Instead of focusing on truly protecting children, white Christian nationalists are focused on banning books. Politicians are quick to say they want to protect children but spend legislative sessions focused on culture war issues like books and anti-LGBTQIA+ bills. If they were really in the business of protecting children, they would take steps to stop child abuse and neglect.

When I traveled to the Louisiana State Capitol to speak against anti-library legislation this spring, I noted that a member of the Republican Party State Central Committee named John Raymond was speaking at several hearings in favor of the bills. I was shocked because, according to the *Shreveport Times*, this pastor from Slidell was facing charges for beating one student and duct-taping the mouths of three other children at the Christian school he presided over. Raymond, who was on season 5 of the

CBS show *Survivor*, was also arrested for allegedly covering the mouth of a four-year-old until he could no longer breathe and went limp. If it were possible to vote out someone from speaking at the legislature, I would have been the first in line to cast my vote against him.

He spoke in support of SB7, dubbed the "protecting minors from libraries bill," and said that anyone who was against the bill was for the abuse of children. Let me repeat, the man who allegedly abused multiple children on several different occasions claimed that people who opposed the anti-library bill were in favor of child abuse. The irony was not lost on me that a man accused of duct-taping children thought library books were what hurt children. Books or a librarian did not cover a kid's mouth until he couldn't breathe. It was a pastor. Allegedly.

John Raymond then announced his intent to run for state office on the campaign promise to "reject the woke trans-agenda." It all became a little clearer to me. He was running for office so of course he picked up the basic culture-war nonsense and ran with it like a good white Christian nationalist. In an interview with *USA Today*, he said, "I feel it's important that people who believe in conservative Christian principles hold positions to create laws to direct our state properly. I've spent 23 years serving St. Tammany Parish in promoting Christian conservative values, and I feel compelled to run to bring those values into law." No, thanks, sir. We don't all agree with your idea of values because your values apparently don't see anything wrong with taping shut the mouths of children. After all, when asked about the allegations against him, he said, "but tape isn't a crime." Lovely fella.

The old saying "The call is coming from inside the house" keeps playing in my mind when I think about the people who trash-talk our libraries in the guise of protecting the children. A Grant Parish resident, Daryl Stagg, joined citizens at public library board meetings in Rapides Parish to voice concern over such picture books as *Pride Puppy!* Not long after, this same man was arrested and charged with three counts each of oral sexual battery, first-degree rape, aggravated crimes against nature, and indecent behavior with a juvenile, according to the *Baptist Press*. Stagg was a Southern Baptist associational mission strategist serving dozens of churches in north-central Louisiana. So, while he was allegedly sexually assaulting children in private, in public his mission was to get a children's book about a puppy in a Pride parade removed from library shelves—because it was the books that hurt the children. (At the time of this writing, charges against Raymond and Stagg are still pending.)

Then there's U.S. representative Clay Higgins from Louisiana. Around here, we call him Couyon Clay. *Couyon* is Cajun French slang for a crazy, foolish imbecile. Representative Higgins is known for his unhinged Twitter posts. Clay decided to throw his hat in the ring and pander to his radical followers with some anti-library propaganda. In March 2023, he tweeted, "Over time, American communities will build beautiful, church owned public-access libraries. I'm going to help these churches get funding. We will change the whole public library paradigm. The libraries regular Americans recall are gone. They've become liberal grooming centers." According to Clay, it is libraries that are grooming children for sexual abuse. Not the church, where abuse is actually happening. No, we're going to make THOSE the libraries. I did say he was unhinged. It makes no sense whatsoever and ignores actual abuse.

According to the Centers for Disease Control and Prevention, sexual abuse affects 1 in 4 girls and 1 in 13 boys in their childhood. In June 2022,

> **Rep. Clay Higgins** ✅
> @RepClayHiggins   ...
>
> Over time, American communities will build beautiful, church owned public-access libraries. I'm going to help these churches get funding. We will change the whole public library paradigm.
>
> The libraries regular Americans recall are gone. They've become liberal grooming centers.
>
> 12:53 PM · Mar 23, 2023 · **1.7M** Views
>
> **295** Retweets   **1,093** Quotes   **1,072** Likes   **107** Bookmarks

the FBI opened investigations into over a dozen sexual abuse claims in the Roman Catholic Church in New Orleans. Our Louisiana attorney general and my elected officials have decided that the bigger fish to fry is not sexual abuse, neglect, rates of foster care, and so forth. No, they want to save children by taking away library books. I have never heard a single elected official in my state decry the number of child abuse cases our state sees as a result of sexual abuse from pastors and other religious leaders. On the other hand, I see ad upon ad about the "woke left" and the need to protect children from libraries. Maybe I'm missing their outrage on actual abuse between the rants about librarians and teachers. Many people in my state continue to stick their heads in the sand and refuse to acknowledge the real problems in our state. We don't need to create a pretend moral panic in Louisiana, or across the nation, when there are actual people harming children, and it's not the drag queens during story hour.

Politicians like Clay Higgins, Valarie Hodges, and Jeff Landry are too busy maligning libraries and those evil people with the books to address real issues in Louisiana, and this is something I am seeing in almost every state in the United States. Unless these politicians become distracted by some other baloney beyond "porn in the libraries," and unless more people start speaking out against their efforts to destroy one of our last great, free-to-the-public, democratic institutions, we will see the complete erasure of public and school libraries. When people ask me why I keep speaking out against censorship and why I keep standing up for our libraries, I tell them it's because I'm thinking of the children. The difference is that I am sincere.

Chapter 13

It's Raining Sin, Hallelujah

The self-righteous scream judgments against others to hide the noise of skeletons dancing in their own closets.

—John Mark Green

If you were a child of the '80s like I was, you most likely remember *Bop* or *Teen Beat* magazines at the local grocery store. My mom would leave us to stare at these magazines full of teenage stars like Ricky Schroder, Fred Savage, Ralph Macchio, and the Two Coreys while she shopped blissfully child-free a few rows over at the local Delchamps. One of the biggest heart-throbs at the time was Kirk Cameron, and I asked my mom to buy me one of those magazines every time they featured him on the mini-posters inside. My wall was covered with Kirk's face, artfully hung with Scotch tape and love. Sometimes I drew hearts around his picture. He was my favorite.

I never missed an episode of *Growing Pains*, featuring Kirk Cameron as son Mike Seaver, and his best friend, Richard Milhous "Boner" Stabone. I was too young to understand why my mother made a noise every time "Mike" said his best friend's name. The joke went over my head. I'm surprised my mom let us watch *Growing Pains*, because the kids were pretty much back-talking jerks, but it was the '80s and that's about all we had to watch on Tuesdays at 7:30 P.M. before the days of cable TV, the internet, and streaming services. I would sit glued to the television while my mom sat on the matching love seat and my dad in his La-Z-Boy recliner, blowing smoke rings as he smoked, probably wondering why we liked that show.

I can still sing every word of the song that played over the opening credits. Like Mike Seaver, I was also the oldest child, saddled with the unfairness of two younger siblings. I imagined that I was as cool as him, or hoped I was. Over the few seasons the show aired, my love for Kirk Cameron only grew. He was my first real crush. As I became an adult, I still looked back fondly on old Kirk until I was into my thirties and heard him speak about his Christian faith. It seems that Kirk had found God. Good for him, I thought. Everyone needs a little Jesus, or so I'd been raised to believe. Then, as the years went by, I would occasionally see him in interviews, and I started to think that my beloved Kirk was a bit of a jerk. He still looked handsome, but the words coming out of his mouth were not.

Kirk's views on marriage, the LGBTQIA+ community, the public school system, and his talk of "assaults on traditional family" seemed obviously false and harmful to me. He seemed to be following the alt-right conspiracy playbook of using COVID to promote himself and perpetuate fear, like when he hosted a "sing-along" to protest COVID restrictions. Kirk appeared on CNN to promote his pro-life stance and insinuated that rape victims who make the heartrending decision to terminate pregnancies are murderers. "Someone who is ultimately willing to murder a child, even to fix another tragic and devastating situation like rape or incest or things like that, is not taking the moral high road." He then furthered the insane notion that public educators have hidden agendas and that we are groomers. He told Fox News that "public school systems have become so bad it's sad to say that they're doing more for grooming for sexual chaos and the progressive left than any real educating about the things that most of us want to teach our kids." He went on to say, "The school system is holding them back from being a 'light in the darkness,' [and from passing] on the kinds of values and virtues that made this the freest, strongest, most prosperous nation in the whole world."

In my humble opinion, Kirk has it exactly wrong. It is white Christian nationalists who are keeping us from prospering. They focus on hate and made-up culture war issues instead of solving real problems. White Christian nationalism is the MAGA phenomenon in which white, often poor citizens are being led to believe that their lives are bad because there's a war on religion and morals. They love using perceived threats against the Christian religion and America as excuses for hate. They want to build walls and bring back God in schools. They don't see that it's the hate they perpetuate that's infiltrating homes and schools but think it's illegal immigrants and the teachers who are "indoctrinating" their children. White Christian nationalists strive for male dominance, obedient wives, and same-sex marriage. They don't recognize that our country is composed of many religions. They think that our government and its citizens should all be Christians. Or at least the people in charge should be. If you show empathy for anyone who is different from the white Christian nationalist, you are a commie leftist nut job to them. They do not practice what they preach.

Kirk is obviously a white Christian nationalist. Kirk sure had a lot to say about our education system, but when was the last time he was in a public school? Kirk was revealing himself to be more than a bit of a jerk. These types of statements, uttered by people selfishly trying to further their own agendas, are extremely harmful. I read a *New York Post* headline that called him a "Growing Pain in the Butt," and I concurred. Another piece of my childhood died with my love of Kirk Cameron. The fear of our country being taken over by white Christian nationalists began to haunt me.

The illusion that Kirk was a good person faded quickly. Good people don't use Christianity as a weapon to sell books or further marginalize others. Kirk released his children's book *Pride Comes Before the Fall* on the first day of Pride Month in 2023. This was no mere coincidence but an obvious attack on the LGBTQIA+ community. The book is published by Brave Books, whose website states, "We founded Brave Books because while we were trying to raise our children to love their God and country, we became more and more aware that there is a real war being waged for the hearts and minds of the next generation. There is an agenda to confuse and demoralize our children and make them hate their country and the values that it was founded upon." Why is there always an insistence that some type of war is being waged on children? Brave Books also published *Elephants Are Not Birds*, a book about "traditional" gender identity, and *Little Lives Matter*, a title that obviously mocks the Black Lives Matter movement.

To promote his books, Kirk launched a campaign designed to promote values. He told Fox News, "Your kids are being force-fed this trans agenda and so much corruption and immorality in their schools and in their libraries. Why don't you let parents bring their kids up for air and talk to them about faith, hope and love, and read them some books at the library?" When he didn't follow a library's meeting room policy for booking events, and his event wasn't accepted, he claimed that there was some type of elaborate plot by the American Library Association to destroy America's social fabric. I wasn't surprised he jumped on the bandwagon to insinuate that public libraries are part of some plot in the downfall of America. It's as if he were willing to latch onto anything that helped him promote his own brand. Kirk's claims are strong accusations without a shred of evidence to back them up. However, white Christian nationalists are quick to pick up this mantra, and many people fall for it.

These book-banning efforts, and the insistence that libraries are "of the devil," are flying the flag of Christianity, but their actions and words do not reflect the teachings of Jesus. As a Christian, I take issue with that. I was taught to never use my faith to harm others or promote myself or an agenda. Pro-censors twist the narrative and use the Bible as a weapon to get Christians on their side, but it's a deception. Librarians are not evil, libraries aren't giving pornography to children, and no one is plotting to ruin the moral fabric of society. White Christian nationalists have been organizing for years and have taken over school and library boards across the nation to push ideals that have nothing to do with Christ. It's a movement with ulterior motives, more political than religious, truth be told. It revolves around promoting politicians, money, and assertions of control. It enrages me the way they use God to suit their needs. It's not the way, I feel, God wants us to act.

————

Speaking of the Bible, have you ever had a prayer group meet to pray about you? I've heard that people have gathered to pray against me, but that's all hearsay because I've never witnessed it myself. What I can confirm is a post made about me by Ryan Thames and his wife where he encouraged people to donate to them "as the Lord leads you" and told the story of David and Goliath. Now, I'd like to preface this by saying that neither I or my husband has ever once posted about these people. However, Ryan and his wife have made multiple posts about me and like to use Bible stories and verses. They tried to make excuses for Ryan's behavior and twist the facts. They once posted:

> My faith has been like the faith and confidence of David. As the opposition raises [money] on their GoFundMe under the guise of fighting censorship . . . over a meme that was my interpretation of what was said at a public meeting.

> As the army of Philistine gathered ready for war . . . a small shepherd boy grabs stone to defeat their mightiest warrior.

> With faith and confidence, the would be King David, who stands without a sword, tells Goliath he's going to cut off his head.

> After 1 stone hurled in the face of Goliath, he was defeated . . . David then used Goliath's own sword to cut off his head for all of Philistine to see, deterring them from advancing attack.

> I'm confident that our state and our parish will regain control of our libraries as they are subject to the will of the people and the laws of decency in the name of the protection of our children.

I have to hand it to them: the misdirection here is prizeworthy, as is the audacity. Apparently, I am Goliath and Ryan is David, and we are allegedly fighting over censorship in some great war. Yes, I did speak about censorship, but that's not what the lawsuit is about. Our lawsuit was about defamation and targeted harassment from a man who is an online bully. Do they believe their own attempts at gaslighting? Even if they did, they have the story backward. I am a middle school librarian who was targeted by multiple people in a smear campaign and, against all odds and personal attacks, decided to fight back. If anything, I am David in the scenario, but I try not to put myself in three-thousand-year-old Bible stories to achieve my own personal ends.

Then I wondered why the state and parish would have to gain control of our libraries when they already are in control and was confused as to what the "will of the people" meant. Do they mean the will of Christians? because according to a poll by Bestplaces.net, only 51.4 percent of the residents in our parish identify as religious. Did they mean Republicans? Eighty-four percent of the parish voted Republican in the last presidential election; however, libraries serve the needs of ALL patrons.

I must have been making them nervous if they compared me to a "mighty warrior," but the whole "David is going to cut off Goliath's head with his own sword" thing was disconcerting. Once again, Christians use Bible stories and talk of war, albeit a culture war, to further their own agendas. I simply can't respect that. I don't recall reading in the Bible where it was okay to make veiled threats against people just because you don't like their stance on an issue.

I have tried hard not to judge their posts that quote the Bible. Matthew 7:1 states, "Judge not, that ye be not judged." I don't set out to make judgments on the whys of these kinds of posts, but I often do. I am human, after all, and the Bible says, "for all have sinned, and come short of the glory of God" (Romans 3:23). But then again, I don't purport to be a Christian warrior, doing the Lord's work. I am a person who happens to be a Christian just trying to live a noble, emphatic life. I will not use God or my religion as a tool against anyone.

Around the same time, a local self-professed child of God decided to join the fray. She's also a fan of posting Bible verses to justify her hate and get ahead in the game of who can be the better Christian. First, she shared a friend's post supporting me and wrote, "Insane. 1000%. Media loving. Attention seeking. Vile. She is insulting as she preys on minority communities by twisting the story so they back her up." I have never met this woman in my life, and she has continued to post on my friend's and family's pages. Can you imagine going onto a perfect stranger's family's socials to intimidate or harass them because you don't like one of their relatives?

One of my sisters, a former missionary and lifelong Christian, posted, "It's not the loudest prayers heard. It's the pure in heart. The position of your heart as you pray matters most." Now, this woman doesn't know my sister from Adam but decided that she needed to go on her social media and teach her some godly lessons. On my sister's post she wrote, "Can't love God and condone sin boo. Jesus would condone anal sex teachings and exposure to sexually pleasurable acts to 8-12 year olds? You're on a slippery slope in what you defend and condone, then speak about prayers."

So not only were these people posting on their own pages and in community forums, they woke up and thought to themselves, "Let me go teach about Christ by attacking people online that I don't know." It boggles the mind. There's a saying that goes, "There's no hate like Christian love." As a Christian myself, I really can't stand that quote, but there's truth in it when you see the venom people spew in the name of God. They wonder why more and more people are leaving church, but they'd see why if they just took a long look at themselves and how they behave. Incidentally, my sister is a Christian counselor. I'd like to suggest that this woman book an appointment.

I frequently see videos of people using these tactics at school and library boards across my state and our country and have even seen them at the legislature. It's a common move to use Christianity to attack librarians and library boards. In neighboring St. Tammany Parish, one woman recently attended a public library board meeting and attempted to proselytize as she shouted at the board, "Oh God break their fangs, shatter the teeth of the ravenous lions. Let them disappear like water falling on thirsty ground. Let them be like snails dissolving into the slime. Let them be cut off never seeing the light of day. God will sweep them away so fast they'll never know what hit them. The godly will celebrate in the triumph of good over evil." I watched that video and wondered what horrible crime had been committed by the library. The answer was that they had Ellen Hopkins's book *Tricks* in the adult section.

White Christian nationalists seem to want so badly to imagine that they are oppressed and victims. When looking at the video from the St. Tammany Parish Public Library Board meeting, I saw a white self-professed Christian issuing threats and then saying that she would be celebrating the library board's demise. From my point of view, it's the Christians doing most of the oppressing. White people in general have not been systematically marginalized in our country, and nobody is trying to take churches or God away from anyone. There is no attack on Christian values. People are free to pray and worship in our country wherever they see fit. If you want to see a group of people who are attacked for their beliefs, look at the rise in antisemitism in our country, and then come back and tell me that it's Christians who are hated.

The world can be pretty confusing these days. What I see is a society growing more open-minded to people who are different from them, and a backlash from a segment of people who are uncomfortable with this. These folks see it as a zero-sum game. Any movement toward openness and acceptance somehow takes something away from them. This is where all the victim talk comes from, and the steady raising of volume and distortion in their claims as the truth fails them and they reach for fearmongering. America was founded not as a Christian nation, as they like to believe, but as a pluralistic democracy guaranteeing freedom of worship and the promise of equality. We still have a long way to go in the equality department, but the progress we have made should be celebrated, not feared. White Christian nationalists want nothing to do with this celebration. They want to turn back the clock to a time and a place that never was. It's sad and too bad. All it would take is a bit of courage, positivity, and generosity. True Christian values. But fear, hate, and intolerance are easier and maybe more emotionally satisfying in the short term. Indeed, they're playing the short game, and it won't end well.

———

Speaking about the hate directed toward me is incredibly painful, almost debilitating. It's also hard to let things go and not hold hate in my own heart about how some in my community have treated me. I remember telling Hannah Allam of the *Washington Post* about the time someone told me that Ryan Thames was selling mugs with the words "librarian tears" on them. That wasn't the painful part. I just felt pity toward him for letting his hatred define his whole personality. The sad part was in the comment section. The father of one of my daughter's friends had commented that he needed a mug and laughed about it. I taught that man's two children and had shown them nothing but kindness. His wife substitute-taught at my school, and our kids are in band together. On that man's social media pages was post after post about being a good Christian.

"Before I am anything else," he writes, "I am a follower of Jesus Christ. As a Christian, I'm called to love God and love others," and "Love one another." It's yet another case of someone failing to practice what he preaches. Another Christian who mocks others and then pretends that they're godly. I've thought about giving him one of those WWJD brace-lets. If you have never seen one, it's a bracelet that Christians sometimes wear to help guide them toward moral decisions. WWJD stands for "What would Jesus do?" I'd like to think that if Jesus were living in the age of social media, he wouldn't dogpile on someone who's been kind and caring toward his own children. I have fantasies of gifting a bracelet to this father after watching our children perform together in the band. But that wouldn't really accomplish anything. It would only be me being petty. Besides, I do like his wife and adore his children. I don't need to perpetuate hate.

I really do try not to hate people like Michael Lunsford and Ryan Thames. What I mainly feel toward them is secondhand embarrassment for their actions, but I do resent them. I'm working on that, I promise. A few months ago, I learned that Ryan had suffered a heart attack. I'm ashamed to admit it, but my first thought was "Karma is a bitch." My second thought was to wonder if he'd now leave me alone. (Spoiler alert: It didn't slow him down from hating on me.) Like I said, I don't claim to be a perfect person. I don't like that those were my first thoughts, because he has children and a family. I would never want someone to think that about me, and I wouldn't want anyone to lose their spouse or father. I prayed about it, asking God to help me be a better person than that, to be the kind of person my parents raised me to be.

I spent a lot of time talking to my therapist about this. My feelings, I learned, were valid. This is a man who has become seemingly obsessed with me and who is intent on destroying our public library system. It's natural to have the thoughts I had, but I realized right off the bat that I was wrong. This is what sets me apart from these people. The quick recognition. But of course I then had to talk to my therapist about feeling superior to them. I don't think I'm better than anyone, but I damn sure know that I have a stronger moral compass.

———

I had a personal revelation when I taught a student of the Sikh faith in my fifth year of teaching. I realized that she was forced to listen to Christian prayer after morning announcements, as well as participate in Christmas and Easter events, and I once intervened when I heard students tell her she smelled like curry. For the first time in my life, I was around someone of a different faith, and it forced me to think of how I'd feel if I were a Christian at a mostly Sikh school and forced to participate in events possibly against my religion.

It's not an exaggeration to say that most people in my community tend to sway the way of the evangelical and have not been exposed to other faiths. Evangelicals come in different stripes and are not necessarily white Christian nationalists. For one, there are plenty of Black evangelical churches. But evangelicals are committed to a conservative reading of the Bible and may even share the belief that the separation of church and state is a mistake that needs to be remedied. If you're a Christian, the idea of giving the church more authority in our society may sound appealing. But the potential downsides of a more authoritarian, less tolerant, less inclusive society were apparent enough to our nation's founders that they nixed the idea. Separation allows for a plurality of faiths and a civil society that can embrace a plurality of peoples and viewpoints. This is fundamental to democracy and especially critical in our public institutions, which need to serve the entire community. Our representative government is meant to represent all society, and anyone can run and hold elected office. The separation of church and state is just as important in our public school and library systems. These institutions are perhaps the best embodiment of the democratic idea. And they need to serve the entire community, not just Christians. It's important to me that everyone understands that distinction.

I grapple with my own faith sometimes. I try to be a decent human being, and I try to avoid thinking about the Bible's many different translations over the years. I know that the Bible is not necessarily a book we can take at face value. However, I do believe in God, and I do believe that Jesus is my savior. I have felt his love. Even if I hadn't, I would still admire the teachings of Jesus. The stories may not be literally true, but they contain worthy lessons and so much beauty. Jesus is kind to sinners. He devotes time to the outcasts of society and is always merciful and loving. In my mind, it's not a great leap. Even if you feel that members of the LGBTQIA+ community are sinners, that doesn't give you reason, at least according to the God of the Bible, to cast them out or judge them. Even Pope Francis has said, "If they [gay priests] accept the Lord and have goodwill, who am I to judge them? They shouldn't be marginalized. The tendency [same-sex attraction] is not the problem . . . they're our brothers." A lot of people would be much happier in life if they worried about themselves and their own sins instead of concerning themselves with others and what constitutes *their* sins.

Promote the true teachings of God if you say that you are a Christian. I wish more of the loving, compassionate Christians would denounce hate speech and those of our faith who speak it. Many Christians do not speak against it, and their silence speaks volumes to everyone watching.

We need fewer pastors denouncing the LGBTQIA+ community and more pastors speaking out about acceptance. We need more "God is love" and less "You're going to hell." We also need to recognize that not everyone shares our views or the tenets of our faith. In my opinion, that's okay as long as they aren't harming anyone.

Nothing solidified those thoughts to me more than the way I saw people treat Dylan Mulvaney. I had followed Dylan on TikTok for a year, watching her speak about her gender transition. Her videos are all about positivity, and she is always focused on love. Dylan's videos sparked joy in a world full of negativity. To celebrate the one-year anniversary of her publicly coming out as transgender, Bud Light sent Dylan one of their cans with her face on it. I thought it was really nice of the company and a cool way to promote inclusivity. Pretty soon, the white Christian nationalists decided that Dylan was too happy and that they needed to break her spirit. What ensued were calls for a boycott of Bud Light and a pile-on for the "crime" of being a happy trans woman. We can't have anyone actively trying to make the world a better place or living their best life, can we now?

I was dismayed at what played out on television and social media. People posted video ranting about wokeism while pouring Bud Light down the drain, and alt-right crazy-train Kid Rock offered up a curse-filled video of himself shooting cans of Bud Light.

What a violent, unhinged response. Dylan showed grace and love, despite the hate thrown her way. She set an example for us all in the way she handled it, but I could relate when she reported that she was having trouble sleeping. Her questions and thoughts were the right ones. "What I'm struggling to understand is the need to dehumanize and to be cruel. I don't think that's right. Dehumanization has never fixed anything in history, ever. And, you know, I'm embarrassed to even tell you this, but I was nervous that you were going to start believing those things that they were saying about me, since it is so loud. But I'm just gonna go ahead and trust that the people who know me and my heart won't listen to that noise." I have felt the same way, but it has taken a year for me to block out the noise.

Dylan took a small break to take care of herself. She admitted, "I've chosen to scale back in order to protect my overall well-being, and it works. I am quite happy, but I'm not doing what I love, so it's kind of a bittersweet thing." I felt it. I, too, had to take a step back, even taking a leave of absence from the job I love to protect my own well-being. I had to do what was best for myself when faced with an onslaught of alt-right vitriol. Like Dylan, I tried to show integrity and hold my head up high when being attacked. Dylan has taught me a valuable lesson. We hold the power within ourselves to make the world a better place, and our reactions are key. To choose to perpetuate hate makes that person and everyone around them miserable. I don't feel that acting the way white Christian nationalists do is in line with the tenets of Christianity. In the words of Kesha, "I hope you're somewhere prayin', I hope your soul is changin'. I hope you find your peace falling on your knees, prayin." Be a Dylan Mulvaney and not a Kirk Cameron. Worry about your own sins.

Chapter 14

It Was the Best of Times, It Was the Worst of Times

It was the season of light, it was the season of darkness, it was the spring of hope, it was the winter of despair. —Charles Dickens, *A Tale of Two Cities*

To say the last year has been the worst year of my life doesn't even begin to capture how bad it was. But I would be remiss not to speak about the joy I discovered. I had to see the lows to appreciate the highs and realize just how good I have it. I'd been walking through life without any major traumatic event before I was targeted. I grew up in a two-parent household and was well taken care of. I was able to live at home while I was in college and fortunate to get student loans to make my degrees possible. We were not rich, but I never wanted for much of anything. We were raised with love and we were always safe. I never really thought about that until the past year. Having the metaphorical shit kicked out of you tends to change the way you view life. It forces you to focus on the positive to survive.

I also started to see just how bad some people have it—not just in other countries but here in our own. I realized that while the United States does have a lot going for it, we aren't as wonderful as many would have you believe. However, don't ever say that out loud around some people or suddenly you are unpatriotic and hate the country. What a bunch of baloney. We should be critical about our government or our community when needed and be able to look at the United States and recognize that our country is far from perfect. If you cannot admit that you've made mistakes, you can't expect to learn from them. This really hits home because of my experience as a middle school teacher and school librarian.

Being a middle school educator is the best. The kids are old enough to tackle bigger concepts but still have that little-kid wonder about the world. They will still sit on the carpet for a picture book read aloud but can also read thick novels. One thing middle schoolers also have is that instant deniability when you catch them doing something red-handed. Middle schoolers have the innate ability to completely deny wrongdoing even when they're looking you dead in the eye while doing it. They will stand two feet away from me, smack a kid while very aware that I am watching, and then say, "Miss, it wasn't me! I swear. I don't even have hands!" I usually just stare at them dumbfounded, like Jim Halpert from *The Office*, in complete silence until they get uncomfortable enough to finally squeak out, "Okay, okay. It was me. I'm sorry."

The thing about middle schoolers is that once they realize they've been caught doing something wrong and that you're going to call them out on it, they typically stop, correct it, and apologize. This is unlike so many others in our country today. What is it with people up in arms about teaching real history? We need to admit wrongdoing before we can move forward, but there's a faction of the Far Right that will deny slavery was harmful and even say slaves benefited from slavery. Growing up in southern Louisiana, I often heard the excuse, "The slaves weren't mistreated. They were family." Black people were owned by white people. It was not okay and they did not benefit. Period, the end. They also didn't magically get treated better when the Civil War ended. We as a country keep getting it wrong when it comes to treating people with equality. It's not equal treatment if you're not treating people different from you with respect, kindness, and even brotherly and sisterly love.

Several years ago, I spent an entire summer researching my family ancestry. This was before my paternal grandfather passed away, and he and I went all over north Louisiana and south Arkansas tracking down grave sites and taking pictures of my grandparents' childhood homes, schools, and churches. I found his great-great-grandfather's headstone and took him there. I remember him smiling with a glisten in his eye because he had never known where it was located. Those were memories I hold dear, but also during this research, I found muster rolls, which are basically attendance records, from the Civil War and Revolutionary War with my ancestors' signatures, excerpts from diaries, and last wills and testaments. Through these I discovered that I had seven great-great-great-grandfathers who fought for the Confederacy and several who owned enslaved people. They listed them in their wills alongside their horses and other personal property. I can confirm that my ancestors did not treat these enslaved people as family, and it's a dark part of my family's history that I'm not proud of. It's important to me to acknowledge that this was wrong and learn from my ancestors' mistakes so that we can do better.

It's time we admit that the United States has had an ominous history that hasn't always been fireworks and "Yankee Doodle." Our country has some awesome ideals but has a history of not living up to them—of mistreating women, children, people of color, and the LGBTQIA+ community. Admitting the dark side of our country's history doesn't mean we hate our country. It is the opposite. If you love someone, you want them to shine and be the best they can be, and the same goes for our country. I don't want to live in a place where people treat others as less-than because of the color of their skin, their gender, or whom they love. I want to live in a country that earns its title of being the best until it is no longer a delusion or a lofty idea but a fact. Instead, I live in a country whose current politicians are too busy dragging us through the mud with manufactured outrage over teaching real history and including books in our libraries that speak the truth and feature all members of society. I would love to stand in front of people like Marjorie Taylor Greene and Matt Gaetz and ask them what in God's name they think they are doing besides causing us to backslide as a country.

This is not to say I am a wonderful person or know everything about our country's history, but I do try. I listen and I try to educate myself. While I was out on medical leave this past year, I read articles to learn more to try and be a better person. I learned about the high fetal mortality rate in Black pregnant women, particularly in Louisiana. I read about the Stonewall Uprising of 1969, looked up statistics on child abuse in the U.S., researched the Civil Rights movement, analyzed drug abuse statistics, and read about homelessness. I started watching the news more and reading seven or eight news apps each day to be better informed about what was happening in the world. Fox News has always been annoying with its one-sidedness, but I would even watch Fox News to see what the far-right talking points of the moment were. It really solidified in my mind that if we want to proclaim ourselves the greatest nation on the planet, we should probably get educated about our past and our present and then start acting like it.

It doesn't seem like the book banners, the alt-right, and the white Christian nationalists are interested in being educated. Education is about knowledge, facts, truth, and what they're pushing isn't about these things. What they stand behind is really a belief system, which happens to be profoundly undemocratic and exclusionary. In truth, it's a belief system based in nostalgia, a longing to turn back the clock to a time when Christianity was more universal, when whites ruled society, when women were subservient to men, and when gay people stayed closeted. It certainly doesn't appeal to me, but for those feeling economically or socially "left behind," or perhaps, simply out of step, it may be a kind of a lifeline. It bestows meaning, belonging, identity. It creates an us-versus-them world, at the heart of which is fear of difference and fear of change. Hate is its by-product. It's powerful stuff and what makes it so miserable to be targeted by them, and so frustrating to go up against. Do they believe the lies about this book or that book being inappropriate? I'm not sure, but I'm sure that they need to believe what they believe to maintain their good standing with others in their communities.

There really is no arguing with these people. They will believe what they want to believe, even when shown the truth, and, when shown the truth, they will often lash out with hate.

Anyone who stands up to them is said to be unpatriotic or doesn't love the U.S., or God, or children. How absurd! The alt-right is filled with hate and they need an enemy because they cannot hate themselves. At the same time, we have to realize that progressives also frame things as "us versus them." Polarization is definitely a two-way street, even if one side of the street seems a lot busier than the other. There is so much history here, including unprecedented income inequality, which is probably behind a lot of it. Regardless, we must learn to work together without smearing one another if we ever want to move forward. It's like I tell my students when I assign group work. You don't have to like each other, but you have to work together to get the job done. That's easier said than done when you're under constant attack just for existing, and I admit I struggle with this.

We desperately need to find a way to turn the temperature down. Fear is a powerful motivator, and people need reassurance that there's a place

for everyone. We need to be able to talk to one another, to listen to one another, to see one another. Unfortunately, that's not the script that the right wing is reading from these days.

As I faced a very personal campaign meant to bring me down, I also discovered the incredible side of humanity and just how loving people can be toward one another. There are truly more wonderful people in the world than there are haters. One of the first messages I received was from a former student whose mother was maligning me online. She reached out to apologize for her mother's behavior, even though I would never hold her mother's actions against her. She told me that she was a proud member of the LGBTQIA+ community and felt bad for the things her mother was posting. I felt awful when I received that message, not because of what the mother said but because she was openly posting vitriol about the LGBTQIA+ community, and people speaking out for them, when her own child was gay. I don't understand how mothers can be so oblivious and cruel toward their own children. That was the first time I realized just how many people were affected by this hate. I thanked my former student for reaching out to me and kept that message to remind me how not to behave toward my own child.

My friend and co-worker Jenny recently told me that she read the court filings, and it's pretty cut-and-dry what these people have done. My neighbor told me the same thing, and I'm grateful to those who take the time to read up on the facts. The problem is that too many people are quick to believe what they see on Facebook, and they don't take the time to find out the truth. It's very difficult to put on a brave face when I venture out into my community, knowing that some people believe the lies that I am a detriment to children. I am not a danger to children. Anyone who knows me knows the truth in this statement. It has gotten better, but it's still hard to go out in public. I still can't wrap my brain around the fact that I have worked my butt off for my school and community, and a few posts by some evil people who don't even know me changed the whole perception that people have of me. I do realize that it's just a select few who think this, but it's hard to know who believes what, so I'm on constant guard.

The lows of the past year have been really low. At one point, I was like a zombie from *The Walking Dead*. I shut down almost completely. I didn't want to leave my home, I was worthless in my job because I couldn't focus, and my health suffered. I have overcome the hurdles thrown my way, but it was a long road to recovery both physically and mentally. In the midst of being defamed, I also faced COVID, shingles, and an emergency hysterectomy. My body was reacting physically and was almost shutting itself down. I spent hours each day working over scenarios of me being vindicated in the public eye, knowing that would never happen. I cried countless hours to my therapist.

It was very hard to hide my pain from my child and try to convince her that I was okay. I was not present for several months, and these people robbed me of that time with my child. I will never get that time back, and while I was struggling, I failed to be a good parent. I also failed to be a good wife, because all I could think about was the attacks on my reputation. My attention was elsewhere, and the trauma was all-consuming. I've spoken to countless librarians who have felt the same way. It's almost impossible to turn off the hate at first. I assure them that it does get better, but it's a hard journey and they can't do it alone. Several of us have a Facebook support group to help each other, and all our stories, while different, have the same ring to them. Having people say that you give children erotica, advocate teaching children how to perform anal sex, and have the word *groomer* attached to your name is not fun. It's life-altering and hard to describe unless it has happened to you. There are too many of us that it has happened to.

At the same time I was being barraged with hate, I was also inundated with positivity via countless messages, emails, and physical letters. People I didn't know were sending flowers to me at my school and letters to our local bookstore on my behalf. One person wrote, "I know that you've heard several negative messages, vitriolic comments and personal attacks regarding your role in fighting censorship. I hope that you are equally receiving messages of support for what you are standing for and for being an advocate for information access for readers, for our communities, for our libraries and for our profession." These messages of support meant the world to me. Every time I started to despair, another message would arrive like the one that said, "Reading all about what you've been through and what you continue to go through in the face of some truly horrible bullshit from some terrible humans. Stay strong sister, we are with you!!!"

I wondered if the haters were getting messages like this. What did they say? Ryan Thames posted online that he didn't care what "1000 ignorant nerds" said about him. Obviously it bothered him that I was getting support, which leads me to believe that he was not as supported as he thought he was. Were the haters being congratulated for spewing lies? It was probably nonsense about protecting children from the evil librarian. If they did receive support, I can't imagine that it wasn't anything other than hate-filled rants, and who wants to receive messages like that? There's no way they received hundreds of kind words like I was getting, and that speaks volumes to me of the difference in the type of people we are, the type of people we attract, and the difference in the way we conduct ourselves.

Each new message helped me heal, and I appreciated each and every one. I tried to reply as much as possible, but at one point I was getting so many that it was hard to keep up. One educator wrote, "Dear Ms. Jones, I'm a teacher at an international school and our mission is inclusivity. What has happened to you is so wrong. You are a brave warrior!" Words like those helped me remember why I had spoken in the first place and why it was important to keep speaking out. The messages were fortifying when I needed them the most.

Not only was I receiving words of kindness and encouragement from strangers, but my friends were constantly checking on me. I received text messages daily from friends reminding me that I was conducting myself with integrity in the face of hate, friends praying for me, and friends offering different ways of support. I attended several conferences over the past year, and librarians would approach me to hug me and thank me. I wasn't doing anything that they weren't doing. We were all standing up for our communities and defending our libraries, but hearing from those colleagues was healing. Some librarians would approach with stories similar to mine, and I tried my best to help them like others were helping me.

When put to the test, I passed with flying colors, and I am proud to be a librarian who practices what I preach. I continue to speak out at our public library board meetings. After all of this has gone down, I still go back to where it all started for the same reasons, to uphold readers' rights, despite putting myself at the same risk of criticism and attack. It's the right thing to do, and I stand by it. I work with the members of our public library alliance for the betterment of my own community and have forged lifelong bonds with like-minded individuals in my parish. I discovered I have more friends than I ever imagined I'd have.

―――――

Aside from the support I received from friends, family, and the kindness of strangers, the support that mattered most came from the library community and those dedicated to safeguarding its health and integrity. Really, what I discovered was a very lively and dedicated activist community that invited me into its ranks and embraced me. Not only did this allay some of my personal anguish, but it gave structure, direction, and larger meaning to what I was going through.

I really wasn't a single wheel spinning, though. I had the constant support of my friends on the LASL Executive Board. I also had the support of our former library director Giovanni Tairov and I tried to return the support when he was targeted. Together we were eighteen wheels spinning, trying to find the road to helping libraries and librarians in both my parish and our state.

Things began to change several months after my ordeal began when my friend Vicki, a retired school librarian, reached out in support. She was joined by a new friend I made named Marla, a like-minded woman who is steeped in common sense, empathy, and wisdom. Vicki, Marla, and I message each other constantly, and their support often gets me through each week. We were joined by Lori and Elise, two other women in the community who saw the truth of the situation. Together, we began working together to bring awareness to our public library situation.

Around the same time, I found out from Lori, who lives in my parish, about a group in my state called 10,000 Women of Louisiana. I attended a meeting and was instantly enthralled with this group of women dedicated to making our state a better place. They spoke about becoming informed about legislation, people running for office, and upcoming elections. They invited me to speak about what was happening to libraries not only in my parish but across the state. I shared with them my fears about a statewide push for censorship, and they offered suggestions. Melissa Flournoy and Angela Adkins, two of their leaders, welcomed me with open arms.

Through my connections with 10,000 Women of Louisiana, I was introduced to a woman named Peyton Rose Michelle, executive director of Louisiana Trans Advocates, who also helps lead the Legislative Organizing Coalition for All LGBTQ+ Louisianans (LocALL). Peyton hosts weekly LocALL meetings to share resources and to strategize state legislation and issues across Louisiana. Peyton often works with SarahJane Guidry, executive director for Forum for Equality, a human rights organization in Louisiana dedicated to eradicating discrimination. Peyton and SarahJane work tirelessly during legislative sessions and help others speak out. I was beginning to learn the ins and outs of our state and local government, along with the players.

My life was profoundly altered when I met Lynette Mejia and Melanie Brevis of Lafayette. These two are the strongest women I know and the founders of Louisiana Citizens Against Censorship. I am lucky enough that they let me hitch a ride with them on their journey to save Louisiana from the anti-library crowd, and I thank God every day for putting them in my path. We instantly bonded and had some of the same haters—the same ones working in both of our parishes to cause chaos in our library systems. Lynette and Melanie had created Lafayette Citizens Against Censorship, and I reached out with questions in forming our own parish alliance. They were extremely supportive, and we forged a bond rooted in our love of libraries, our shared dream of an equitable society, and the trauma of being targeted by some of the same people.

I had been working tirelessly to unite my own community and drum up support for the Livingston Parish Library Alliance, a citizens' alliance I founded with the help of EveryLibrary. Lynette and Melanie were invaluable at helping us in Livingston and shared some of their strategies and successes. I cannot express enough how important it is to create a community alliance for your libraries and unite with surrounding-area alliances before the shit hits the fan. I formed our alliance, and our mission, which was written by member Kelci Sibley, states, "LPL Alliance is a coalition of Livingston Parish community members whose mission is to support and amplify the work of the Livingston Parish Library system. Members live, learn and work in the parish and recognize the importance of preserving the freedom of the library to provide services to all patrons no matter their ethnicity, religion, gender identity, education status, political affiliation, socioeconomic status or any other diversity of life and thought."

As censorship attempts started cropping up across the state, fueled by hysteria caused by our former attorney general Jeff Landry's rhetoric, more alliances were formed in neighboring parishes. Lynette started a private social media channel for us to communicate with each other and strategize together. As they say, two heads are better than one. We have strength

Louisiana Citizens Against Censorship

Fighting for Free Speech in the Bayou State

in numbers that far outweigh those of the white Christian nationalists targeting our libraries. Lynette, Melanie, and I also discussed the need for an organization to unite us all, and she created a website and social media for Louisiana Citizens Against Censorship (LaCAC). I have never seen someone so devoted to a cause as Lynette, and I wholeheartedly believe that once we conquer the censors, it will be in large part to Lynette. The website she created is a work of art and includes videos, calls for actions across the state, a newsletter, and petitions when needed. Lynette reaches out to other parishes and offers guidance. LaCAC's resources have been referenced by the ACLU of Louisiana and have a far reach on social media.

I feel less alone knowing that these women are willing to speak up for intellectual freedom and against the hate and censorship in our state. Lynette, Melanie, and I are able to channel our rage into actions through our work in our individual parish alliances and together with LaCAC. Lynette and I joined forces with the other parish alliances, and we sent thousands of emails to Louisiana state representatives and senators. We also joined our other comrades in arms to speak out in committee hearings. We were trained by 10,000 Women of Louisiana on where to go, what to fill out, and how to speak at these hearings, and we all showed up in force. We were able to "kill" two of the bills, but two did eventually pass into law. We now work to mitigate the fallout from these bills across the state.

I could have just crawled into a hole and disappeared after being targeted, but I was determined to find the positives and seek change. I don't know if it was due to my upbringing or my stubborn personality or a bit of both, but I was determined to fight back. These ladies helped give me a purpose and focus, which guided me in healing and helped channel my energy into a cause for good. It is all about taking the lemons dealt to us in life and making lemonade out of them. It does nothing to just talk about our grievances. We must take action if we want change, and Lynette and Melanie helped me see that. Melanie once gave me a necklace with the word *hope* on it, and I really have hope for a better future because of people like Lynette and Melanie.

———

After my initial court case was dismissed, we requested a new trial, but the judge denied that request and upheld the dismissal. It was a devastating blow, but one that was expected. I am not one to give up lightly, and neither is my attorney, Alysson Mills. In fact, when I first met with Alysson, she was very up-front about the uphill battle that my case would face. When I hired her, the case had been dismissed by the local court, but Alysson strategically asked for a new trial, knowing that the judge would not be reversing her decision. I was under no illusion that the judge was going to admit she was wrong, but I did have a tiny sliver of hope. When you look at the case law and how well Alysson put together the request for retrial, it is glaringly obvious. I was glad it went into public record because I wanted the truth to be accessible to anyone who wanted it. I'm aware that several community members did seek out the court documents.

We filed an appeal, and oral arguments were heard in the First Circuit, Louisiana Court of Appeal, on September 19, 2023. My attorney wrote in the brief, "This appeal does not ask this Court to pick a side in any debate. It does not ask this Court to decide the merits of any book ban. It does not ask this Court to hold Defendants are wrong and Jones is right. All it asks is for permission for Jones to proceed with her case. The law entitles her to that. This lawsuit is not meritless. Jones can prove each element of her defamation claim: defamatory words, falsity, malice, and injury. A trial judge deciding a special motion to strike cannot weigh evidence, assess credibility, or resolve disputed issues of material fact. The trial judge erroneously did that here, crediting Defendants' own representations of disputed facts and forming her own opinions on how a reasonable person might understand Defendants' words. The trial judge impermissibly resolved in Defendants' favor questions that belong to a jury."

For the first time, I had more supporters than the opposition did at the hearing. My family and friends sat beside me quietly as Alysson pled my case before three judges instead of just one. This court was a lot more relaxed than the local court system, but I still couldn't stop the tears from falling down my face as the opposition tried to distort the truth. My sister Melanie and my friend Tiffany were on either side of me, making the process a little easier. My friend Vicki was there, along with my parents. I felt very supported.

I've written about the difficulties in proving defamation cases, but that will not deter me from trying to obtain a fair trial. In dismissing the case, the local judge didn't even give my case the opportunity to enter the discovery phase or have it heard by a jury of my peers.

All I want is a shot at a trial. To me that is only fair. Admittedly, life is not always fair and neither is the judicial system. I am prepared for either outcome, as much as one can be. A victory in court would just be the icing on the cake in taking back my life, but the cake by itself still tastes pretty delicious. I've already accomplished what I set out to do, and that is to not just take the hand that was dealt to me. Not only have I not accepted it by filing my initial suit, but I am actively working to make the world a better place by bringing awareness to situations like mine through interviews, public speaking, this book, and speaking my truth.

I've discussed the emotional and physical tolls this has taken on myself and my family, but the monetary cost involved in these cases is staggering. If it weren't for the kindness of strangers on the internet, who graciously donated to my GoFundMe, I'd never have been able to file suit. It's no wonder why very few people stand up for themselves through legal means when the money and politics involved can be huge obstacles.

I had almost given up before fortuitously finding a new legal team, with Alysson Mills at the helm. My new attorneys lit a fire under me with their legal strategies and views on the case. Being able to turn it over to them and to trust them to really *get it* has been a relief. I'm happy to have found a kindred spirit such as Alysson, and I hope that after this is all over, we can become friends and not just attorney and client. She understands why standing up for myself is important and how I have essentially already won in my own way.

―――――

Throughout this whole time of alliances, public speaking, and a trial, I have discovered that I have a newfound purpose in life besides my job as a school librarian, and that is to inspire and support others like me and speak out against injustice. I'm still young and will only be in my mid-fifties upon retirement from the public school system. It's my hope that one day I can work with an organization to promote online safety, help students and educators combat cyberbullying, and help our school and public libraries remain safe, equitable, and inclusive spaces. I discovered this desire over the past year through many conversations at conferences and over messages and phone calls from supportive librarians across the country.

I was finally over that hump of despair in the spring of 2023. I no longer felt like the world was about to come crashing down around me. I also no longer felt the anger I once had for the people who chose to bully me online. There's peace in finding a way to forgive people who have wronged you. I won't go so far to say I forgive them, but their actions no longer dictate my state of mind. I learned to let go and no longer worry what they were doing and saying. It took a lot of therapy to get to that point, so I thank my therapist, Bella. I promised her I would no longer look at their social media, and I haven't since that day. Several times a week, people will message me to see if I've seen the latest posts from the haters. Now I politely tell them I'm not interested. I'm truly not. I made a promise to myself that I will never again look at their social media, and I meant it.

During the summer of 2023, I realized that I had come full circle and was "back to normal" when I attended the American Library Association's annual conference in Chicago. I stayed with my close friends Andrea, Amy, and Wenndy in Andrea's home. The eight days hanging out with my friends at this conference were the final piece of the puzzle of putting my life back together. We went sightseeing and celebrated Emily Drabinski's inauguration as ALA president and my friend Courtney Pentland's inauguration as AASL president. I saw Judy Blume speak in person, got to speak with author Nikki Grimes, attended the Newbery-Caldecott Gala, met ALA executive director Tracie D. Hall, and received two awards. I even was lucky enough to meet Librarian of Congress Dr. Carla Hayden while waiting in line to have our photographs taken for *American Libraries* magazine. Fellowship with friends was just what I needed to get back on track.

Also over this summer I was able to reflect on my own behavior from the past year. I say I have no regrets, but I do have one, and that is the fact that, try as I might, I didn't always take the high road. I was bothered by something I posted out of anger back in the fall. When our public library director was being targeted, I was very angry on his behalf, particularly by the way he was treated by one of our parish councilmen, Garry Talbert. In anger, I openly posted on Facebook that Garry was an asshole. Having taught his children, I look back on doing that with regret. No child, even as an adult, should have to see their former teacher call their parent a name on social media, even if I did feel justified. I resorted to behavior that was no better than the attacks that I myself had received. I recently reached out to Garry to apologize, and he accepted it. It is my hope that he will one day reach out to our former public library director Giovanni Tairov with an apology of his own. Giovanni deserves it. And I will strive to avoid that type of behavior and focus on being a good example for my own child and the children of our community.

I have learned that there's always room for improvement in our lives, and when we're wrong, we need to own up to it. I doubt that I will ever receive an apology from the two people who chose to target me, but that's on them. I'm working hard to spread love and cannot worry about them any longer. Writing this book is one of the many ways I've used what happened to me to spread my story and help others facing similar issues in their communities. I know that there will continue to be many ups and downs, but I'm not going to let the downs stop me from helping others or stop me from speaking my truth.

I have received a lot of praise over the past year, and I don't know how to react to people who praise me. I don't think I deserve it. All I did was speak out in my community the same as the other twenty or so residents did that fateful night on July 19, 2022. I was targeted, and I refused to back down. There are hundreds of other librarians and educators just like me who refuse to cower who are also being defamed. I am no different except that I already had a platform in the public eye, and I chose to use it. I was able to make that decision because of my strong professional learning network and my many privileges. There are thousands of residents in their own communities like me who have formed grassroots alliances to protect our public institutions, and countless librarians who work to protect the First Amendment and our students' and patrons' right to read and access accurate information. I am proud to join their ranks. A win for one of us is a win for all.

When I visit public libraries across the country, staff members will often stop to thank and encourage me. Even though I lost a few friends along the way, I gained many new ones and grew stronger bonds with my true friends. At a conference, my friend Tom introduced me for a keynote and said sometimes our friends become family, and I gained many new "family" members in this journey, whose strength helped me in some very dark times.

I also had so many authors reach out to me, which for a librarian is like winning the lottery. Authors whom I have admired for years were emailing me, and I was in awe that they even knew who I was. I met Kwame Alexander, who made a video with me at our public library; received personal messages from the amazing Nikki Grimes, whom I finally got to meet in person at an American Library Association conference; and got to have dinner with the legendary Ellen Oh. I was even invited by Phil Bildner to join the Author Village, which still blows my mind, and have received encouragement from authors I love, like Jo Hackl and Barbara Dee.

So in spite of a year filled with turdtastic crappery, there were some very positive moments in my life. Through this journey, I have learned that we must dwell on the highs and not the lows. I learned that I am made of strong moral stuff and that, when faced with adversity, I didn't shrink away. I have always said I stand for what is right and just, and I proved it to myself. Many people often say this and then do the exact opposite when put to the test. I'm proud to say I walked the walk when I had to and never backed down. I stood up to the bullies, didn't allow them to silence me, and spoke out about injustices. I can say I was on the right side of history in a moment that tested many Americans, and not only did I survive but I persevered and came out swinging.

I am often reminded of the Anne Frank quote "In spite of everything I still believe that people are really good at heart." In times of crisis, people will show you their true colors, and a plethora of people showed me that their souls radiate with kindness. At the end of the day, that is what matters—that there are more people in the world willing to stand up for truth and righteousness than there are those who exist solely to tear others down. Karma is a bitch, and the haters will get what is coming to them whether it comes from me or not. I will no longer dwell on revenge and bitterness. I choose to ruminate on the joy in life. In the darkest of times,

I hope others can find comfort with family and friends like I have been able to do. I encourage others to reach out in support when they see people dragging others down, as friends and strangers alike, did for me.

It's not what other people say about us that determines whether we are winners or losers, but rather our reactions and what we stand for. My daughter thinks I am a badass, and that is everything to me. In the worst of times, I found out that with the help of my friends and family, I could be the best possible version of myself. There's nobody in the world who can take that from me.

Chapter 15

What You Can Do in Your
Own Community

She's a sparrow when she's broken
But she's an eagle when she flies

—DOLLY PARTON, "EAGLE WHEN SHE FLIES"

Every day for the past twenty-two years, I've left my house and traveled the same route to work. It takes exactly six minutes from the time I leave until the moment I open the door of my SUV to walk inside my school. Every day I walk to the passenger side to get my purse, school bag, and thermos of iced tea to drink at work and then look at the large cutout of an eagle over the gym on my way into school. I attended Live Oak schools from elementary through high school, and the eagle has always been our mascot. After I graduated college, I went back to work at the school I attended as a child, once more an eagle. I have been an eagle for thirty-five of the forty-five years that I have been alive, in more ways than one.

A few years ago, I took an online test that compares personalities to animals, and I had to laugh when my results came back as an eagle. Eagle personalities were described as being goal-driven, bold, action-oriented, and not afraid of a challenge. Eagle personalities, much like the actual bird of prey, are daring, persistent, savage yet nurturing, resilient. Upon reflection, I wouldn't say that I am naturally a courageous person, but I will go toe to toe with someone, regardless of who they are or how dangerous, if they try to harm me or someone I love. Like an eagle, I can be ferocious when needed.

After July 2022, when both I and my community's library system became targets, I decided to show the haters just how ferocious I could be. I never thought that attending a public library board meeting to speak against censorship would make me a target, but I wasn't going to take it lying down. I set forth to create a game plan to help my parish that included getting to know the players, gathering allies, and creating alliances, and the determination that while we might lose some skirmishes along the way, we would win the big game no matter what. I am playing chess to their checkers.

The pro-censors are loud and obnoxious, and they're only growing bolder. They'll continue their rampage unless rational people speak out against them. This movement could have detrimental effects on our schools and libraries for decades to come if we don't consistently confront them. People who believe in inclusivity, the freedom to read, and the public good need to be even louder and more active than the book banners. They post about saving children but provide no evidence that children are in danger. It's not about kids for them. We all want to protect children. That has never been the difference between us and them. Their agenda is all about silencing voices, politics, and money. It's very important in the quest for intellectual freedom that we get to know our foes.

I highly recommend that everyone take the following steps to stay informed within your community:

- **Attend school board, library board, and local governance meetings.**
  Take notes on which officials use words like *woke* and *indoctrination*.
  If they use words like *gender ideology* and *sexually explicit material*,
  chances are they are pro-censorship. Hate and oppression is a

running theme, and you will find that they all post the same ridiculous memes filled with lies and conspiracy theories.

- **Follow the social media accounts of elected officials and take screenshots to document any extremist views.** Share the knowledge with others in your community.
- **Use a website like https://pluralpolicy.com/ to track legislation and your elected officials.** In Louisiana, we have our own Geaux-Vote app and legislative website to follow bills and officials. Stay in the know.
- **Use your state government's website to look up politicians and their donors.** Follow the money and you will find the motives.
- **Vote in every election.**

I try to know not only the players in my own parish but also the players in the surrounding parishes, as they often join forces. It's important for us to join forces as well. Keeping tabs on the pro-censors in other areas allows you to prepare for their hateful antics. From following the push to censor materials in St. Tammany Parish, I took note of some issues they had with their library signs. The St. Tammany Library Alliance, a group of citizens devoted to protecting the library, posted signs around town that said TRUST OUR LIBRARIANS. A group of local far-right ideologues then purchased nearly identical signs that said NO ONE TRUSTS OUR LIBRARIANS. I made a mental note to be sure that our future signs were harder to mock.

I also found out about an email that a woman named Connie sent the director of the St. Tammany Parish Public Library that said, among other things, "My ultimate goal is to make sure that you are not there," and "We will see who ultimately prevails but remember I have God on my side, God always wins, and if you underestimate me you do so at your own peril." I checked in with our director to make sure she was okay, and she told me a man called the library to tell her she was a cunt. The types of people who call and email librarians with threats and inappropriate comments are vile. Be sure you counteract the hate by emailing positivity to your library staff to help counter the negativity they hear too often.

After the attacks on me, I was helped by continued messages of support from across my state and the country. People I had never met were sending me postcards, letters, and gifts to my school, our local library, and the local bookstore. Hundreds of supportive emails were sent my way, and it made me feel less alone. I looked for ways to pay those messages forward and started combing through social media posts in communities where I knew librarians and educators were also being attacked. I would see the same disgusting comments over and over, but occasionally I would see someone defend the librarian or educator. I would then private-message those people and share how supportive emails had helped me and ask them to consider sending one to their local librarian. Who knows if the librarian would see the social media post, but a personal email can make a real positive impact. It's one small way I have tried to help others.

I then discovered that the school librarian Christopher Harris has made the process a little easier with his website We the Librarians: Honoring Librarians with Message of Resilience. The website can be found at https:// wethelibrarians.org/ and anyone can donate. This amazing website allows you to sign up so that you can mail messages of support to librarians across the country. You can also send them names of librarians under attack so that they will receive letters, and you can even donate to this website to help support their work. A letter may seem like such a small thing, but it can mean the world to somebody who is being bombarded with hate.

A bigger step to support your library, and stand up for intellectual freedom, is to create a solid community alliance for your school and public libraries. I have found that the vast majority of people are against censorship, but sometimes they can easily fall for lies posted on social media. A solid alliance can dispel lies and promote the truth. Alliances also act as support for the librarians and a common place where like-minded individuals can gather to plan and show solidarity. Many people want to help, but they don't know how. Alliances can keep residents informed about public meetings, agenda items, and politicians, as well as promote positivity. The citizen alliances joined forces during the 2023 Louisiana legislative session, and we were able to send thousands of emails and letters to legislators about the four anti-library bills.

Consider forming an alliance before things go south, because then you won't be playing catch-up. With an alliance in place, you can play offense rather than defense. When I was first targeted, I was blessed to have personal support from the EveryLibrary organization; our community was fortunate to have their help in creating a citizen alliance for our parish's entire public library system. EveryLibrary was key in helping our residents set up a game plan for success, and with their help we steadily held off the censors. Consider contacting EveryLibrary for assistance getting started on an alliance.

Alliances offer support to our librarians. Whether it's an email, the sharing of a post, or attending a public meeting, we want them to know that there's an entire army behind them in the community. Here are a few of the activities that the Livingston Parish Library Alliance has focused on to support librarians and intellectual freedom.

- **Utilize social media.** We created a Livingston Parish Library Alliance Facebook and Instagram page. We post meeting dates, ways to contact local governance, issues facing our library, and how people can stay involved and aware. We post election information and actively promoted our library millage tax renewal.
- **Create a website.** During the legislative session, we posted templates for emailing legislators, displayed legislative contact information, gave tutorials for speaking out in the legislature, and kept the community informed about each step of every anti-library bill. We also posted a censorship tool kit and graphics for residents to use and informed the community on the importance of our library tax millage renewal.
- **Be aware of public meetings.** Keep the community aware of important agenda items for upcoming meetings and alert them when we need resident support for the library. We even offer talking points and sample speeches for anyone who wishes to speak but doesn't quite know what to say.
- **Write letters of recommendation.** When it's time for our local governing board to appoint new members to our Library Board of Control, our alliance has written letters of recommendation for potential appointees. We help the appointees craft a statement and

gather signatures. Our last letter of recommendation had over 120 signatures from business owners, influential community members, and politicians. These can make a huge difference!

- **Send emails.** We regularly post information for community members to email local governance. We thank local leaders when they are supportive, condemn behavior that is damaging to our library, and send them other information. For example, during one meeting, a library board member and parish council person said that books being challenged should be removed from the shelves while under review. We were able to ask the help of a local law clinic to send them a letter on how this could potentially violate laws and the First Amendment.
- **Submit public records requests.** We use our alliance to request public records from our public library. We often request book challenge information and emails. We cannot request emails of private residents, but we can request the emails they send to our library board and library workers. This helps us know if they are receiving any hate mail or need our support standing up against book challenges.
- **Rally support through signs, billboards, and buttons.** Funding can be difficult to find. You can try crowdsourcing or asking for help from EveryLibrary. I have even seen alliances create their own political action committees (PACs) and nonprofits to find donors and create fundraisers. Through the help of donors in our parish, we were able to provide buttons and bookmarks at library board meetings, yard signs, and billboards to push the library millage tax renewal.
- **Establish partnerships.** Our alliance has partnered with the Unite Against Book Bans, Louisiana Citizens Against Censorship, EveryLibrary, and the National Coalition Against Censorship. There is strength in partnerships and the sharing of resources.

If you are alone and don't know where to start, create an alliance Facebook page and invite your friends and family who support libraries. Ask them to invite their library-supporting friends. At each public meeting,

pass out flyers with the name of your Facebook page and a little bit about your alliance. It's amazing how quickly it will grow. We allow anyone to follow our Facebook page, but we will block anyone who posts hate speech or starts arguments. Don't hesitate to block anyone on your personal page. You do NOT have to put up with hate on your own social media pages. Eventually, you can start a private discussion group within that page and invite trusted individuals. You want to keep strategy close to the vest, but acknowledge that even private discussion groups can probably be infiltrated. Ask others in the group to share administrator duties for the page as it grows.

I am proud to have founded a grassroots alliance of residents from across our parish that has helped our public library system. Should we start having issues in our school libraries, the alliance is ready to go. We started out as a very small group but found dozens of people willing to help over time. We also started out with only social media but grew over the course of a year. You can put as much or as little as you want into an alliance, but make no mistake: your community needs one.

While larger groups like the American Library Association, PEN America, and EveryLibrary can help with the big picture, campaigns, and resources, the real work is at the local level with grassroots efforts. It takes members of the community to stand up, speak out, and stick together as a cohesive unit. You are better together in numbers. Hold regular meetings via Zoom, or meet thirty minutes before a public meeting to pass out buttons and strategize. One thing I love about the St. Tammany Parish

Library Alliance is that the members of the alliance show up very early to pack the front of the meeting space as much as possible.

Eventually, if you have it in you, consider forming a statewide alliance, or team up with your state's library or school library association. Lynette Mejia and Melanie Brevis had already formed a solid community alliance in neighboring Lafayette. They wanted to unify the many parish alliances under one banner, and we formed Louisiana Citizens Against Censorship. Lynette works tirelessly to update the LaCAC website with a newsletter, calls to action, resource guides, election information, and videos to share with the public, and her legislative resource guide was even shared across the state by the ACLU of Louisiana. All it takes is one person, or a small group, to get the ball rolling.

When, inevitably, you have people in your community who try to say that there are sexually explicit materials in your school or public library, first and foremost it's important to remind them about collection development and reconsideration policies. After that, prove their lies wrong. Our grassroots alliance posted the following message on social media and our website, and emailed it to local governing boards. We also created handouts with this message to pass out at library board meetings. It has made a real difference in helping combat the lies told across our community:

> The next time you hear someone say there are sexually explicit materials in children's sections of your library (which is not true), here are some suggestions:
>
> 1. **Ask this person to give you a title of an actual book.** Look on your library's catalog to see if the book even exists and/or if it is even in the children's section. You can usually see for yourself that their claim is false. Then YOU don't have to perpetuate the rumor and can stop it in its tracks.
>
> 2. **Check out the book and read it for yourself.** Remember that every book might not be your cup of tea, but that doesn't mean

the book is sexually explicit. If you object to a title, fill out a formal request for reconsideration if you feel that is necessary. Keep in mind that a book in the adult section must fail the Miller test to be considered obscene and sexually explicit. Books are taken as a whole and based on literary merit—not just one page out of context.

3. **Ask yourself if they have a hidden motive.** Once you can prove to them that their claims are false and they continue to spread the lie, ask yourself why. You'd be amazed at how many people simply want to spread lies, even if they know they are lies. That's called chasing clout. They want to feel important and/or were fed disinformation that they did not take the time to verify.

4. **See if they or a family member is running for office.** Are they just jumping on the bandwagon of using the library as a punching bag to stir up drama so that they can say they will swoop in and save the day from that fake issue? This is called pandering for votes.

5. **They might need attention because something is missing in their life.** Be a good friend. Invite them to lunch and then swing by the library to pick up free books, magazines, movies, or music for checkout. The library also contains self-help books!

5. **Ask your friendly neighborhood librarian or email the alliance, and we will help prove it for you!**

Before diving into defending intellectual freedom, libraries, and your community, I also implore you to visit PEN America's Online Harassment Field Manual to prepare and check in often with Kelly Jensen's censorship articles. Kelly, a former librarian, is a journalist for Book Riot. Her coverage of censorship activities has been commended by the American Association

KNOW THE FACTS.
FIGHT THE LIES.
STAND WITH THE LIBRARY.

LPLALLIANCE.COM

of School Librarians as well as the Louisiana Library Association. She covers censorship stories for both school and public libraries. Through her coverage, we have been able to be informed on practices and tactics used in other states but have also helped share awareness of censorship in Louisiana through her coverage of our state. The more prepared and knowledgeable you are, the better able you will be to defeat bad actors who want to destroy libraries and librarians.

It is also important that, if you decide to take any type of stand against hate, you take advance precautions to protect yourself. Online trolls and keyboard warriors consider anyone and everyone fair game, even your family. Nobody is off-limits to their garbage, and safety is key. You also need to know that no matter how many safety measures you take, they will find a way to come at you. The truth doesn't matter to them, and they will openly lie in seeking to destroy you. Be prepared as much as you can and consider the following:

- **Remove any references to your job from personal and professional websites and social media.** Do this with every app that you use. There were some I didn't even think about, like Goodreads, the app I use to track my reading.

- **Work emails are for work. Personal emails are for personal use. Don't confuse the two.** Make sure all apps, websites, and social media only contain your personal emails. Your work emails could be subject to public records requests. Now, that's not to insinuate that you are doing anything wrong on your work emails! I just know from personal experience that these people will take screenshots out of context and twist words. Be careful.
- **You can retroactively set all previous Facebook posts to private or friends-only viewing with the click of a button. Do it.** You should also remove or hide pictures of your children and other family members and fix your privacy settings on all social media to allow minimal commenting from people you aren't "friends" with on the platforms.
- **Change your passwords often on all accounts.**
- **Use an app like Slack, with channels for different topics, to help your cause.** Only invite the "inner circle" of trusted leaders in these communications.
- **If you are a librarian, use an app like Signal to communicate with each other.** This app is less likely to be hacked, and you can set messages to disappear after a few minutes.
- **Don't engage with online trolls.** You will only stress yourself out, and you're not going to change their minds. The best thing to do is block and ignore.
- **You can also report harassment or misinformation on most social media platforms.**
- **If you receive a threatening email, do not forward it, as you can potentially mess with the email's code.** Print it out, save it, and report it to law enforcement immediately.
- **Document every link, screenshot, and email.** Save the information in multiple secure places. You never know when it will come in handy.

Back in July 2022, I went to a public library board meeting thinking I would do my part to give one speech, sit down, and life would go on. Instead,

I became a target. I could have chosen to ignore the online lies and hate being told about me, but why should I have stayed silent when I had done nothing wrong? In fact, they probably would have forgotten about me in a few weeks or months. Would I still be looking over my shoulder today had I chosen to do nothing?

Probably not. I chose to take a stand, and that decision changed the trajectory of my life. I chose to fight back. It was a hard decision that I did not take lightly. It has taken an emotional, physical, and mental toll on me and my family. I would not change a single thing I have done and think this is all a part of God's plan for my life. I have zero regrets. This has become a purpose in my life—to stick up for librarians and libraries, speak out for historically marginalized students and authors, fight back against online bullying, and help others find their voices to do the same. However, I want others to understand that it is okay to walk away. There is no shame in taking care of yourself and your family first.

Over the past year, other librarians have reached out to me because they, too, have been targeted online or at public meetings. I am always very up-front about the personal toll, as well as all the other issues one can face when fighting back. For starters, I have a very strong support system, which is key. I have not walked this journey alone. I spent the past several years working hard to build up my professional learning network. I never knew why I was doing it other than I just like making connections with librarians across the country. My network helped keep me strong when I needed it. I was also blessed with a school system that was supportive. While I wish my colleagues had been more vocal, their support behind the scenes never wavered. Most important, I had the support of my husband, child, and family. I am also fortunate to have a GoFundMe account that has helped offset the costs of litigation. Suing for defamation is extremely difficult and costly. If you cannot find someone to take your case pro bono, or if you do not have tens of thousands of dollars to spare, I would encourage you to think long and hard about the possibility of going into debt if you decide to fight back through legal means. Defamation cases are incredibly hard to prove. You also have to consider the court system. Most local judges are elected. If you are in a far-right area, your chances of winning become slimmer. In a perfect world, judges should know the letter of the law in these types of cases, but First Amendment and defamation cases are intricate, and your average local judge is probably not familiar with the specifics of these cases. Because they are elected, it also weighs in their minds, no matter how hard they try not to, that they themselves will be judged on their decisions. I knew all of this going in and still made the decision to file suit. To me, just standing up for myself and filing the lawsuit was worth it, even if I didn't win in court. That might not be enough for you.

Regardless of my lawsuit, I will continue to speak out against censorship. Even if it takes years, we will win in the long run. I am an eagle through and through. An eagle will protect its territory by flying around it or by perching conspicuously near the top of a nearby tree. I will attend every local meeting with a watchful eye. I will continue to speak out. Like an eagle protecting her nest, I will help protect my community and myself from those who threaten us. I will circle above, going high instead of low, until the threat leaves the area.

Chapter 16

Don't Let Anyone Dull Your Sparkle

But you see in dealing with me, the relatives didn't know that they were dealing with a staunch character and I tell you if there's anything worse than dealing with a staunch woman . . . S-T-A-U-N-C-H. There's nothing worse, I'm telling you. They don't weaken, no matter what.

—EDITH "LITTLE EDIE" BOUVIER BEALE, *GREY GARDENS*

My last year in the classroom, teaching eighth-grade English Language Arts, I had a sweet student named Alanna. She was wise beyond her years, always polite, and a model student. I also taught her sister in the library and counted her mother as a friend. When I taught Alanna, she, like many eighth-grade students, was on the receiving end of some unkind remarks from other students. I used to tell her, "Don't let anyone dull your sparkle," and it became our mantra. Whenever I would see her looking sad, I'd remind her. A few years later, her mother bought me a sign that featured the phrase, and it's proudly displayed in our school library to remind me and the students to not let the words of others affect the way we live our lives. I occasionally run into Alanna, who is now an adult, and still remind her not to let anyone dull her sparkle.

I have thought long and hard about that phrase over the past year and have decided to practice what I preach. I have decided that I will not allow the people who harass and seek to destroy me the pleasure of dulling my sparkle. If anything, I have decided that the best revenge is to sparkle even brighter. I'll sparkle bright like Edward Cullen in the sunlight.

Sometimes I think about my haters, although less each day. When I do think about them, sometimes I compare our lives. I have a job I love, a supportive family, and friends beyond measure, and I am a leader in my field because I work hard at what I do. I am proud of my accomplishments, my dedication to our community, the lives I've shaped, and the way I have endured the past year with grace and integrity. On the flip side, the haters don't have much going for them besides ruminating in their own hate, if you can count that as an accomplishment. They have little to show for their lives in this "work" they do. Are they approached by people who said they've made a difference in their lives for the better? Doubtful. I will continue to think about them less and less, and that is success for me. However, I think they will continue to think of me for the rest of their lives and wish they had not chosen to pick a fight with me. That's the nature of hate.

I have been accused of being woke. It seems to me that the people labeled woke are those who are empathetic, are open-minded, and challenge the world to be a better place. If they want to call me woke, I will wear it like a badge of honor, because the opposite would be to say I'm "asleep." My eyes have been opened over the past year, and I have taken my head out of the sand. Politicians, especially our local ones, tend to lie and pander as if their constituents were idiots. Unfortunately, few seek out the truth and instead fall for the nonsense. I'm also more aware that online bullying is harmful to everyone involved, many believe everything they see on social media, and there are people who seek to destroy others simply for existing. While we must fight these evil forces with all we have, we must also realize that there are many good people in the world and that all it takes is one voice, taking one positive action at a time, to show the world we can do better. I was fortunate to hear the author Kekla Magoon speak at a conference, and she said that we are like raindrops. Individually, we are just one drop, but together we can be a storm. I am proud to join others to make a difference and thunder loudly to anyone who will listen.

I've also been labeled a radical leftist. Funnily enough, I've been a lifelong registered Republican or Independent. I have historically voted for the Republican Party, or candidates I feel would be the best fit for the job. It has only been in the past few years that I have leaned more left of center and voted Democrat, but I've often wondered if maybe that is not the case. Maybe it is that the center shifted, and Republicans, in my state at least, don't represent the ideals I hold important and want as a voter. I still consider myself a moderate on most issues, with the exception of human rights issues that I believe should not be political. On those, I stand proudly to the left. If people feel better about themselves calling me a radical, then that's on them and it doesn't bother me. Human rights should not be political. We should all want to show empathy and kindness to everyone regardless of party lines. I often wonder where we have gone wrong as a country when people who believe that the LGBTQIA+ community should be allowed the same rights as everyone are labeled radicals. It's basic human decency, but the United States seems to be lacking that. We should all want to have truth taught to our children and libraries that are inclusive to people from all walks of life. We should be able to have open conversations without name-calling and personal attacks just because we disagree with someone.

I have been disheartened over the past year to also have been labeled as some type of degenerate or have my Christianity called into question. For starters, my religion is between myself and God. I also know that my religion is mine. I don't need to walk around shoving it down anyone else's throat or attack people who don't believe in God. I don't need to prove it to anyone. I believe in the separation of church and state and the notion that government institutions should be free of religion. That doesn't mean I'm not a Christian. It means I recognize that not everyone else is and that libraries should have no role in furthering any one religion by excluding everyone who doesn't follow the main religion of a community. Libraries are for everyone—the nonreligious, the woke, and the radical leftists, but also for the Christians, Republicans, and the alt-right extremists. Libraries provide resources for an entire community but should not push one religion or one viewpoint or exclude anyone.

This notion that white Christians are being oppressed or persecuted is asinine. They want so badly to be victims when they are the ones doing the oppressing. Christianity is not under attack. White people are not being persecuted for being white. I see a concerted effort by white Christian nationalists to oppress anyone who is not them, while the "other side" simply wants to exist, be afforded the same rights, and to be left alone. Libraries should include all religions and serve every member. What I see is an effort to ban books by specific authors, or with characters, who are not white Christians. More specifically, pro-censors are going after stories with characters and authors from the LGBTQIA+ and BIPOC communities. They do this by saying they aren't trying to ban books and that they're trying to protect children. They imply that there is sexually explicit material in children's sections of public libraries or in school libraries. This is not true. They'll trot out the same two-page spread from *Gender Queer* as if that is the whole story or it's floating around next to *The Very Hungry Caterpillar*. People need to wake up and see through these attempts to push an agenda of far-right ideology into our libraries. The pro-censors use shock-and-awe tactics via social media to push their hatred. The books they challenge aren't typically books with sexually explicit material. The book challenges are focused on books from LGBTQIA+ and BIPOC authors and characters.

Freedom and parental rights are a rallying cry, but the same people who say this are trying to take away the rights of young adult readers, their parents, and others. The people who say they are for small government are pushing governmental control over what we the people have access to, and not just children. We should ALL want the freedom to read what we want to read and have access to reading materials from a variety of viewpoints. Protecting our libraries is exactly how we do that. The attack on librarians and libraries is shameful and something everyone should fear. Once they destroy our libraries and schools, what will be next? Where will it end? We must continue to speak up. That's all we can really do. We must stand up for what is right and good, regardless of what is said about us. The book banners, the people who attacked me for daring to disagree with them, wanted to silence me. I didn't let them. I did the opposite. For the past year, I have agreed to almost every interview requested of me to help spread the word across the nation about what is happening in our libraries and to librarians. It has been exhausting, but necessary. I will continue to speak out when asked. We have to not just for the sake of libraries but for real freedom. Everyone who can needs to speak out on behalf of those who cannot. People who are rational need to take a stand against the irrational. We must do so with grace and truth, never stooping to the tactics the pro-censors use. We are the real patriots.

Our politicians need to stop creating fake issues and promoting false-hoods. If not, we need to vote them out. We need to stop the political divide and have rational conversations for the betterment of society. People must turn off Fox News, stop believing everything they see online, and be wary of any politician or political pundit who targets people for the sake of votes or clicks. When the "news" you watch is just commentary, false outrage, and the disparaging of others, you need to branch out. Try watching a variety of channels. Try striking up conversations with people who are different from you, or have differing views, to learn understanding. Put yourself in others' shoes and think about what you would do if you were them. Having empathy for others is a remedy for hate. Make no mistake—we all have work to do and none of us is perfect. Take a deep breath and think before you believe everything your cousin's girlfriend's neighbor posts on Facebook.

Not every gesture has to be grand. If you're not comfortable speaking at public meetings, don't. You do need to show up, though. Stay aware of what is happening in your community. Not every conversation has to be life changing. Start small and point out lies and hypocrisy with your family and friends. Provide the truth, because it is the truth that will eventually set us free. Encourage others to seek out and understand perspectives that differ from their own. You don't have to show up with signs to protest. Standing in solidarity by reaching out in support, and showing up just to be a presence, can be supportive. Just don't be apathetic. Indifference, and thinking it could never happen, is what got us into this mess while the pro-censors were strategizing and forming a plan of fascism.

———————

On August 11, 2023, I woke up and chose my return-to-school outfit care-fully like it was my first day of school as a kid and not as a school librarian returning for my twenty-third year. I asked my husband if I looked okay, and he gave me a reassuring hug before I got in the car with my school bag and travel mug of coffee. I double-checked to make sure my school keys were back in my purse after having been on my home computer desk for the past eight months. I searched Spotify for the right song, "I'm Still Standing," by Elton John, and slowly backed out of the driveway.

As I drove the two miles to work, I took slow, deep breaths and prayed for a good year. I'm already planning to make this year better than ever and have pages of notes for new programs and ideas that I cannot wait to share with the kids. I parked in my old familiar parking spot and made my way inside, stopping to talk to Mr. Victor, our custodian, whom I missed. I walked into the library, away from the one-hundred-degree heat outside, and back into my home away from home, thinking, "I've got this."

I have done a lot of soul-searching this past year. I found out I'm stronger than I ever thought I could be. I learned I have weaknesses as a human. I found out I am not immune to online bullying and discovered that this is an area we as educators need to work on with the kids. I spoke at the legislature, helped form grassroots alliances, and made national headlines. I learned to use my voice and my privileges to make the world a better place in my small corner of the world. I took a stand for something I believe in and will continue to stand up for intellectual freedom. I realized that I have a whole army of friends and supporters who have helped me succeed and I am blessed beyond measure. It was a life-changing year.

The road to overcoming my fear and trauma was a winding one. There were ups and downs. I took medical leave from school for a semester, and I'm glad I did. It's okay to admit you need to take a break or need help. We need to take care of ourselves. I journaled, went to therapy, wrote this book, and slowly weaned myself off the anxiety medication. My hair has begun to grow back in from the patches I lost to stress. I won't mind if the weight stays off. I grew stronger in my faith and in the bonds with my family. I became the kind of person I hope my daughter and my students can admire.

This ordeal could have defeated me. It didn't. I wouldn't let it.

Alysson, my attorney, just filed our first brief in the appeal process. Over a year ago, the judge dismissed my case, twice, but my appeal is before the First Circuit, Louisiana Court of Appeal, where it will be heard by three judges. If we should not prevail, I will file a further appeal with the Louisiana Supreme Court. All I'm hoping for is a fair shot at a jury trial. All I am asking, should the dismissal be overturned and we actually get to try the case, is one dollar and a public apology. That's it. Maybe I will win, maybe I won't, but at least I tried. I am grateful for every word of encouragement and every penny donated to help me and my case.

Before school started for the day on August 11, the faculty stood together in the cafeteria taking selfies before the kids arrived. Administration came on the intercom to wish everyone a great first day of school. I waited for the bell, catching up with co-workers I hadn't seen in months. When the bell rang that morning to start school, a rush of kids came bounding off the buses and into the school. I stood there ready to greet them for a brand-new school year. Student after student stopped to hug me and tell me they're glad I'm back. I am glad too. I will never again let anyone dull my sparkle. I am, after all, "that librarian," the exact staunch character that my parents raised me to be.

MY JULY 19, 2022, SPEECH TO THE LIVINGSTON PARISH LIBRARY BOARD OF CONTROL

My name is Amanda Jones. I am the 2021 *School Library Journal* National Librarian of the Year, an international speaker and advocate on behalf of libraries, and am president of the Louisiana Association of School Librarians. I am here as a representative of that organization, but more importantly as a lifelong resident of Livingston Parish, parent of a child in this district, and taxpayer. I am here tonight because book content and book signage have been listed on tonight's agenda. I hope that what I am about to say is not needed, and that my fear that a member of the board is trying to censor books and signage is unfounded.

While book challenges are often done with the best intentions, and in the name of age appropriateness, they often target marginalized communities such as BIPOC and the LGBTQ community. They also target books on sexual health and reproduction. Considering that Livingston Parish has the highest rate of children in foster care per capita in Louisiana, and that number has doubled over the past few years, I find it ironic that any member of the community would want to limit access to any book on reproduction or relocate it away from our children who need it the most. Once you start relocating and banning one topic, it becomes a slippery slope and where does it end?

All members of our community deserve to be seen, have access to information, and see themselves, in our PUBLIC library collection. Censoring and relocating books and displays is harmful to our community, but will be extremely harmful to our most vulnerable—our children. According to the Trevor Project, "LGBTQ youth are not inherently prone to suicide risk because of their sexual orientation or gender identity but rather placed at higher risk because of how they are mistreated and stigmatized in society."

Libraries are for everyone. According to the American Library Association, of which I am a member,

> LIBRARIES ARE A cornerstone of the community dedicated to serving the information needs of everyone. As such, they collect and make available a wide variety of information resources representing the range of human thought and experience. With such a broad spectrum of ideas and information available, it is inevitable that people will occasionally encounter resources they believe to be inappropriate for their family.

Just because you enter a library, it does not mean that you will not see something you don't like. Libraries have diverse collections with resources from many points of view, and a library's mission is to provide access to information for all users. All library users have the First Amendment right to borrow, read, view, and listen to library resources, according to the ALA. If an individual is concerned about a children's or young adult's resource or its location in the library, that individual has the right to go through the library's reconsideration policy that is already in place. Each family has the right to determine which library resources are acceptable for its own children, but individuals must also realize that they must afford the same rights to all other parents.

The citizens of our parish consist of taxpayers who are white, Black, brown, gay, straight, Christian, non-Christian—people from all backgrounds and walks of life, and no one portion of the community should dictate what the rest of the citizens have access to. Just because you don't want to read it or see it, it doesn't give you the right to deny others or demand its relocation. If we remove or relocate books with LGBTQ or sexual health content, what message is that sending to our community members? Why is your belief system any more important than others'? What will be next if you accomplish your mission? Parents have a personal responsibility to monitor their own child's reading and nobody else's.

The LPL director Giovanni Tairov has accomplished wonders for our public library and made it into an award-winning system. There's a reason the Louisiana Library Association named him the 2019 Public Library Director of the Year. Trust his judgment and those of the other dedicated LPL employees. There is a solid collection development policy in place. Nobody is putting pornography in children's sections of the library. Stop that false narrative. The librarians over the collection have library science degrees and use professional reviews, which list ages of relevancy and age appropriateness, before deciding where to place them in the library. There is already a book challenge process if a community member does not like a particular book or location of a book in the library. As board members, I would hope you already know that.

To board member Erin Sandefur, who placed this item on the agenda, I will say this: you once posted on social media that there are folks who do not agree with you and that we can be one of your greatest teachers. That is an admirable statement. I would love to teach you about how harmful censorship, book policing, and agenda items like these affect our youth and historically marginalized community members.

To the entire board, I will say this: I grew up in this parish being taught that God is love. What I've come to realize is that what many people mean is that God is love only if you have the same religious and political beliefs as them. I have lived in our parish for forty-four years. I am a mother of a child in our school system. I have been an LPL card holder since 1983. I have watched our public library grow to be one of our parish's biggest assets—something we can be proud of. I will remind board members that regardless of your own beliefs on the topic of book content and location, to think about this: no one on the right side of history has ever been on the side of censorship and hiding books. In the words of author Stephen Chbosky: "Banning books gives us silence when we need speech. It closes our ears when we need to listen. It makes us blind when we need sight." Hate and fear disguised as moral outrage have no place in Livingston Parish.

Thank you for allowing me to speak tonight.

ACKNOWLEDGMENTS

Anything is possible when you have the right people there to support you.

—MISTY COPELAND

Thank you to Jason, Josie, Momma, Daddy, Bookie (my ninety-seven-year-old grandmother), the siblings and their spouses, and all my nieces and nephews for being my family.

In December 2022, I bid on a We Need Diverse Books auction item, which happened to be a thirty-minute session with a literary agent. I wanted to ask how the whole process worked. I won the auction and learned so much from my session with Sarah Fisk. Imagine my surprise when the next day, Sarah and Tobias Literary Agency offered to sign me. Thank you, Sarah!

Two days after I signed with Sarah, I received an email out of the blue from a man named Anton Mueller, an editor at Bloomsbury, telling me he had heard me on the *New York Times First Person* podcast and asking if I had ever considered writing a book. I thought it had to be fate, since I had just acquired an agent! I owe you big-time, Anton. Thank you to Anton and the team at Bloomsbury for taking a chance on a first-time writer, and scorned school librarian, who decided it was time to tell my story.

Words are hard and I am not a skilled storyteller. Thank you to Tom Bober, who gave me notes on this entire book and helped shape it into something I'm proud of. Tom taught me about back matter, forced me to dig deeper, and made the writing better with his feedback. This book would totally suck without his guidance. It's an honor to be included at the Tom Bober and Friends table of life.

To Puff. For all of it. For every single thing and then some. I don't think I'd still be here without you.

Melanie and Colleen. Thank you for standing by me. This doesn't mean we need to hug, but I'll admit now that I love you.

Thank you Kelsye, Tam Tam, Kristy, Lovie, and AB for guiding me through the dark, all the times you cheered me up, and for listening to me yammer. And to our silent friend Shark—I appreciate you very much.

To Bonnie—thank you for implanting this idea in my head. I can't believe I actually did it, because I was kind of joking when I said I was going to, but then it just happened.

To the bravest person I know, Lynette Mejia. She's changing the world for the better. Her picture should be in the dictionary beside the word *legend*.

The queso to my chip, Heather. You just get me and I thank you for it.

For Melanie B. I have hope.

To 18-18-18. I didn't purposely pick all of these twists and turns for my Choose Your Own Adventure, but I'm thankful you were in it pretty much every step of the way since birth.

Thank you to Jen M and Rachelle for allowing me to gripe and grumble, for boosting me up, and for our shared political stances.

To the League of Ladies, Clubhouse Crew, FReadom Fighters, Chapter Assembly, and Garden Club. We are #BetterTogether and you have made my life richer.

Thank you to Andrea, Amy, and Wenndy. I love you guys.

To K.C., I hope one day I am as fabulous as you. You truly are The Boss.

Marla and Vicki, whom I can't thank enough. LP owes you big-time and they don't even know it.

Thank you to Mr. Tom Aswell of Louisiana Voice for keeping our local community informed on the real story.

Thank you to Courtney, Momo, and Pepper. Every day should be "Caturday" and everyone should be blessed to have a friend like Courtney.

To Ellen Oh and WNDB. You had the auction that started this whole ball rolling. I never imagined this would happen when I bid, but I'm sure glad it did. Thank you for ensuring diverse literature is written and gets into the hands of students.

I'd like to thank Alysson Mills. She's more than my attorney. She's a fierce woman who is helping right the wrongs of the world, and I would have spiraled into despair had she not walked into my life.

To Kelly Jensen—she was there almost from the start for me and the rest of us. She knew it was coming and we were all slow to listen. Keep fighting the good fight. You are needed and appreciated. When it's over, it will be in part because of you, even if it doesn't say it in the history books. But it better say your name in the history books or I'm going to be super pissed.

John Chrastka and EveryLibrary—you swooped in and offered support right from the get-go. None of my success would have happened without you. Your help to librarians and citizens all across the country, real plans of action when we need it, are vital. Thank you.

Giovanni Tairov—what they did to you was horrible. My final chess move will be in your honor, but you might have to wait one more year. I told you I was playing the long game. I'm sorry I couldn't do more.

To Reverend Doctor Andrea T—I'd like to think I am a more empathetic person due to your influence. Your mere presence in this world makes it better and I thank you for all of the pep talks.

Thank you to Kiesha, who is the personification of love and light. She is a true friend who I admire and I thank you for everything.

Thank you to Katie Schwartzmann, Andrew Perry, and the Tulane First Amendment Law Clinic. It's good to know there are people like you who fight so diligently for the rights of Louisiana citizens.

To all of my friends in Livingston, St. Tammany, Lafayette, Jefferson, and Rapides Parishes who refuse to see their libraries go down without a fight. They won't because of you. You matter and you're making a difference.

To the activists in Louisiana, particularly the LGBTQIA+ community. You taught me how to speak out and have shown me more empathy and kindness than any member of my church. Melissa, Lori, Angela, Peyton, and SarahJane—a thousand thank-yous.

Thank you to Kara, Kathy, and the team at *School Library Journal* for covering my story. *SLJ* changed my life back in 2021. I hope I can one day return the favor.

Thank you to Dr. Heather Harding, Rachel, and the team at Campaign for Our Shared Future—a better day for our children really is in reach because of people like you.

To Emily Drabinski, a leader in our field, who does not deserve the hate flung at her from the Far Right, I would like to let you know that your kindness to me did not go unnoticed. Thank you.

Thank you to my high school BFF, Eddie Joseph Rogers, for teaching me empathy and acceptance (and also putting up with my crap) and for kicking off my legal fund with that first donation.

To John and Michelle Cavalier of Cavalier House Books for allowing me to use your store for numerous photo shoots. Thank you for your friendship and for providing a local, independent bookstore (and safe zone) for our community.

My school librarian PLN and friends—I started to list you all and I'm afraid to leave someone out. You all know who you are. You are in the hundreds if not thousands. I appreciate each and every one of you.

To Phil Bildner and The Author Village. To be among you is surreal.

To everyone out there fighting the good fight, know this: you are not alone. Grassroots alliances, parents, librarians, and other members of society are dedicated to combat this pro-censorship movement that seeks to destroy our nation's libraries, marginalize members of society, and defund our public institutions. I believe in my soul that those of us who stand for freedom far outnumber the extremists who seek to destroy. I hope that each of you in your own states find your Lynettes, your Vickis, and your Marlas, your 10K Women and LoCALL, and join together to form your own coalitions for the greater good.

To Mikey and Ry—in the words of Gwyneth Paltrow, I wish you well.

And none for Kirk Cameron. Bye.

BIBLIOGRAPHY

ALA Office for Intellectual Freedom. "About Banned and Challenged Books." Banned and Challenged Books. Accessed June 12, 2023. https://www.ala.org /advocacy/bbooks/aboutbannedbooks.

Antone, Tiffany. "Kirk Cameron Has Caused Controversial Debates Many Times— 15, to Be Exact." She Knows, May 13, 2016. https://www.sheknows.com/enter tainment/slideshow/6101/15-times-kirk-cameron-was-the-absolute-worst/.

"Ben Shapiro Challenges Biden Admin to Read from Sexually Explicit Book Found in School Libraries." *Daily Wire*, June 9, 2023. https://www.dailywire.com/news /ben-shapiro-challenges-biden-admin-to-read-from-sexually-explicit-book -found-in-school-libraries.

Best Places. "Religion in Livingston Parish, LA." Livingston Parish, LA. https://www .bestplaces.net/religion/county/louisiana/livingston.

Block, Melissa. "Accusations of 'Grooming' Are the Latest Political Attack—with Homophobic Origins." NPR, May 11, 2022. https://www.npr.org/2022/05/11 /1096623939/accusations-grooming-political-attack-homophobic-origins.

Carter, Madeline, and Mark Vanderhoff. "JCPS Board Votes Unanimously to Keep 'Gender Queer' Book in School Libraries." WLKY News, September 26, 2022. https://www.wlky.com/article/gender-queer-book-louisville-jcps-libraries /41393659#.

Centers for Disease Control and Prevention. "Fast Facts: Preventing Child Abuse & Neglect." https://www.cdc.gov/violenceprevention/childabuseandneglect /fastfact.html.

Chavez, Roby. "Librarians in Louisiana at Odds with Conservative Activists Working to Ban Books." *PBS News Hour*, March 2, 2023. https://www.pbs.org /newshour/show/librarians-in-louisiana-at-odds-with-conservative-activists -working-to-ban-books.

Clark, Jess. "Judge Dismisses Suit Against JCPS Librarian over Books Centering LGBTQ Voices." Louisville Public Media, January 18, 2023. https://www.lpm .org/news/2023-01-18/judge-dismisses-suit-against-jcps-librarian-over-books -centering-lgbtq-voices.

Cobabe, Aimee, Daniella Rivera, and Emiley M. Dewey. "Utah Book Challenges by the Numbers: A KSL Investigation." KSL News Radio 102.7 FM, June 21, 2023. https://kslnewsradio.com/2013792/utah-book-challenges/.

Cohen, Jenna, and Joshua Barajas. "How Many Book Bans Were Attempted in Your State? Use This Map to Find Out." *PBS News Hour*, April 24, 2023. https://www.pbs.org/newshour/arts/how-many-book-bans-were-attempted -in-your-state-use-this-map-to-find-out#:~:text=The%20association%20said%20 its%20data,%2C%20in%20different%20library%20districts).

Garcia, Raymond. "American Library Association Reports Record Number of Demands to Censor Library Books and Materials in 2022." ALA News, March 22, 2023. https://www.ala.org/news/press-releases/2023/03/record-book -bans-2022.

Grossman, Hannah. "Kirk Cameron: Public Schools Grooming Kids with Critical Race Theory, 'Sexual Chaos,' and 'Racial Confusion.'" Fox News, May 31, 2022. https://www.foxnews.com/media/kirk-cameron-public-schools-grooming -kids-critical-race-theory-sexual-chaos-racial-confusion.

Hale-Shelton, Debra, and Austin Bailey. "Secret Moms for Liberty Audio Captures Threatening Rhetoric Targeting a School Librarian." *Arkansas Times*, June 16, 2022. https://arktimes.com/arkansas-blog/2022/06/16/secret-moms-for-liberty -audio-captures-threatening-rhetoric-targeting-a-school-librarian.

Harris, Martha. "She's a 2nd-Generation Utah School Librarian. But After 10 Years, She Needs a Break." KUER 90.1 Radio, July 6, 2023. https://www.kuer.org /education/2023-07-06/shes-a-2nd-generation-utah-school-librarian-but-after -10-years-she-needs-a-break.

Hickson, Martha. "What It's Like to Be the Target of a Book Banning Effort? School Librarian Martha Hickson Tells Her Story." *School Library Journal*, February 3, 2022. https://www.slj.com/story/from-the-breaking-point-to-fighting-anew -school-librarian-martha-hickson-shares-her-story-of-battling-book-banning -censorship.

Hilburn, Greg. "Louisiana GOP Official, Pastor Charged with Juvenile Cruelty Running for State House Seat." *Shreveport Times*, May 26, 2023. https://www .shreveporttimes.com/story/news/2023/05/26/louisiana-republican-official -charged-with-juvenile-cruelty-running-for-house-of-representatives/70258 303007/.

Hutchinson, Piper. "Landry's 'Protecting Minors' Tip Line Flooded with Thousands of Spam Complaints." Louisiana Illuminator, February 20, 2023. https:// lailluminator.com/2023/01/20/landrys-protecting-minors-tip-line-flooded -with-thousands-of-spam-complaints/.

——. "Livingston Parish Council Member Hired Private Investigator to Check for Porn in Libraries." Louisiana Illuminator, February 13, 2023. https:// lailluminator.com/briefs/livingston-parish-council-member-hired-private -investigator-to-check-for-porn-in-libraries/.

——. "St. Tammany Library Board Weighs Policy Changes in the Wake of New Law." Louisiana Illuminator, July 13, 2023. https://lailluminator.com/2023 /07/13/st-tammany-library-board-weighs-policy-changes-in-the-wake-of -new-law/?fbclid=IwAR2p3NN6i5446cSaXjCl9QzJupfIC4uEroRsNcp _HnBXuXiaNFa7QKwJilo_aem_AS9fzwUhPM5h7u2HP9T5ePm8nnGd_lzD QhG6KZrpbK2BY47JdNvbKYddsGejQCiazTk&mibextid=Zxz2cZ.

Idaho Judge Sentences 5 from White Nationalist Group to Jail for Conspiracy to Riot at Pride Event." Associated Press, July 21, 2023. https://apnews.com/article /patriot-front-riot-charges-idaho-pride-320afcd56c122e34d3884628fe358da5

Jensen, Kelly. "Louisiana School Librarian of the Year Seeking Legal Action After Slander Campaign." Book Riot, August 2, 2022. https://bookriot.com/louisiana -school-librarian-of-the-year-seeking-legal-action-after-slander-campaign/.

Kingkade, Tyler. "In Rare Move, School Librarian Fights Back in Court Against Conservative Activists." NBC News, August 13, 2022. https://www.nbcnews

.com/news/us-news/rare-move-school-librarian-fights-back-court-conservative
-activists-rcna42800.

Lavandera, Ed, Andy Rose, and Ashley Killough. "Texas County Commission Votes to Keep Library in Operation After Threat of Closure over Banned Books." CNN, April 13, 2023. https://www.cnn.com/2023/04/13/us/texas-llano -county-shut-down-libraries-banned-books-vote/index.html.

"Louisiana Associational Mission Strategist Arrested on Sex Crime Charges." *Baptist Press*, June 10, 2023. https://www.baptistpress.com/resource-library/news /louisiana-associational-mission-strategist-arrested-on-sex-crime-charges/.

Malden, Cheryl. "Denise Neujahr Wins the 2023 Lemony Snicket Prize for Noble Librarians Faced with Adversity." *ALA Member News*, March 27, 2023. https://www.ala.org/news/member-news/2023/03/denise-neujahr-wins-2023 -lemony-snicket-prize-noble-librarians-faced-adversity.

Maldonado, Mia. "North Idaho Librarian Wins National Award for Supporting LGBTQ+ Youth Despite Backlash." *Idaho Capital Sun*, April 27, 2023. https:// idahocapitalsun.com/2023/04/27/north-idaho-librarian-wins-national-award -for-supporting-lgbtq-youth-despite-backlash/.

"Marley Dias Talks Encouraging Kids to Read, Getting Kids Involved in Activism." ABC News, February 18, 2018. https://abcnews.go.com/US/video/marley-dias -talks-encouraging-kids-read-kids-involved-52938642?fbclid=IwAR3xGYp5 3slSeBBkGwelntrTrcoYwQJyJbiTmDConQCY82a3bsFlYv2VpJY.

Marnan, Julia. "Librarian Says She's Being Called a Child Predator over Books at School. She's Suing." *Miami Herald*, May 2, 2023. https://www.miamiherald .com/news/nation-world/national/article274932056.html.

McElfresh, Amanda. "Lafayette's Drag Queen Story Time: A Timeline of Events." *Daily Advertiser* (Lafayette), October 5, 2018. https://www.theadvertiser.com /story/news/local/2018/09/04/lafayettes-drag-queen-story-time-timeline -events/1191355002/.

Michigan Library Association. Millages and Tax Capture—MLA Advocacy Priority Area. Accessed July 14, 2023. https://www.milibraries.org/millages -and-tax-capture#:~:text=Everyone%20is%20familiar%20with%20how%20

property%20taxes%20have,through%20a%20popular%20vote%20on%20
a%20ballot%20initiative.

"Michigan State Senator Pushes Back on GOP Colleague Who Accused Her of Wanting to 'Groom' Children." Yahoo News video, April 20, 2022. https://news .yahoo.com/michigan-state-senator-pushes-back-143048001.html.

Murray, Conor. "How Trans TikTok Star Dylan Mulvaney Became a Far-Right Target After Scoring Deals with Bud Light and Nike." *Forbes*, updated April 14, 2023. https://www.forbes.com/sites/conormurray/2023/04/07/how-trans-tiktok -star-dylan-mulvaney-became-a-far-right-target-after-scoring-deals-with -bud-light-and-nike/?sh=519b8a9f26ee.

Mustian, Jim. "FBI Opens Investigation into Sex Abuse in the Roman Catholic Church in New Orleans." *PBS News Hour*, June 29, 2022. https://www.pbs.org /newshour/nation/fbi-opens-investigation-into-sex-abuse-in-the-roman -catholic-church-in-new-orleans.

National Children's Alliance. "National Statistics on Child Abuse." Accessed July 9, 2023. https://www.nationalchildrensalliance.org/media-room/national -statistics-on-child-abuse/.

Oleksinski, Johnny. "Why Kirk Cameron Is a Growing Pain in the Butt." *New York Post*, December 23, 2023. https://nypost.com/2020/12/23/why-kirk-cameron-is -a-growing-pain-in-the-butt/.

Pagones, Sara. "Billboards Are the Latest Front in St. Tammany's Battle over Library Content." Nola.com, April 12, 2023. https://www.nola.com/news/northshore /st-tammany-library-battle-taking-to-billboards/article_4dd6349c-d974-11ed -9dfb-9b53c0856a38.amp.html.

"Right-Wing Extremists Amp up Anti-LGBTQ Rhetoric Online." WFSB Channel 3, June 13, 2022. https://www.wfsb.com/2022/06/13/right-wing-extremists-amp -up-anti-lgbtq-rhetoric-online/.

Roth, Andrew. "Michigan Sen. Lana Theis Joins the Growing Conservative Trend of Baselessly Accusing Political Opponents of Being Pedophiles/Groomers." Twitter, April 18, 2022. https://twitter.com/RothTheReporter/status/15160943311 94650629.

Scipioni, Jade. "Michelle Obama: Why Going 'High' When Faced with a Challenge Is So Important to Her." CNBC, July 26, 2016. https://www.cnbc.com/2020/02/12/michelle-obama-on-famous-catchphrase-when-they-go-low-we-go-high.html.

Sentell, Will. "Jeff Landry Wades into Library Controversies, Suggesting Need for Law on 'Sexual' Material." Nola.com, December 2, 2022. https://www.nola.com/news/politics/ag-jeff-landry-says-pornography-in-libraries-merit-action/article_3949d798-71c5-11ed-9986-8f07149db4a2.html.

Serrano, Alejandro. "Llano County Libraries Case Has Lawyers and Publishers Worried About Existing Legal Precedents." *Texas Tribune*, June 19, 2023. https://www.texastribune.org/2023/06/19/llano-county-books-legal/.

Southern Poverty Law Center. "Moms for Liberty." Accessed August 12, 2023. https://www.splcenter.org/fighting-hate/extremist-files/group/moms-liberty?gclid=CjwKCAjwq4imBhBQEiwA9Nx1BqFGxdychY5QeBM_UtlixAqurFUkV-wl_dkcLaD8kNi3PjsJ-3zCDxoCjbcQAvD_BwE.

Sullivan, Becky, and Neda Ulaby. "Penguin Random House and 5 Authors Are Suing a Florida School Board over Book Bans." NPR, May 18, 2023. https://www.npr.org/2023/05/18/1176879171/florida-book-ban-lawsuit.

Taylor, Claire. "Drag Queen Story Time Opponent Elected President of Lafayette Library Board." *Acadiana Advocate* (Lafayette), October 21, 2021. https://www.theadvocate.com/acadiana/news/drag-queen-story-time-opponent-elected-president-of-lafayette-library-board/article_6fe8969c-3277-11ec-8375-5fbb7fb6f56e.html.

Taylor, Claire. "Lafayette Library Board President, LCG Sued for Stifling Free Speech over Censorship." *Advocate*, March 7, 2023. https://www.theadvocate.com/acadiana/news/anti-censorship-pair-sue-lafayette-library-board-president/article_8b303c1a-bd28-11ed-8a27-8f9e0b9abea8.html.

Travers, Mark. "Why We Tend to See the Best in People." *Psychology Today*, January 24, 2020. https://www.psychologytoday.com/us/blog/social-instincts/202001/why-we-tend-see-the-best-in-people.

"What Is Your Life's Blueprint?" *Seattle Times*. Accessed April 22, 2023. https://projects.seattletimes.com/mlk/words-blueprint.html.

Widick, Mark. "Rosie and JK Rowling." YouTube, January 24, 2007. https://www.youtube.com/watch?v=hKQpCNIyLmE.

Woodward, Alex. "The School Librarian in the Middle of Louisiana's War on Libraries." *Independent* (UK), April 24, 2023. https://www.independent.co.uk/news/world/americas/louisiana-banned-books-library-jeff-landry-b2324440.html.

Yorio, Kara. "After Her Book Displays Drew Criticism, Librarian Elissa Malespina Lost Her Job. She's Here to Say 'I'm Not OK with This.'" *School Library Journal*, October 18, 2022. https://www.slj.com/story/After-Her-Book-Displays-Drew-Criticism-Librarian-Elissa-Malespina-Lost-Her-Job-Shes-Here-to-Say-Im-Not-OK-with-This.

A NOTE ON THE AUTHOR

AMANDA JONES has been an educator for twenty-three years, at the same middle school she attended as a child. She has served as president of the Louisiana Association of School Librarians and won numerous awards for her work in school libraries, including *School Library Journal* Librarian of the Year. A sought-after keynote speaker, Amanda is a frequent volunteer for state and national library associations as well as founder of the Livingston Parish Library Alliance and founding member of Louisiana Citizens Against Censorship. She lives in Livingston Parish, Louisiana. You can find out more about her at librarianjones.com.